Icons of FASHION

THE 20TH CENTURY

Icons of FASHION

THE 20TH CENTURY

Edited by Gerda Buxbaum

With contributions by

Andrea Affaticati, Rebecca Arnold,
Christopher Breward, Gerda Buxbaum,
Joëlle Chariau, Farid Chenoune, Elizabeth
Ann Coleman, Carlo Ducci, Caroline Evans,
Deanna Farneti Cera, Anna Gloria Forti,
Gisela Framke, Robin Givhan, Ingrid
Loschek, Margit J. Mayer, Patricia Mears,
Jane C. Milosch, Jane Mulvagh, Alexandra
Palmer, Jan Glier Reeder, Caroline Rennolds
Milbank, Birgit Richard, Beate Dorothea
Schmid, Valerie Steele, Julia Szabo,
Elizabeth Wilson and Gundula Wolter

PRESTEL
Munich · Berlin · London · New York

BETWEEN DREAM AND REALITY

New ideas emerge that challenge the monopoly of a greedy clothing industry—which, according to reformers, had never understood the female body and viewed it only as an erotic and decorative object—and contribute to fashion and lifestyle reforms.

CONTENTS

left to right: Paul Poiret, 1908 (P. Iribe) / E. Wimmer-Wisgrill, "Tango" ensemble, 1913

Robes et Femmes, 1913 (E. Sacchetti)

Jeanne Paquin, 1919 / Georges Lepape, 1921

 Shoes, 1925/30

CRINOLINES AND MASCULINE CLOTHING

The first new looks of the century are characterized by retro-elements and symbols of prewar fashion. Although anachronistic, these fashions are extremely luxurious, despite economic depression, galloping inflation, and extreme shortages of materials, fabric, and accessories.

A STYLIZED MASQUERADE

Following wartime shortages that make practicality a priority, tunic dresses, tailored blouses, and sporty suits yield to sumptuously decorated dresses, fur-trimmed, wraparound coats, and coquettish, gored skirts in bold color combinations, cut and draped along sophisticated lines.

1915–1921

4|025 **The Wartime Crinoline**
Optimistic designs despite fabric shortages—full, gathered skirts—peplums—the "barrel" shape, a romantic look

6|027 **Coco Chanel**
Sporty, jersey dresses—unisex—Chanel No. 5—tweed—the *tailleur*—faux jewelry

8|029 **Avant-Garde Clothing**
Sonja Delaunay—the Russian Constructivists—the Italian Futurists—practical clothes

0|031 **Erté: Art Deco Master**
Decadent, idiosyncratic drawings—theater and ballet decor and fashions—1913 model for Mata Hari—notoriously influential drawings for *Harper's Bazaar*

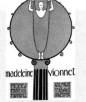

1922–1929

032|033 **Feminine and Masculine**
The princess-line dress and the coat-dress—the cloche and slouch hats—permanents and cropped hair—frilly dresses and pants—the *robe de style* and tailored suits

034|035 **Sportswear**
The pullover—jumpers—pleated skirts—knitted cardigans—the "Norwegian" look—knitted swimwear

036|037 **Fashion in Motion**
Fringe—tassels—long shawls—ropes of beads—the Charleston and the Shimmy

038|039 **Madeleine Vionnet**
The bias cut—asymmetrical draping—crisscrossed stitching—the fluidity of ancient Greek drapery

040|041 **The Little Black Dress**
Sophisticated, black, cocktail dresses by Chanel and Patou—simplicity and adaptability

Les Bijoux, 1920 (G. Barbier)

top to bottom: Sonja Delaunay, 1922
Madeleine Vionnet, Logo

Charleston dress, 1925/26
American *Vogue*, July 1927

Arpège perfume, Lanvin, 1927
Jean Patou, sweater, 1930

NEW ILLUSIONS

In 1932 Joan Crawford is dubbed the world's most emulated woman, and in 1934 Marlene Dietrich succeeds her. The actresses' star status helps to popularize slender jacket dresses with nipped-in waists and crisp, white trim, rakish, little, daytime hats, soft, womanly dresses made of charmeuse—a coquettishly romantic look for afternoon—and chiffon evening dresses with fitted bodices and gracefully floating skirts.

BETWEEN UNIFORMITY AND GLAMOUR

Wartime creates a gap between the European and U.S. fashion industries. Designers compensate by harmonizing subdued colors and classic, practical silhouettes with style and originality via striking hats, unconventional accessories, and emphatically cheerful fabrics.

1930—1938

1939—1946

Lacoste, Polo shirt

top to bottom: Worth, 1937/Lady Mendl, 1939/glitzy stairs at Chanel, 1937/Duke and Duchess of Windsor, 1937

top to bottom: Paquin, 1938/Pierre Balr 1946/Théâtre de la Mode: Lucile Mangu and Dupouy-Magnin, 1946/Bette Davis 1940s/Carmen Miranda with necklace b M. Boucher, 1940

Chanel, 2/1955 bag

THE "NEW LOOK"

Christian Dior's success is guaranteed when he "propositions" women with fashions that they cannot refuse. Following years of austere fashion, he presents tightly fitted bodices which are difficult to move in, long, full skirts—or pencil-slim ones—which are utterly unsuitable for work, and accessories that have no function. Dior states simply: "I wanted to make women beautiful again."

NEW DEPARTURES AND REDISCOVERIES

The fashion industry advocates "be beautiful" and "have fun" attitudes. This is the era of the German Economic Miracle and the golden age of lamé and gold brocade in a fashion scene that courts elegance. Cocktail and evening dresses, in particular, are made from "gold" fabrics.

top to bottom: feathered hat, 1948/Christian Dior, 1948/ Dior, "Bar" suit (Gruau)

left to right: Diorissimo perfume (Gruau)/ pastel tones, 1952/Lanvin – Castillo, 1951/Jacques Fath, 1954

POP MUSIC, SPACE RACE, BODYSUITS, AND SECONDHAND

Fashion sheds its elitist image and gives way to change. For the first time in history, fashion is centered around young people who call for fewer undergarments and visible underwear designs. Clothing for women consists of little more than what were once elements of underwear.

1961–1967

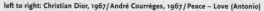

left to right: Christian Dior, 1967 / André Courrèges, 1967 / Peace – Love (Antonio)

Yves Saint Laurent, 1965/66

THE LOOKS

From the 1970s on, military pants and camouflage jackets are among the classics of almost all youth cultures whose anti-establishment protests demonstrate a readiness for combat.

1968–1979

100 | 101 **Radical Chic**
The "Hippie" look and secondhand clothes—anti-fashion—countercul-ture—alternative lifestyles

102 | 103 **The Folkloric Look**
The "Noble Peasant" look with sheep-skin coats—the "Gypsy," "Carmen," "Bedouin," "Mongol," and "Zhivago" looks—fashions from India and Africa

104 | 105 **Yves Saint Laurent**
The Trapeze line—the "Beat" look—ladies' smoking jackets—navy blazers and white silk pants—the see-through blouse—evening Bermudas—the gilt leather trenchcoat

106 | 107 **Military Style**
Fake uniforms and army surplus—oversized parkas—cartridge belts—Gestapo trenchcoats—olive green and khaki colors—camouflage—military badges—ideological T-shirts

108 | 109 **Fashion Gets Physical**
Jogging and aerobics—sneakers—new fabrics: fleece, Lycra, sweatshirt jersey

110 | 111 **Geoffrey Beene**
The basics—multipurpose clothes—casual-looking evening dresses in classic, sumptuous fabrics

112 | 113 **Kenzo: East Meets West**
Asian folklore heightened to fantasy—cotton patchwork—sumptuous colors—fun clothes at affordable prices

114 | 115 **United Colors of Benetton**
A new lifestyle and world view—young fashion in a broad range of colors—controversial advertising campaign by Oliviero Toscani

116 | 117 **Disco**
Dressing for effect—shiny, reflective fabrics—glamorous styling—skintight spandex

118 | 119 **Vivienne Westwood**
Bondage—Rococo and demi-monde—traditional tailoring techniques—designs that border on bad taste

120 | 121 **Punk**
Vivienne Westwood and Malcolm McLaren—Seditionaries—the Sex Pistols—body piercing—slit skirts—safety pins—dyed hair

left to right: Missoni, 1973 (Brunetta) / Hot pants, c. 1970s / Patchwork, American *Vogue*, 1970

left to right: Jean Claude Montana, Fall/Winter 1983/84
Gianfranco Ferré, Fall/Winter 1982/83

left to right: Katherine Hamnett, Fall/Winter 1984/85
Escada, Spring/Summer 1983 / Christian Lacroix, Fall/Winter 1987/88

DRESSING FOR SUCCESS/NO FUTURE

The glitz and glamour of the fashion world set the stage for the emergence of the celebrity supermodel, whose ever-radiant, perfect face and body transform the female physiognomy into a brand name and a fashion industry label.

1980–1990

Masako, Romeo Gigli, 1989

Romeo Gigli, 1990 (Mats Gustafson) / Gianfranco Ferré, 1982 (Antonio)

THE GLOBAL VILLAGE AT THE END OF THE MILLENNIUM

Today the dominant influence in fashion seems to be an archaic, classical model that, apart from mixed, retro-styles, advocates blonde fairies, dark Circes, and ethereal queens of the night—as opposed to the creation of functioning concepts of life for the new millennium.

1991–2000

Manolo Blahnik, Fall/Winter 1998/99

top to bottom: Calvin Klein underwear
Isabella Blow wearing Julien McDonald
Philip Treacy, Fall/Winter 1999/2000
Alexander McQueen, Spring/Summer 1999

FASHION MARKS TIME (YOHJI YAMAMOTO)

This book is an invitation to peruse, discover, and revisit the highlights of the history of twentieth-century fashion. By focusing on and restricting the century in book form, it is possible to see its fashion as a phenomenon of communication, social development, and reflection of aesthetic values—an entire universe concentrated in the distinct appearance of a skirt, a shirt, or a pair of pants.

Icons of Fashion is a collection of the "big names," those who had the ability, stamina, and good fortune to establish themselves successfully. It would be impossible to list all of the diverse individuals and companies who contributed to the fashion of this century, the names of the many unknown—perhaps "true"—initiators or the "skilled hands" of the numerous workshops and technical laboratories. It is the undiminished presence of such great European and American couturiers as Madeleine Vionnet, Christian Dior, Salvatore Ferragamo, Cristobal Balenciaga, Claire McCardell, and Charles James, the continued topicality of "perfect" clothes and revolutionary fashion innovations, and the trends such as Grunge that reveal fashion's power to distill the ideas of a specific historical moment through clothing. Movements are always challenged by countermovements; the familiar and the alien crop up, form a scenario, and together contribute to the drama of the twentieth century.

It is not only fashion designers and cult clothing that count as fashion icons. In this century, as never before, other emblematic influences—fine art, music, subcultures, youth culture, distant lands, and simply *individuals*—have marked the development of fashion. This diversity is reflected in the varied perspectives and professions of the twenty-seven authors who have contributed to the contents of this book.

What did the *nouveautés de la mode* look like? What was *en vogue, très chic,* all the rage, "in" and then immediately "out" again? How "cool" or "hip" was something perceived to be? What became an absolute "must"? How similar is John Galliano's *femme fatale* to the flower-like Art Nouveau beauty? These questions have cropped up repeatedly throughout the century and do so again in this book. Have we perhaps been going round and round in circles?

In particular, two trends dominate the end of the millennium. One is reduction—a tendency toward abstraction, light, pure energy, and articulation of perfect form. The other phenomenon is something that the philosopher Jean Baudrillard calls the "dance of the fossils," a phrase he uses to describe the need to free things from their contexts, in order to lay them bare and give them cultural value.

Fashion borrows from art and vice versa; they both operate in terms of illusion, displacement, the virtual, multiple layers, and interweavings. Often it is increasingly difficult to differentiate between them. Or, as Barbara Vinken has expressed it, "At the end of the twentieth century fashion has become what art wanted to be: the spirit of the age is manifested in it."   *Gerda Buxbaum*

01

"HOW OFTEN HAS ART INSPIRED FASHION, AND DOES NOT THE NEW ART MOVEMENT—THE VIENNESE SECESSION—HAVE A SOURCE IN FASHION?" (*WIENER MODE*, 1898)

WOMAN AS A FLOWER

At the beginning of this century, Woman stood conscious of her dignity wrapped in the opulent armor of her robe, her figure pressed into a grotesque S-bend: breasts pushed outward into a sweeping curve, while an exaggerated, projecting bottom curved in the opposite direction as a counterweight beneath the tightly corseted waist and flat abdomen. This look included hip-hugging skirts which fanned out toward the ground, very long and narrow sleeves, extremely high stand-up collars, trains, well-coifed hair and rolls of pinned-up, wavy hair beneath overly decorated, dramatically draped hats made of chiffon, chiné fabrics, silk alpaca, velvet, and lace.

The greatest innovations in the ball gowns of 1898 were long-stemmed, stylized flowers, colorfully embroidered borders and decorations that had an upward movement. An unprecedented passion for decoration characterized this time: corded embroidery, appliqué, lace inserts, glass beads, sequins, frills, and pleats covered women like a glossy, flickering web.

Another newly formulated inspiration shared by art and fashion surely lay in the erotic images and new ideals of feminine beauty: thick, flowing hair was replete with symbolic meaning for the Secessionists, and fashion, too, laid great stock in full-bodied, curly hair tied into a loose knot and pinned at the back of the head. The Viennese artist Gustav Klimt (1862–1918) painted portraits of women that symbolically united art and life through a feminine yearning to stand above everyday concerns in a Madonna-like attitude wrapped in untouchable beauty. Klimt's images seamlessly merged ladylike dignity and sexual availability.

Around 1900, the entire female body was treated like a decorative or bejeweled object—erotically stylized, deformed, and estranged from its biological function by a profit-seeking clothing industry. Fashion and femininity were inextricably linked. Already in the 1890s, designers had tried to establish the aesthetic principles of asymmetrical composition in ladies' fashion. Fashion not only expressed the asymmetries between social classes; it also mediated the inequalities between men and women.

Surveying the history of twentieth-century fashion in 1993, fashion historian Barbara Vinken defined a "fashion after fashion" which subscribed to an aesthetic of poverty, of the sentimental, of kitsch, or of poor taste: "While fashion had invented 'the woman' for over a hundred years, a 'fashion after fashion' began to deconstruct that self-same woman; while fashion initially hid its art, it now begins to also display its bag of tricks."

Gerda Buxbaum

02
03
04

05

RATIONAL DRESS

01

Dress reform movements emerged in reaction to the elaborate, fitted dresses and tight lacing of the mid- and late-nineteenth century. In the 1850s, Amelia Jencks Bloomer of New York advocated functional clothing and wore "Turkish" pants—a version of these became known as bloomers—with a knee-length dress, as a hygienic and sensible alternative to corseted fashions and long skirts. In England dress reform followed two veins: aesthetic and medical. A medieval model was proposed by the Pre-Raphaelite Brotherhood (1848–53), a group of artists whose ideals of natural feminine beauty and dress were synthesized in their paintings of Jane Morris: she wore draped, loose-fitting dresses that permitted freedom of movement, and no lacing or corset was visible.

The debate over dress reform peaked in the 1880s. The Rational Dress Society, founded in 1881, drew social and medical attention to restrictive dress. In 1884, London hosted an International Health Exhibition that included displays of hygienic dress. One exhibitor was Dr. Gustav Jaeger, a German professor of Zoology and Physiology, who had developed theories about healthful dress that involved wearing only natural fibers, such as wool, next to the body. Commercial dissemination of reform and aesthetic dress ideals was realized through the dress department of Liberty of London, established in 1884. Liberty's produced loose-fitting and flowing designs that could be worn with or without a corset. Typical features of early reform and aesthetic dress included a loose-cut design, muted colors, smocking (identified with peasant dress), and embroidery.

In the twentieth century, reform and aesthetic dress styles continued to seek solutions to dress that would liberate fashion from Paris couture dominated designs and obsolete seasonal models. Belgian designer and architect Henry Van de Velde (1863–1957), who advocated unity in the fine and applied arts in everyday life, first designed dresses for his wife Maria that were inspired by the ideas put forth in Liberty's catalogues and the children's illustrations of British artist Kate Greenaway (1846–1901). His designs were realized in heavy, plain fabrics, such as velvet, trimmed with lace and appliquéd with curvilinear forms typical of the Art Nouveau style.

The Secessionist movement in Vienna brought about the founding of the Wiener Werkstätte in 1903 by painter Koloman Moser (1868–1918) and architect Josef Hoffmann (1870–1956). This avant-garde design group opened a textile workshop and fashion department that aimed to harmonize dress and interior design as well as to free design from the foliate forms associated with Art Nouveau. Design influences came from the Glasgow Arts and Crafts practitioners in Scotland, especially Charles Rennie Mackintosh (1863–1928), and from Dutch Art Nouveau designers, particularly Jan Theodoor Toorop (1858–1928). Their designs drew upon Asian graphic and textile design, folk art, and contemporary abstract art. Dress design followed a vertical, high-waisted *directoire* line that was later made popular by Paul Poiret. In Italy the ideas of aesthetic dress were pursued by Mariano Fortuny and Maria Monaci Gallenga (1880–1944), artists who became designers and followed classical and medieval models mixed with ethnographic inspiration. *Alexandra Palmer*

"THE 'UNFASHIONABLE' IDEAS OF RATIONAL DRESS ... ATTEMPTED TO RECONCILE ART
AND LIFE ... WITHOUT REALIZING THAT THE BASIC SOCIAL PRECONDITIONS FOR AES-
THETIC EMANCIPATION FROM THE TYRANNY OF PROFESSIONAL FASHION DESIGNERS ...
HAD NOT YET BEEN ACHIEVED." (HANEL KOECK, 1986)

03
04

01

"A CULTURED ÉLITE DRESSED WITH DISTURBING OPULENCE. JAPONISME SUPERSEDED THE POTPOURRI THAT WAS HISTORICISM ..."
(URSULA VOSS, 1986)

The Orient has been a source of inspiration for fashion designers since the seventeenth century, when the wares of India, China, and Turkey were first widely seen in Western Europe. While the use of the term "Orientalism" has changed over time, around 1900 it referred to the appropriation by western designers of exotic stylistic conventions from diverse cultures spanning the Asian continent. This trend reached an apex in the early twentieth century, and the sources for this mania for "all things oriental" ranged from a nostalgia for the legends of Persia and Arabia, as popularized by *A Thousand and One Nights,* to the Paris debut of Sergei Diaghilev's Ballets Russes in 1909. This burst of Orient-inspired creativity in the realm of fashion also had lesser-known sources, including the avant-garde art movement Fauvism and Japanese kimonos made expressly for the western market.

French couturiers, such as Paul Poiret and Jeanne Paquin, were inspired by the Ballets Russes' performances of *Cléopâtre, Schéhérazade,* and *Le Dieu Bleu.* This Russian dance company took Paris by storm with their revolutionary choreography, music, and costume and set designs by the Russian artist Léon Bakst (1866–1924). In addition to these fantastic costume shapes and opulent decorative elements, couturiers incorporated the vibrant color palette of Fauve artists such as Henri Matisse. Not only did designers create garments with Orientalist influences, so did the modistes: turbans topped with aigrette or ostrich plumes and secured with jeweled ornaments were paired with neo-classic and exotic silhouettes.

The modern couturiers' adoption of the construction elements in East Asian garments was another crucial innovation in twentieth-century fashion. One prime source was the flowing Japanese kimono, a garment that began to be exported to the West after 1854, when this island-nation was opened to the West. The reverence for textiles held by the Japanese (and many other non-western cultures) discouraged the cutting of fabric necessary for European, body-fitting fashions that divided the female form into a corseted bodice on top and a full, floor-length skirt below. In the decade prior to the onset of World War I, the demise of the corset was imminent. Revolutionary couturiers like Marie Callot Gerber (1895–1937), for the House of Callot, found inspiration in the drapery-like quality of kimonos. Loosely cut sleeves and crossed bodices were incorporated into evening dresses while opera coats swathed the body like batwinged cocoons.

Madame Gerber created some of the earliest versions of the harem pants, "Turkish" pants. From 1910 to the outbreak of World War I, acclaimed beauty and woman of style, Rita de Acosta Lydig, worked with Gerber to create versions of Oriental costumes that were composed of vests made from seventeenth-century needle lace or one-piece garments that were made like pants instead of skirts. Often called the tango dress, after the new dance craze imported from Argentina, this style was popularized by couturiers like Lucile (Lady Duff Gordon, 1863–1935) and by fashion illustrators Paul Iribe (1883–1935), Georges Barbier (1882–1932), and Georges Lepape (1887–1971).   *Patricia Mears*

02

05

ORIENTALISM AND OPULENCE

03
04

"WHEN I PUT MY SIGNATURE ON A DRESS, I REGARD MYSELF AS THE CREATOR
OF A WORK OF ART." (PAUL POIRET)

01
02

PAUL POIRET

Paul Poiret is ranked among the outstanding artistic personalities in fashion history. With his new lines, developed in the first two decades of the twentieth century, he pointed the way towards a modern era. He was not only a couturier for the avant-garde but also a visionary and entrepreneur, one who was prepared to take risks, pressed forward into foreign territory, and won a great deal, but, in the end, also lost everything.

Poiret began his career with a commercial apprenticeship, while sketching and drawing in his spare time. Madame Chéruit—who bought fashion sketches from him—introduced him to Jacques Doucet (1853–1929) who gave him the opportunity to learn the basics of haute couture while working in his studio. There he learned Doucet's technique of designing directly on the body, a method which he was to retain all his life. In 1899 Poiret was entrusted with the task of designing a coat for the famous actress Réjane, and his design caused a furor. When Poiret parted company with Doucet because of conflicts of loyalty, Poiret used the opportunity to develop his *esprit nouveau* for the House of Worth, which he did for two years prior to opening his own haute couture salon in 1903.

His fashion boutique, with its extravagant ambience and theatrical models in exotic, expressive, and colorful designs, found a favorable response among the avant-garde. Poiret's creations were often worn by his wife, Denise Boulet. In 1906 she appeared in one of his first, corset-free dresses, and photos taken around 1910 show her in thin chemises *à la Grèce*. Dressed in an Orient-inspired costume, she caused a huge sensation at the "A Thousand and One Nights" party organized by Poiret. Poiret's "lampshade" tunics and "Turkish" harem pants were also a media event—the scandal of the 1910/11 season.

Poiret saw himself as an artist and considered the fine and applied arts as parts of a unified entity. He had an excellent understanding of how to spotlight his fashions through social events: his models made public appearances, and he hosted tours, showed films of fashion parades, and initiated book projects with Paul Iribe and Georges Lepape. All of which had the intention of not only illustrating his modish creations but also of interpreting fashion in a free and artistic manner. He commissioned Erté to do drawings for him, and in 1911 he collaborated with the painter Raoul Dufy (1877–1953) to design fabrics. These activities were decidedly innovative, as was his penchant for starting businesses: he established a perfume factory with a couturier (Rosine, 1911), set up a craft school and craft shop (Ecole Martine, 1911), and opened a workshop for packaging design (Collin, 1912). With his instinctive feel for the wishes of his chic female clientele he became highly successful and was soon the owner of a complex of houses in the heart of Paris.

During World War I, Poiret's fashion house was closed, and after its reopening he had difficulties adjusting to the new conditions. By 1925 he was in financial ruin, his businesses were sold, his painting collection was auctioned off, and in 1929 his salon was declared bankrupt.   *Gundula Wolter*

PAUL POIRET

1879	Born on April 20 in Paris, France
1896	Works as a salesman in a shoe shop
1898–1903	Trains with Jacques Doucet and Charles Frederick Worth (1901–03)
1903	Opens haute couture salon at Rue Auber 5, Paris
1905	Presents "Nouvelle Vague" line, dresses which no longer require corsets
1908	Publishes *Les Robes de Paul Poiret*, illustrated by Paul Iribe
1909–24	Opens further shops in Paris; designs clothes inspired by the Far Eastern costumes of the Ballets Russes—tunics, "Turkish" harem pants, turbans, kimono sleeves, flat slip-on shoes
1910	Hobble skirt
1910–11	Textile designs by Raoul Dufy
1911	Long trousers, overalls, and culottes for women; hosts his "A Thousand and One Nights" party; founds Ecole Martine, a school for applied art, where he, Erté, and Paul Iribe teach; has models photographed by Edward Steichen; *Les Choses de Paul Poiret* published by Georges Lepape
FROM 1911	Overseas tours of London (1911), Berlin, Vienna, Brussels, Moscow, St. Petersburg (1912), New York (1913)
1914	Encourages the founding of the Syndicat de Défense de la Grande Couture Française
1921–25	Opens shops in Cannes, Deauville, Biarritz, and La Boule
1925	Last major success at the *Exposition des Arts Décoratifs*, Paris; exhibitions and fashion shows held on three boats
1929	Declares bankruptcy
1944	Dies on April 28 in Paris

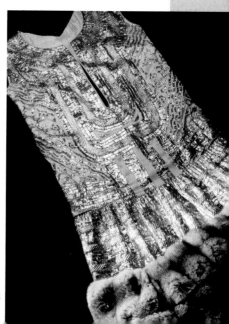

"CHARM IS, IN ITS ESSENCE, PREFERABLY AN ELEMENT OF FEMININITY."
(*DIE DAME*, 1937)

FEMMES DE LA MODE

In the last decade of the nineteenth century, a number of women designers launched businesses that were to have a major influence on early twentieth-century fashion. The House of Callot Soeurs, founded in Paris in 1893 by four sisters, began as a lace shop that quickly developed into a full couture house renowned for exquisite garments incorporating lace and embroidery. Jeanne Lanvin built her house of couture around beautifully crafted garments designed with a unique aesthetic that combined simplicity and naiveté with romanticism. She enjoyed particular prominence after World War I and into the 1930s. Lady Duff Gordon, alias Lucile, was the first English couturière to achieve worldwide success. Her design aesthetic incorporated a sense of high drama with seductive femininity. In 1891, on the Rue de la Paix, Jeanne Paquin and her husband, Isidore, opened the House of Paquin. It soon became the largest and most stylistically influential couture house of the Belle Époque, attracting forward-looking women aspiring to a new fashion image at the end of the Victorian era. The press coined the term "Paquinesque" to signify youth, modernity, and the height of sophistication.

Just eight years after beginning her career, Paquin was chosen by other leading couturiers to head the first collective exhibition of couture at the Paris Universal Exhibition in 1900. For her display, she chose to exhibit a wax mannequin of herself sitting at a dressing table and attired in a sumptuous blue velvet teagown embroidered with gold roses and trimmed with Alençon lace. Paquin always wore her own designs and, as an active career woman, was naturally concerned with matters of comfort, function, and versatility. While she created opulent gowns, her work also provided a vital link in the evolution from the restrictive fashions of the past to the comfort and freedom that constitutes our modern way of dressing—earning her the title "The Mother of Modern Dress."

From 1905, Paquin persistently promoted the high-waisted *directoire* line, which required an upright, natural posture and fewer underpinnings, establishing a context for Paul Poiret's similar but more extreme "Hellenic" designs of 1908. In 1912, she created a line of clothing designed specifically for sports as well as a dress that combined tailoring with draping for day into evening wear. Paquin herself frequently wore an ankle-length suit of functional, yet chic, blue serge—a perennial favorite. In response to the tango dance craze, she designed a tango dress constructed with hidden pleats that allowed for ease of movement while retaining the fashionable narrow silhouette popularized by the hobble skirt. This led to similarly designed suits and day dresses.

Paquin was the first couturière to become a fashion icon. She was the personification of her own style, and her popularity prepared the way for the rise of the next great fashion personality—Coco Chanel.   *Jan Glier Reeder*

01

02
03

01
02

THE WARTIME CRINOLINE

03

"ROMANTICISM IS A SIGN OF CRISIS, THE LONGING FOR TRADITION, FOR BETTER TIMES. WHEN TOMORROW HAS NO APPEAL, TWO DIRECTIONS REMAIN: THE PATH INWARD AND THE PATH BACK." (BARBARA VINKEN, 1993)

At a time when people had little money to spare, fabric was a luxury, and women had to work jobs previously done by men—precisely in these conditions—there was an increased expenditure on clothing which seemed to contradict all logic. *Kriegskrinoline* (wartime crinoline) is the German term for the dress and suit silhouette that became the dominant fashion throughout Europe from 1915 to early 1917, when women wore extremely wide skirts supported by numerous petticoats but without a hooped underskirt. Such ample, bell-shaped skirts were in fashion despite the difficult demands placed on women because of wartime and economic hardships; the high cost of the skirt, which used lavish amounts of material, was contradicted by the poor quality of fabrics and modest trimmings.

During World War I, the emphasis on traditional female forms gained new importance. At the same time that the "pannier" skirt (a skirt that widened greatly at the hips by the addition of inverted cones that opened at the top) and the "barrel" shape (a full skirt that was gathered at the ankles) were introduced, Biedermeier curves as well as the lines worn during the reign of Louis XV became popular. Voluminous skirts were worn with bodices, and peplums were attached to the sides of the skirt, thereby emphasizing the shape of the hips. For the first time, day dresses were barely calf-length, though worn with high lace-up boots. Interestingly, in contrast to the romantic skirt shapes, jackets often displayed military decoration—lacing, high uniform collars, severe lapels, metal buttons—and were in metallic colors or named after generals or seamen, such as Tegetthoff (a famous Austrian admiral) blue.

Haute couture, too, was preoccupied with the wartime crinoline, but the designs were softer and daintier, and skirt hems were longer. The full skirt survived in the *robe de style* of the 1920s. It is interesting that the Austrian dirndl costume emerged in 1916, completely in the style of the times, with a high waist, rounded bustline, and a wide, calf-length skirt.

Times of crisis usually act like catalysts on fashion as regards new materials, but also significant is the sentimental, backward look to seemingly secure, harmonious times. Veils on enormous straw hats, bodices, broad belts in corselet form, and the wide skirts of the "Winterhalter" look are known from countless historical films, while poke bonnets and waltz gowns (as an expression of operetta's soulfullness) are known from films of musicals. A preference for lace, chiffon printed with a gossamery profusion of flowers and leaves, and rippling floods of black tulle is evident in the costumes of 1930s Hollywood films, as are skirts incorporating extravagant amounts of material, puffed sleeves to emphasize the shoulders, hip-shaping flounces, and evening gowns with clouds of skirts.

Gerda Buxbaum

04
05

"FASHION IS AT ONCE BOTH CATERPILLAR AND BUTTERFLY. BE A CATERPILLAR BY DAY AND A BUTTERFLY AT NIGHT ... THERE MUST BE DRESSES THAT CRAWL AND DRESSES THAT FLY." (COCO CHANEL)

COCO CHANEL

01
02

03

With a simple, characteristic line—sweaters, sailors' pea jackets, calf-length, pleated skirts, and straight chemise frocks made from cheap, cream-colored, cotton knit fabric that was originally intended for underwear—Gabrielle "Coco" Chanel unseated the most influential couturier of the day, Paul Poiret, whose expressive, rebellious creations had made the erotic aura of the exotic socially acceptable at the beginning of the twentieth century.

Almost all women's wear today, no matter what kind it is, is essentially the result of Chanel's ideas, experiments, and "clean outs." She ruthlessly discarded everything which she considered superfluous in order to expose the substance of a garment that modern women could wear. Chanel was also her own best mannequin—boyishly slender, sporting a healthy tan to an advanced age, and, since 1917, wore her hair extremely short.

After initially designing hats, Chanel opened a shop in Paris at Rue Cambon 21. She attracted a wealthy clientele of women who praised her groundbreaking pants designs, which gave them more freedom of movement, and her overall simple, but nevertheless extremely expensive, fashions. She reinvented the pajamas so as to make them socially acceptable, propagated the unisex style with great matter-of-factness, made opulent jewelry—both genuine and costume—an essential element of attire, and, in the late 1930s, created gowns with outrageous sex appeal on a gypsy theme.

As early as 1920 she introduced specific sportswear garments: sporty jersey frocks and costumes, pullovers, and pleated skirts were worn in combination with triangular scarves and long strings of faux pearls—all these things made her into an international celebrity. Her famous Chanel No. 5 perfume appeared on the market in 1921, since Mademoiselle was of the opinion that true elegance always involved a perfume.

In 1926 she declared black to be the only appropriate color for a standardized, economically perfect attire, and in the 1930s she stated that white was "most important." In her 1932 collection, she made exclusive use of cotton fabrics and presented a range of evening dresses full of refreshing charm. The "Chanel in Hollywood" project—MGM wanted Chanel to reform the taste of Hollywood stars—failed because of the diametrically opposed interpretations of elegance and glamour. She once told the Surrealist painter Salvador Dalí (1904–89) that she "took the English masculine and made it feminine," and that all her life she did "nothing more than transform men's clothing into women's jackets, haircuts, ties, and cuffs."

Chanel closed her business in 1939. However in 1954, at the age of seventy, while perched at the top of the legendary curved staircase of her salon, watching unseen as her models made their entry, she celebrated a sensational comeback. Her strictly tailored tweed suit—a style which every woman could copy—caused a sensation. As Maurice Sachs said: "She was like a general, obsessed by the desire to win."

Gerda Buxbaum

GABRIELLE "COCO" CHANEL

1883	Born on August 19 in Saumur, France
1909	Establishes hat workshop in House of Etienne Balsan
1910	Opens first shop at Rue Cambon 21, Paris; from 1920, also at Rue Cambon 31
1913	Opens boutique in Deauville
1914–15	Sweaters, pea jackets, calf-length pleated skirts, straight frocks, and shirtwaists made from inexpensive cotton-knit fabric
1915	Boutique in Biarritz (with Boy Capel)
1918	Pajamas for women
1920–21	Russian-influenced work: furs, ornaments, and peasant blouses; costumes for Jean Cocteau's *Antigone*
1924	Shows first costume jewelry collection; founds perfume company under the management of the Wertheimer brothers
1926	Creates the "little black dress"
1926–31	Designs "English" style clothing and jewelry in collaboration with Fulco di Verdura
1928	Haute couture on the first floor at Rue Cambon 31
1931	"Unisex" style; trousers for women
1938	Dresses in "Gypsy" style
1939	Closes shop and studio
1953	Reopens shop at old address
1954	Makes a comeback with the tweed suit and two-tone pumps with ankle straps
1957	The Chanel bag—shoulder bag of quilted leather; Neiman Marcus Award; first and only visit to the United States
1971	Dies on January 10 in Paris; business placed under the artistic direction of Yvonne Dudel and Jean Cazaubon; from 1978 prêt-à-porter under Philippe Guibourg
FROM 1983	Karl Lagerfeld responsible for haute couture and prêt-à-porter from 1984
PERFUMES	Chanel No. 5 (1921), Chanel No. 19 (1970), Cristalle (1974), Coco (1984), Egoïste (1990), Pour Monsieur (1991), Allure (1993)

04
05

"THE ITALIAN FUTURISTS, THE RUSSIAN SUPREMATISTS AND CONSTRUCTIVISTS, AS WELL AS EXPONENTS OF THE BAUHAUS MOVEMENT ARE INVENTING A NEW WAY OF DRESSING. THEIR APPROACH IS RADICAL: THE NEW PERSON DESERVES ENTIRELY NEW, REVOLUTION- ARY CLOTHING." (FRANÇOIS SCHEER)

AVANT-GARDE CLOTHING

01
02

Prior to World War I, and especially during the 1920s, artists throughout Europe were attempting to redefine the clothing of modern men and women. These avant-garde artists wanted to bridge the gap between art and life. They believed that there was no division between the so-called fine and applied arts; on the contrary, the creative permeation of everyday life was part of their understanding of art. They wanted to break with the past and called for a revolutionary reorganization of every genre of art; they also glorified the modern world of machines and technology. However, they differed in their degree of radicalness and followed divergent paths, particularly in their political affiliations.

Filippo Tommaso Marinetti (1876–1944) provided the impetus for the European avant-garde with his Futurist manifesto of 1909. In order to "reinvent" clothing, the Italian Futurists placed themselves in the spotlight, dressing as though for a theatrical performance. Giacomo Balla (1871–1958) summarized their thoughts in his 1914 manifesto *Il Vestito antineutrale* (Anti-Neutral Clothing), in which he advocated simple, practical, and reusable clothing. The artists showcased their nonconformity at regional and international congresses and exhibitions using asymmetrical cuts, bright "muscular" colors, striking waistcoats, accessories with flashing lights, "anti-neckties" made from aluminum, and shirts made out of metal. These designs and prototypes for women's and menswear only entered the regional Futurist *Case d'Arte* series to a limited extent.

In 1919 the Futurist Ernesto Michahelles (1893–1959, known as Thayaht) developed a unisex "uniform garment." This radical design, similar to overalls, was comfortable and inexpensive; it consisted of a one- or two-piece, *T*-shaped suit which he called a *tuta* (jumper). Similar, counter-designs were being developed in the 1920s by Russian artists such as Varvara Stepanova (1894–1958), Alexander Rodchenko (1891–1954), and Vladimir Tatlin (1885–1953). During this time, Thayaht also designed the logo for Madeleine Vionnet's fashion salon. Vionnet was his partner in Paris for a few years from 1922. Thayaht's designs reflected classical models from antiquity, which was in complete contrast to the demands of the futuristic avant-garde of that time.

In 1925 the Italian artists encountered avant-garde movements from other European countries at the *Exposition Internationale des Arts Décoratifs et Industriels Modernes* in Paris. The Russian Constructivists and Suprematists triumphed there with their textile creations. During the 1920s, the Russian female artists Stepanova, Lyubov Popova (1889–1924), and Ludmilla Mayakovskaya actually worked in textile factories in order to further technical and aesthetic developments in fabric production.

Whereas Thayaht and other Italian artists were only intermittently active in the fashion world in Paris, innumerable Russian emigrés settled there permanently and became involved in the industry. Among those artists who developed new concepts of clothing using artistic expression, special mention must be made of Natalia Goncharova (1881–1962) and her work for the "Salon Myrbor," as well as Sonja Delaunay (1885–1979) and her "Boutique Simultanée." *Gisela Framke*

03

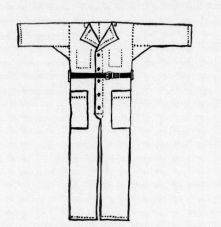

04

TAGLIO DELLA TUTA

— MODELLO DI THAYAHT —

QUESTO MODELLO È TOTALMENTE TAGLIATO A LINEE RETTE.— PER LA PERSONA DI ALTEZ MEDIA CI VOGLIONO METRI 4.50 di stoffa ALTA CENTIMETRI 70 (COSTA 7 LIRE AL METRO).— TELA D'AFRICA, TELA DI CANAPA O COTONE

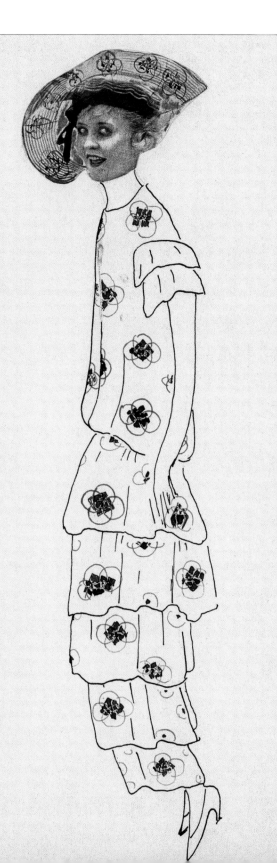

05

"ERTÉ'S MYTHOLOGY IS SO COMPLETE AND CONVINCING THAT ONE NO LONGER KNOWS WHETHER HE CREATED THE WOMAN OF HIS ERA OR SIMPLY UNDERSTOOD HER IN A STROKE OF GENIUS." (ROLAND BARTHES, 1985)

01
02

ERTÉ

1892	Born Romain de Tirtoff on November 23 in St. Petersburg, Russia
1906	Studies at the Academy of Fine Arts, St. Petersburg
1912	Works with Paul Poiret in Paris
1913	Designs costumes for dancer Mata Hari in *Le Minaret*
1914	Studies at the Académie Julian, Paris
1915–36	First fashion sketches for *Harper's Bazaar* (until 1936); also does drawings for *Vogue, Cosmopolitan, Delineator, Sketch*, and others
1916	First music hall designs for Mistinguette at Bataclan and for Gaby Deslys at the Théâtre Femina, Paris
1917–30	Designs costumes for the Folies-Bergère, Paris
1921	Dress with asymmetric décolleté
1922–29	Designs for George White's *Scandals*; the Ziegfeld Follies, Wintergarden, and French Casino
1933–52	Designs for the *Bal Tabarin*, Paris
1950–58	Designs for *La Nouvelle Eve*, Paris
1960	Designs costumes for Racine's *Phèdre*, Paris
1967	"Flying Colours," Expo '67, Montreal; costumes for "Silent Night," ABC Television
1970–72	Designs stage sets and costumes for Roland Petit's shows at the Casino, Paris
1990	Dies on April 24 in Paris

ERTÉ: ART DECO MASTER

03

The name Erté evokes the very image of Art Deco opulence. His work as a fashion illustrator and costume designer made him one of the most acclaimed artists of the twentieth century. Highly stylized designs of sinuous bodies swathed in fabric and fur, ornamented with endless strings of beads and pearls, and topped with fantastic and towering headwear, are his signature images. Although Erté—whose name derived from the French pronunciation of the initials of his real name, Romain de Tirtoff—worked until his death in 1990 at the age of ninety-seven, the genesis of his acclaimed style began before World War I.

Born to an aristocratic family in St. Petersburg in 1892, Erté demonstrated an early talent for art and design as well as for dance and theater. In 1912 he moved to Paris where his first notable employ-ment was a brief stint as an illustrator for the couturier, Paul Poiret. It was during this period that Erté designed costumes for a play entitled, *Le Minaret* (1913). One of the cast members, who gained infamy for her exotic dress and daring performances, was the Dutch-born Mata Hari (1876–1917). Also known as "The Red Dancer," she became legendary after the Germans shot her for espionage during World War I.

When Erté left the House of Poiret in 1914, his work was in great demand for opera, theater, and ballet productions in Paris, Monte Carlo, New York, Chicago, and Glyndebourne. His most memo-rable stage work was done for music hall productions—enormously popular at the time. He designed sets and costumes for Irving Berlin's *Music Box Review*, George White's *Scandals* and *Manhattan Mary*, and numerous productions of the Ziegfeld Follies, as well as for shows at the Folies-Bergère, Casino de Paris, and London Palladium. In 1925 Erté also created costumes for a small number of Hollywood films produced by MGM; these designs were extremely influential on later costume designers such as Gilbert Adrian (1903–59).

Erté's contribution to the world of fashion illustration was also substantial. Although he worked for *Gazette du Bon Ton* and *Vogue*, among other publications, it is primarily his work for *Harper's Bazaar* for which he is best remembered today. In 1916 the American publishing tycoon, William Randolph Hearst, offered him an exclusive ten-year contract that was subsequently renewed until 1937. Literally hundreds of Erté's illustrations were exclusively created for, and published in, *Harper's Bazaar*. Erté differed from most other illustrators of the period in that each drawing was his own original creation, not a depiction of another couturier's design.

Though Erté's work flourished during the 1920s, he stated that he lacked sympathy for the *garçonne* or flapper look, with its short skirts and tubular silhouettes ornamented with geometric and abstract designs. In a manner that bridged the styles of Art Nouveau and Art Moderne, Erté produced stunning images that drew upon Greek mythology, Ancient Egypt, Indian miniature paintings, as well as his own Russian heritage.

Patricia Mears

04

05

01

"THE BASIC MASCULINE—FEMININE APPEAL IS IN PEOPLE, NOT IN CLOTHES. WHEN A GARMENT BECOMES SUFFICIENTLY BASIC, IT CAN BE WORN UNISEXUALLY." (RUDI GERNREICH, c. 1965)

FEMININE AND MASCULINE

In 1926 readers of a German women's magazine, *Die Dame*, were informed: "Just now, the struggle between the male and the female principle is most strongly expressed in fashion.... The cloche hat with its supple lines and a sinuous brim that softly shades the face is up against the severe 'flower-pot' hat with a mercilessly hard edge that ends in an abrupt line just above the eyes." The *robe de style*, inspired by the romantic sentimentality of a bygone era, competed with pants; the practical jumper was as much in fashion as were sleek, princess-line dresses; there were floral prints, but also pin-stripes; pastel silk-flower corsages and austere, linear brooches; playful *retro* bracelets and jewelry in Bauhaus style; enameled butterfly pins and chrome-plated "gas pipe" and snake necklaces; mannish suits and ties, but also dainty blouses in transparent gauze or voile; and while the working woman wore a kasha suit (made from a soft woolen material woven from the fleece of Himalayan sheep) by day, she would exchange it for an embroidered, low-cut handkerchief dress in the evening.

Die Dame continued: "For many years we have heard the same message: woman wants to become more masculine! Has she not already cast away her most precious natural adornment by cropping her hair and then taming the charming curls and wisps surrounding her pageboy by smoothly brushing them back—just like a man? Isn't women's fashion cut more and more like men's? How unfeminine!"

In the 1920s designers were not working to create a "freedom suit" as a symbol of liberation from sexual oppression (in the manner of the female novelist George Sand who had "fled" into men's clothing); instead, they worked towards creating an androgynous dress code that would broaden the discussion of the relationship between the sexes. While skirts and hair grew shorter—and consequently revealed more of the body—bosoms became flatter. Greta Garbo and Marlene Dietrich modeled this new and extraordinarily appealing crossover between masculine and feminine, and millions of women followed their example.

"What a strange misconception! Each era has a distinct image of male and female appearance and often mistakes the image for true masculinity and femininity. Looking back, however, ... we realize that the issue remains unresolved: is a taut braid truly a symbol of masculine strength, as contemporaries of the soldier-king Frederick William I believed, or is it inextricably linked to the charming image of a bashful virgin, idolized in the nineteenth-century romance novels of Eugenie Marlitt," concluded *Die Dame*.

In 1928 *Die Dame* reported again: "The jersey or tweed dress is one of the most important fashion trends this summer.... These dresses should not be limited to the golf course, for many a woman will look more attractive in them in the morning or afternoon than she would wearing one of those brightly patterned and overly decorated 'dainty' dresses." *Gerda Buxbaum*

02

Soft, wide-brimmed hat, *Vogue*, September 1929 ••• 02 Annie Offterdinger, cover of *ITZ*, depicting spring suit, January 1927, color lithograph ••• 03 Jeanne Lanvin, day dress, gouache, 1927

Eduard-Josef Wimmer-Wisgrill, "Plaza" dress, ink and watercolor, 1926

"SPORTSWEAR IS 'DRESSING UP' FOR LEISURE." (BIRGIT RICHARD, 1997)

SPORTSWEAR

01
02

03

06

04
05

At the beginning of the 1920s, with the discovery of the health-promoting aspects of sport, women were also permitted to take part in sporting activities. As the tightly laced corsets of the time made movement difficult, lighter fashions were developed that made it easier for women to take long walks and to participate in sports. The pioneer of sportswear designs was Coco Chanel. Her leisure suit made from a light jersey fabric became the socially acceptable fashion for informal wear. In the mid-1920s the "jumper ensemble" (the combination of a knitwear jumper [the original pullover] worn over a long knitted waistcoat) and a below-the-knee, wide-pleated skirt was popular. Women who performed gymnastics wore rather unflattering knickerbockers with a loose top.

When women's swimming, the only socially acceptable type of sport for women, was declared an Olympic discipline in 1912, the extremely impractical long skirt that had been prescribed, gave way to a close-fitting, one-piece swimsuit with knee-length legs. Women who enjoyed swimming as a hobby were, however, expected to wear a short skirt over their suits. They also wore a flat bathing ring around the neck, permitting them to swim without damaging their make-up.

Nevertheless, in other types of sport such as tennis, hiking, or croquet, women's clothing in the early 1920s was still far from adequate: a cumbersome ankle-length skirt was still the prescribed norm. Pants were only allowed for riding but, even then, only in conjunction with a closed coatdress or with a long skirt. For skiing, another sport that became very popular after its introduction at the 1924 Winter Olympics, women wore the so-called Norwegian suit—a knitted pullover with ankle-length knickerbockers worn under a long skirt—an outfit that must have made skiing, even for the most athletic of women, a real challenge. In the mid-1920s, as a result of the overall shortening in the length of daywear, a short skirt was permitted for tennis. This trend was retained even when skirt lengths began to fall again at the end of the 1920s.

Today, the female sportswear of the 1920s still appears restrictive and anti-woman, however, the sportswear developments of that time laid the groundwork for what would be explored in the course of the century. All of our present-day fitness gear—sportswear and swimwear—has developed from the discovery of elastic fibers, which made movement in clothing really possible for the first time. The jumper, in the form of the pullover or sweatshirt, is still a highly popular item of women's casual wear. And pants, first permitted as a revolutionary "undergarment" for women's sportswear, have developed into a standard element of female outerwear. *Beate Dorothea Schmid*

01

02

03

FASHION IN MOTION

In the 1920s fashion was defined by a totally new body awareness, which manifested itself not only in ideals of beauty but also went hand in hand with a more permissive society and new types of sports. This was a golden era for extravagance and, above all, for outrageousness. Flowing fabrics enveloped the extremely stylized female figure—the ideal type being boyishly slim with matchstick-short hair. Jerseys and knits, wide-legged pants, fringed dance dresses, long chains or strings of pearls, called *sautoirs*, and opulent tassels were used to bolster the new lifestyle.

In 1928, a fashion reformer writing for a German fashion magazine remarked: "What I need to see and understand above all else in dressing a person new to me or working with an unfamiliar fabric is the 'movement.' Some fabrics fall stiffly, need to be smoothed out, have a line. Others naturally gather into rounded folds, cling, bunch up, and require fullness. Flowing fabrics demand shape, and the times we live in give movement free reign. The dress no longer has a solid framework as it did in the past, it is no longer a suit of armor; corsets, whalebone stays, or even tightly cut bodice-linings no longer force a change on the body's outline or stylize and constrict movement. Today's ideal is a vibrant body toned through sport and physical training, a body that stretches and moves without constraint. In the past, a dress 'fitted' like a glove—provided you stood stock-still or moved only in the most inhibited manner within the constraints of the body-hugging garment! For any activity that required free movement, you had to quickly step out of the 'good' dress so as to avoid pulling it out of shape."

In a time of greater economy in decoration, the seam was used for both decoration and structure to allow for a more graphic rendering of the body. The faintly diaphanous dance dresses of the 1920s were enriched by yet another effect of partial transparency, revealed only in motion: swinging and fluttering rows of fringe which revealed the outline of the female form.

The 1928 article concluded: "The 'skintight' form was developed for a motionless body, the posed 'figure' at rest.... In the past, even the best-fitting dress displayed unwanted distortions as a result of any sudden and unrestrained movement; but today, the truly well-fitting gown reveals its full beauty in the way it follows movement, translates it into folds and extensions, underlines good lines and softens unflattering ones."

The most interesting feature in fashion was the new preference for unevenness and asymmetry. In contrast to earlier balanced and symmetrical designs, this brought animation and tension into clothing design. Diagonal lines, cloth draped on one side only, pleated skirts, fluttering pieces of fabric as ornamentation, bows and narrow ribbons, loose trim, scarves, and asymmetrically trimmed necklines allowed for considerable scope in individual design.   *Gerda Buxbaum*

04

"FASHION ADJUSTS TO THE SPEED OF THE TRAFFIC, HOLDS ITS OWN IN THE ADAPTATION TO THE RAPID, FLEETING APPEARANCE THAT ALONE PROMISES THE ATTENTION AND THE GAZE OF THOSE PASSING IN CONTINUAL MOTION." (SABINE FABO, 1998)

05

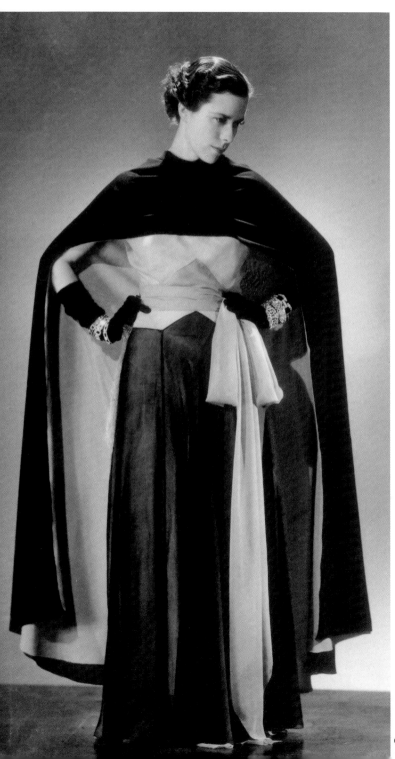

"IT WAS THE BIAS CUT—DISCOVERED BY VIONNET—THAT MADE FREEDOM OF EXPRESSION IN CLOTHING POSSIBLE." (ISSEY MIYAKE)

MADELEINE VIONNET

1876	Born on June 22 in Aubervilliers, France
1888–95	Trains and works in Paris as a seamstress
1896–1901	Manages a dressmaker's shop in London
1901–06	Works as a pattern director at the Paris atelier, House of Callot Sœurs
1907–12	Holds position of director at the House of Jacques Doucet
1912	Opens own salon in Paris
1914	Closes salon due to World War I
1919	Reopens salon
1921	Makes debut in the United States
1922	Extravagant designs inspired by Greek vases and Egyptian frescoes
1923	Invents "bias cut" to make dresses that fit tightly at the waist and flare out into a bell-shape
1925	Designs "seam decorations," decorating visible seams in star or flower shapes
1939	Awarded the Order of the Légion d'Honneur
1940	Closes salon
1975	Dies on March 2 in Paris

01

MADELEINE VIONNET

03

Madeleine Vionnet, sitting in her work chair, a wooden mannequin standing in front of her, arranging a piece of cloth that would become a dress—this is the image that encapsulates the working practices of the high priestess of *cut*. Vionnet is a couturière whose reputation continues to grow. Since the closure of her fashion house in 1940, her fame extends beyond the confines of the respect she has earned from peers such as Jacques Doucet (1853–1929), Cristobal Balenciaga, Christian Dior, and Azzedine Alaïa.

Vionnet did not make sketches of her dress designs. Instead she improvised on her mannequin, spinning it on her piano stool—like a potter at the wheel—working out shapes, volumes, and lines. She treated the mannequin not as a passive object to adorn, but rather as a human subject, a living, moving body. A model wearing a Vionnet design would be photographed at three different angles (from the front, rear, and side) in order to protect it from forgery.

Like Paul Poiret and Coco Chanel, Vionnet belonged to the anti-corset generation that developed around the 1880s. Instead of orientalizing the female body like Poiret, or making it more masculine, like Chanel, she exalted it. She used fabric intelligently, achieving a seamless antique drapery that referred to the Greek *peplos*, a simple rectangular piece of cloth that hung from the shoulders and was belted around the waist. In the 1920s, she fashioned garments from geometrically patterned fabrics which reflected the Futurist or Cubist aesthetics of the time. She used triangles, squares, oblongs, circles, and petal shapes, building them up into layers, balancing them against each other, and cascading them in fluid, waterfall effects. She also used fringe, designed by the embroiderer Albert Lesage, to decorate her gown designs from that period.

The secret to the fluidity of her designs was her use of the bias cut. Formerly used in the making of collars, sleeves, gores, and borders—especially in lingerie—the bias cut is cloth cut across the diagonal. This cut endows it with a flexibility and ease of handling that is impossible using the traditional "cut on the straight." With Vionnet, the bias cut made its debut in the world of dress designing. The fabric as a whole is drawn into a spiraling dynamic which envelops the body, enhancing the fullness and looseness of the serpentine silhouette which became prominent in the 1930s and which blossomed, under the impetus of her collaborator Marcelle Chaumont, into the romantic mousseline, tulle, or crepe evening gowns characteristic of the later stages of her career.   *Farid Chenoune*

04 05 06

01 Coco Chanel, Marion Morehouse in black crepe dress with sequins and fringe, *Vogue*, May 1926 ••• 02 Libiszewski, "Shopping for the Ensemble," watercolor, *Vogue* 1930
03 Moschino, little black dress with teddy bears, advertising campaign, Autumn/Winter 1988–89 ••• 04 Chanel, Autumn/Winter 1995 ••• 05 Audrey Hepburn in *Breakfast at Tiffany's*, 1960

"SHEHERAZADE IS SIMPLE, BUT THE LITTLE BACK DRESS IS COMPLEX." (COCO CHANEL)

THE LITTLE BLACK DRESS

04
05

Should anyone wish to compile a retrospective of the cultural milestones of the twentieth century, one definite inclusion from the world of fashion would be the little black dress.

In this deliberately simple garment—in the color of experience, of independence, and of eroticism—we find the dominant sociocultural trends of this century. It represents modernism in its rejection of sentimentality, feminism in its dignity, and individualism in its resistance to blending in with the colorful mass of humanity. As a wearable equivalent to Le Corbusier's "machine for living," the little black dress is rooted in the democratic utopia of the Bauhaus, but it also takes things a step further. It has what Mies van der Rohe's "Barcelona" chair has—that combination of logical form and sensuality for which this century has coined the word "glamour."

The birth of the "wonder dress" took place, quite traditionally, in Paris; its parents were Jean Patou and Coco Chanel. Patou, a forerunner of Ralph Lauren in his enthusiasm for the sporty/chic lifestyle of Riviera society, provided the architectural line, while Chanel contributed that dash of impertinence, i. e. black—the color traditionally worn by the maidservants of her couture clientele. In 1926 she presented a long-sleeved black crepe dress, with straight stitch seams in an X-shape, which American *Vogue* compared to Henry Ford's classic Model T, and which, it was prophesied, would become "a uniform for all women of taste."

That is exactly what happened, and much more. Whether worn by the Duchess of Windsor or Tina Turner, Martha Graham or Donatella Versace, Elizabeth Taylor as a call girl in *Butterfield Eight* (1960) or Anne Parillaud as a contract assassin in *Nikita* (1990)—the little black dress became a uniform for women who did not fit the conventional cliché of femininity. Practicality or appearance, active subject or passive object, "to be or not to be," the black dress always spoke for the former. Every woman her own Hamlet, a beautiful rebel on the stage of her private and public life.

Fashion consultants have for decades hailed the little black dress as a slimming garment, as a bridge between day and evening wear, and as the ideal backdrop for accessories. One dress, so many possibilities of transformation; but are these qualities still relevant for today's woman? Most recently the little black dress—at Helmut Lang, Calvin Klein, and, of course, Chanel—has really come into itself. By turning up in extravagant fabrics and dramatic shapes, the little dress suddenly seems quite grand, almost triumphal. Karl Lagerfeld's version, for the winter collection of the new millennium, is an adaptation of the evening dress worn by Delphine Seyrig in Alain Resnais's *Last Year at Marienbad* (1961). The merest, fragile wisp of black chiffon and yet a battle dress to be worn with flat black boots. *Les jeux sont faits:* the game of submission beneath the male gaze is over. *Margit J. Mayer*

03

02

ELSA SCHIAPARELLI

1890	Born on September 10 in Rome, Italy
1927	Designs first trompe l'oeil pullovers: black with knitted-in white bow
From 1928	Studio in Paris (Rue de la Paix)
1930	Mermaid line; uses brightly colored zippers as decoration
1931	Beach overalls; broad shoulders
1933	Pagoda sleeves; fashion magazines compare her work to Chanel's
1934	Opens shop in London at Upper Grosvenor Street 36; "Storm" silhouette; synthetics/cellophane shawl; embroidery by Salvador Dalí
1935	Takes over Madame Cheruit's fashion house at Place Vendôme 21 under her own name; designs less expensive ready-to-wear in addition to haute couture; intermittently employs Hubert de Givenchy as her assistant
1936	Smoking jacket; parachute dress; desk suit (with Dalí); airplane silhouettes
1937	Colorful tweed ensembles; "Music" collection: waltz dresses with wide, crinoline-like skirts; "Circus" collection: elephants and circus horses embroidered on boleros
1938	"Astrology/Zodiac" collection: giant suns, sun god with chariot, gold embroidery on evening capes; "Commedia dell'Arte" collection (last major collection): carnival masks, three-cornered hats, Harlequin patterns
1939	Presents "Cash and Carry" collection prior to the outbreak of World War II
1941	Closes salon and moves to the United States
1945	Reopens her house in Paris; "Talleyrand" silhouette
1949	Opens boutique in New York
1954	Closes her salon and retires
1973	Dies on November 14 in Paris
1977	Designer team reopens her fashion house
Perfumes	Shocking (1937), Snuff (1939), Le Roi Soleil (1947), Shocking You (1976), Shocking Schiaparelli (1998)

"The Italian artist who makes clothes," is how the great Coco Chanel described Elsa Schiaparelli, with a forced smile—Coco, the undisputed queen of Parisian haute couture, could not hide the trace of envy. "Schiap," as her friends called her, was born to a well-to-do and cultivated Roman family. She studied philosophy, married young, and moved to New York. In 1920 her husband left her, and she returned to Europe with her daughter and settled in Paris. Despite not having a profession or financial resources, she became involved in fashion, which was to become her lifelong passion. One of her first designs, a black jersey with a white trompe l'oeil bow, was noticed by a department store buyer, who placed a large order with her. The year was 1928, and so began her ascent of the Olympus of Parisian haute couture. One of her great contributions was the introduction of an "Egyptian" style along with the pagoda sleeve, the fundamental silhouette for the postwar "New Look." In 1935 she opened a boutique in the Place Vendôme and before long her clientele included famous names such as Mrs. Wallis Simpson, the Duchess of Windsor.

Her clothes emanated outrageous style, irony, and provocation, all of which distinguished her from her rival, Chanel. Schiaparelli did not want to give women style or elegance—she believed that they already possessed these attributes. Rather, she wanted to attract attention, and to this end she found the Surrealists' ideas to be inspirational. Schiaparelli was acquainted with some of the most important artists of her time, including Salvador Dalí (1904–89), Jean Cocteau (1889–1963) and Man Ray (1890–1977). She found inspiration in their imagery, and her collaborations with them resulted in her famous "Circus" and "Musical Instruments" collections, which used these themes as leitmotifs for the decoration of fabrics and accessories. Some of her more unforgettable items included the "Rococo Mirror Jacket" from 1939, inspired by the paintings of René Magritte (1898–1947), and a jacket she created with Cocteau in 1937, featuring an embroidered hand sensually squeezing the waist. But her most rewarding partnership was the one she had with Dalí. It was Dalí who had the idea for the famous 1937 "Shoe Hat" as well as the subsequent "Hen" and "Squid" hats. They also designed the famous "Lobster Dress" worn by Mrs. Simpson—an extremely elegant dress of white organza from which projected a large red lobster. Everything was meant to be amusing, such as the "Bug" necklace (1937–38), or shocking, such as the "shocking pink" color that would also lend its name to her perfume, Shocking, in 1937. The shape of the small perfume bottle was a reproduction of Mae West's perfect hourglass figure.

Schiaparelli reigned supreme in the world of fashion for a quarter of a century. By mixing art with fashion, she expanded the possibilities of women's choices in clothing. Then, in the 1940s, her star faded, and during World War II she moved back to New York where, in 1949, she opened a boutique. In 1954 she held her last fashion show and then retired. In her autobiography (published in 1954) she gave credence to Chanel's statement: "Dress designing … is to me not a profession but an art."

Andrea Affaticati

01

03

ELSA SCHIAPARELLI

"HER ESTABLISHMENT IN THE PLACE VENDÔME IS
A DEVIL'S LABORATORY. WOMEN WHO GO IN THERE
FALL INTO A TRAP, AND COME OUT MASKED ..."
(JEAN COCTEAU, *HARPER'S BAZAAR*, APRIL 1937)

04
05

01

STIRRUP PANTS, WEDGE HEELS, WEDGE-SHAPED GORES AND INSETS;
V-SHAPED BACK DÉCOLLETAGE, THE TORSO AS A TRIANGLE; COLLARS,
CAPES, CAPE COLLARS, EPAULET-
TES, WING-LIKE ELEMENTS ...

WEDGE AND TRIANGLE

In the 1930s the triangle seemed to be the dominant geometric shape in fashion design. Stirrup pants and wedge heels hit the market at the same time, and both were complete innovations in fashion design. The emphasized shoulder—at first with decorations, then later with shoulder-wide collars, ruffles, flounces, ingenious wrap-tops, and ruffled sleeves—was combined with a narrow waist which shaped the female torso into an inverted triangle.

The deep *V*-shaped back décolletage also presented a triangle of bare skin. The end of the decade saw yet another triangular form, this time in the cut of skirts—short, narrow across the hips, and flared. The famous dress designed by Hollywood couturier Adrian—for Joan Crawford in her title role in *Letty Lynton* (1932)—was copied millionfold, and it is considered to be the catalyst for the emphasis on shoulders which ultimately led to shoulder pads for women. Elsa Schiaparelli's pagoda shoulders of 1933 were similarly influential; her dresses and coats, inspired by the uniforms of British Guardsmen, featured broad shoulders as early as 1931.

"Broad shoulders and narrow hips are emphasized ever more strongly, and one can safely predict that this style won't reach its peak any time soon because ideas for this silhouette still abound. Everything is worked around the shoulders: jackets, coats, dresses, and blouses. Epaulettes, tabs, and rolls are used with amusing inventiveness. Afternoon dresses in soft silky satin are more draped, soft, yet wide collars flow over the shoulders, sometimes looped and other times ending in points," reported the women's magazine *Die Dame* in 1930.

Inset fabric sections—to add width in elegant bias-cut dresses—included flares, also referred to as false or fan pleats, and triangular insets. Stirrup pants—ski pants with legs tapering to the ankle and kept taut by means of a strip of fabric or elastic passed underneath the foot—first surfaced in 1936 at the Winter Olympics in Germany. They were originally made of gabardine with a loose cut around the hips, and a far cry from the Lastex pants, the "Bogners," of the 1950s.

In the same year, 1936, Salvatore Ferragamo invented the high-wedged heel, which was sometimes hollowed out, when used for elegant shoes, and often made of raffia or cork. The wedge heel was to remain in fashion for the next decade. During World War II, it was usually manufactured in cork or plain wood without leather covering, and even the newly invented Plexiglas was used for heels.

Gerda Buxbaum

02

03

228

01 Salvatore Ferragamo with distinguished customers' lasts ••• 02 Salvatore Ferragamo with Audrey Hepburn ••• 03 Salvatore Ferragamo, sandal with platform sole and heel covered with colored suede, 1938 ••• 04 Salvatore Ferragamo, concave wedge heel, 1947 ••• 05 Salvatore Ferragamo, slipper, iridescent silk taffeta embroidered with Swarovski silver crystals designed for the film *Ever After, A Cinderella Story*, directed by Andi Tennant, 1998 ••• 06 Salvatore Ferragamo, "Calypso" sling-back sandal, 1955

SALVATORE FERRAGAMO

01

SALVATORE FERRAGAMO

1898	Born on June 6 in Bonito near Naples, Italy
1914	Moves to the United States; works for the American Film Company: cowboy boots, Cinderella's shoe
1922	Makes shoes for Hollywood stars
1927	Founds a factory in Florence with 100 shoemakers
1929	Declares bankruptcy due to the stock market crash
1930	Strappy sandals with a pyramidal heel
1935	Wedge heels
1936	Patent for cork-soled shoe; shoe of plaited straw
1938	Wedge heeled, platform shoe with brightly colored layers
1947	Wedge heels with a concave curve; Neiman Marcus Award
1955	Steel-reinforced stiletto heels for Marilyn Monroe
1960	Dies on August 7 in Fiumetto, Italy; his wife Wanda takes over as director of women's accessories
From 1967	Daughter Giovanna designs women's prêt-à-porter
From 1968	Handbags
1985	*I protagonisti della moda. Salvatore Ferragamo*, retrospective in the Palazzo Strozzi, Florence
From 1991	Women's prêt-à-porter designed by Steven Slowik
1994	600,000 scarves and ties worldwide
1996	Takeover of the Emanuel Ungaro fashion house
1997	Joint venture with Bulgari regarding perfumes and cosmetic products; shoes for the film *Evita* (based on original shoe design for Evita Perón)
1998	Marco de Micheli becomes chief designer for women's prêt-à-porter
Perfumes	F. de Ferragamo (1973), Monsieur F. (1975), Ferragamo pour Femme (1998)

Salvatore Ferragamo, the "Michelangelo of Shoe Designers" and the "Shoemaker to the Stars," was born in a village near Naples to an extremely poor family for whom shoes were a luxury only for holidays. While still a child, he exhibited an unusual passion for creating footwear. At the age of nine he designed his first shoes, and, following an apprenticeship at twelve, opened his first workshop in Bonito. In 1914 he immigrated to Boston in order to gain experience in machine production methods. As it turned out, however, his talent for handcrafted work was unsuitable for assembly line methods. He later moved to California, where, with two other brothers, he opened a shoe repair shop in Santa Barbara and began to collaborate with Hollywood film studios.

Ferragamo's fame grew rapidly, and within a short time he opened a custom shoe shop in Hollywood, which was frequented by Rudolph Valentino, Mary Pickford, Douglas Fairbanks, Joan Crawford, and Gloria Swanson. He enrolled at the University of California Los Angeles and studied anatomy. With the newly acquired knowledge from his studies, he developed a revolutionary concept that resulted in shoes that were extraordinarily comfortable as well as original and attractive. His success continued and his international clientele grew. He realized that he required highly skilled craftsmen to execute his designs and the highest quality of materials available, but these workers could only be found in Italy, where he returned in 1927. He moved to Florence, where he opened his first shop in Europe.

Following the 1929 crash on Wall Street, combined with some of his shop's own financial mismanagement, a crisis arose which lead Ferragamo to focus on the domestic market. During this period it was also difficult to find high quality materials, so he invented new ones. Tireless research led him to utilize simple materials: he invented "orthopedic wedges" from cork and used transparent paper (the type for wrapping chocolates) with raffia to create "invisible," revolutionary sandals—all became extremely fashionable. His famous clients included Greta Garbo, Evita Perón, the Duchess of Windsor, Queen Maria José, and Imelda Marcos. In 1938 he acquired the Palazzo Feroni-Spini, which became, and still is, the Ferragamo company headquarters.

By 1950 Ferragamo's company had 700 employees and created 350 pairs of shoes a day. The expansion of the market made it necessary to turn to machine production, but all items were, and still are, finished by hand. In 1960, following Ferragamo's death, his wife and children took over the company, which they still manage. The range of products has expanded from shoes to include handbags, scarves, and fur, as well as menswear and women's wear collections. *Gerda Buxbaum*

03

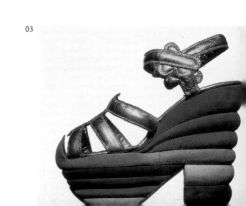

"I AM BLESSED OR CURSED, DEPENDING ON HOW YOU LOOK AT IT, WITH AN INCURABLY RESTLESS SPIRIT AND THE ABILITY TO WORK HARD." (SALVATORE FERRAGAMO)

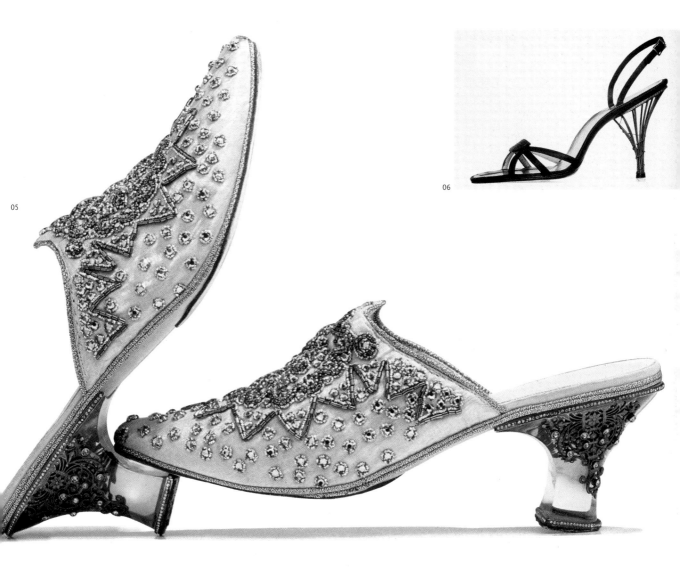

05

06

04

"PLEATS DON'T EXPOSE THE BODY. INSTEAD THEY WRAP IT IN THE DRAPERIES OF
ANTIQUITY ... GREEK AND ROMAN SCULPTURES COME TO LIFE, RECAPTURING AN
EASE OF MOVEMENT."
(BARBARA VINKEN, 1993)

FOLDED, DRAPED, AND GATHERED

01
02

In 1940 the German magazine *Elegante Welt* stated: "Pleated garments have a special charm when they do not fall in straight lines but—in addition to the pleating—are also draped. That means the pleated parts should be laid diagonally over one another, wrapped, puffed, knotted ..." Gathered bodices, a classical fall of folds on skirts, and draped turbans as sculptures made from fabric were the specialty of Madame Grès (1899–1993), who had actually wanted to be a sculptor. In 1931 she opened Maison Alix (from 1939 known as Grès) in Paris and draped her jersey designs directly onto the body of a model or even the client herself; the aim being to keep the number of seams to the absolute minimum.

She was a mistress of draping and gathering. Her garments—usually white—were like the robes of Greek caryatids and were given a modern character by emphasizing the body. Gathered fabric was wound around the body like a snake, and arrangements of folds fell freely down the back. Despite the fluid fall, the gathers were precisely fixed in place with fabric tape so that nothing could slip un-intentionally. Only after 1945 did Madame Grès mount her drapings on silk undergarments. The originals were impossible to copy: usually she used silk jersey, two-meters wide, and sometimes needed up to twenty running meters per gown.

Jean Dessès (1904–70), a Greek brought up in Egypt, opened his own *maison de couture* in Paris in 1937. His unmistakable hand was expressed in complicated chiffon evening gowns; most famous were his dresses of chiffon and silk muslin, which were closely draped on the body. For many designs he used fabrics with gradated color nuances, and he loved soft, powdery colors.

The famous "Delphos" gown by Mariano Fortuny appeared as early as 1907. The Ionian chiton (the basic garment of ancient Greece, usually worn knee-length by men and full-length by women) served as its inspiration, but it was also inspired by the Rational Dress movements of the time. Fortuny did not rely on the accidental drapings of antiquity but created finely pleated garments that required nearly four times the average width of material. Over the following forty years he designed countless variations in thin silk *pongé* or silk satin. The Delphos gown always brushed the ground and gave its female wearer the appearance of a statue rising, flower-like, from the floor. As the pleated fabrics were highly elastic, Fortuny weighted down the hem with hand-blown Murano glass beads affixed to silk cords; these sometimes also replaced shoulder or side seams. Today, there is still disagreement about his famous pleating technique, which he applied not just vertically but also in a secondary, sometimes horizontal, crimping. The brilliant palette of the delicate silk dresses (which weighed about 150 grams each and were stored twisted up like a skein of wool) was produced by repeated dippings in different color baths, thereby achieving an enchanting translucent coloration which seems to change with every alteration in light and every movement of the wearer. *Gerda Buxbaum*

04
05

06

"MR. JAMES IS MADLY IN LOVE WITH CUT ..." (MAINBOCHER)

CHARLES JAMES

01
02

03

British by birth but of American extraction, Charles James is regarded as America's first and most respected designer to work in the haute couture tradition. He spent nearly one-third of his career outside of the United States; during the first decade of his career, in the 1930s, he worked primarily in London, but also in New York, Chicago, and briefly in Paris. His designs are often compared to those of Cristobal Balenciaga, who admirably described James as the "world's best and only dressmaker," responsible for elevating the trade from an applied to a pure art form. A driven man and an extreme perfectionist, James created only about a thousand designs, and it is his exquisite ball gowns for which he is best remembered. Many of his creations were not just designed and constructed, they were engineered. This may be explained by his initial work as a milliner, when he sculpted headwear.

Early on James developed a fascination for mass production. Never a businessman himself, he achieved critical, if not financial success, due to partnerships with various manufacturers. Always demanding the very best materials, however, James found it difficult to accept the cost-cutting steps necessary for mass-produced garments, as these inevitably diminished the overall quality and complexity of his original designs. His most successful association was with Alexis, a producer of infant's garments, while the most important collaboration of his career was with William Popper, a coat and suit manufacturer who managed to tailor the essence of Jamesian cut and color into ready-to-wear garments. The most fraught arrangement, and the one that permanently crippled his career, was with dressmaker Samuel Winston; James accused Winston and his employees of unauthorized adaptations of his designs, and they claimed he did not fulfill his contractual quotas.

Throughout his career James reworked his design models, varying their appearance with certain compositional elements: lobe shapes, intriguing solutions for setting sleeves, subtle adaptations of geometric forms, linings of unexpected brilliance, a predominance of patternless fabrics, and either an exorbitant number of pattern pieces or the bear minimum. His preference for fabric without decorative prints allowed his bravado of cut to be more readily understood, since patterned fabric camouflages seam lines.

Over three decades, James produced different versions of his "Ribbon" dress, famous for its skirt that boasted a multitude of tapered panels. In the mid-1930s, he wrapped the torso in a single piece of cloth, with the exception of an elasticizing diamond at the center-back waistline—creating one of the most dramatic halter-top gowns. He so complexly structured the lobes and layers of his iconic "Cloverleaf" or "Abstract" gown (1953) that, characteristically, it was not ready for the intended event. A careful inspection of his down-filled jacket design, which Salvador Dalí called the first soft sculpture, reveals James's indecision about where the defining stitch lines should fall. More than in the garments of other designers, telltale stitching—a mark of refinement—signifies the work of Charles James.

Elizabeth Ann Coleman

CHARLES JAMES

1906	Born on July 18 in Camberley, Great Britain
1926	Opens millinery under the name Charles Boucheron
1929	Founds fashion house E. Haweis in London
1933	Founds second fashion house in London; designs extravagant evening gowns with sophisticated necklines, sometimes working for years on one gown
1937	Designs down-lined evening jackets made of white silk satin; creates a new, soft silhouette
1940	Founds fashion house in New York; designs for Elizabeth Arden First Floor; customizes manufacture of evening dresses; clients include New York fashion maven Diana Vreeland
1978	Dies impoverished and in obscurity on September 23 in New York; his life's work comprises no more models than produced by a large couture house in a single season

05

04

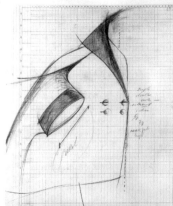

MODISH MAKESHIFT

01
02

The worldwide rationing of textiles imposed in 1940 led many countries to develop economical measures which in turn bolstered creativity and ingenuity. Many fashion houses invented so-called phantom fashions which turned out to be quite fashionable after all. All kinds of substitute fabrics were used, such as fish-skins for blouses, jackets, and belts, or synthetics for shoes and galoshes, and rope, cork, and wood for soles. In 1941 a designer collection was marketed for the British Utility scheme which defined and rationed the use of fabrics and dyes. In the United States, a textile-procuring system called "L-85" was introduced in 1943, and, according to the "L-217" system, leather for ladies' shoes was available in six colors only.

Shortly before the German occupation, Parisian couturiers presented fashions with suggestive titles such as "False Alarm" and "Attack"; these featured a silk blouse, a long woolen skirt, a jacket with silk lapels, and a gas mask in its bag. Pierre Balmain designed an "Occupation" evening gown and an "Underground" dress, while Mainbocher (1891–1976) created the U.S. Navy and Red Cross uniforms for women. Inspired by the traditional saying "old dress, new hat," many women made their own hats and soon began to wear huge paper hats (newsprint was not rationed) or tiny hats made of trim or tulle remnants. In 1942 these were replaced by turbans fashioned from veiling, ribbons, and other less-restricted materials. Hats that looked like large hankies hanging out of small, round boxes were called dusters. Milliners were obliged to design hats that would stay firmly on the head, without the use of elastic, and berets came back into fashion. When even straw was no longer available, crocheted headwear—hairnets and snoods, for instance—replaced straw hats.

Canvas, curtains, and terrycloth were used for sportswear, and coats left behind by the men away at war was also reused. Everybody knitted and people made use of whatever materials came into their hands. One invention was the so-called peasant skirt, a patchwork skirt made from squares of printed fabric and ribbons that had been sewn together. Practically everything was used in the end. As one German women's magazine reported: "A man's suit no longer in top condition was transformed into an attractive tailored suit, while a black riding habit became a black daytime suit. A lady's suit, past its prime, was turned into a coat-dress with velvet collar and pockets, and, finally, an evening dress was fashioned into an afternoon dress delicately trimmed in lace."

Even in these difficult times, the magazines tried to make fashion palatable to women: "Every fashion-conscious woman takes pleasure in transformation—a seductive game of using her clothes to hide or to reveal. Ration-cards have made this game more difficult for women, but surely that's no reason to give up! Our pattern for the truly fashionable basic dress offers many different options of transformation, even though the pattern is restrained in cut and color!"   *Gerda Buxbaum*

"WHAT THE 'UTILITY SUIT' OF ENGLAND, THE 'VICTORY SUIT' OF AMERICA, AND 'EVERYMAN'S CLOTHING' OF GERMANY HAD IN COMMON WAS THEIR ECONOMIC USE OF FABRIC AND SIMPLICITY OF DESIGN." (GERDA BUXBAUM, 1999)

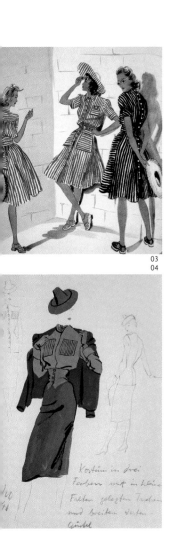

03
04

05

01

HOLLYWOOD SETS THE TRENDS

The tremendous influence that female movie stars—as arbiters and icons of style—once had on fashion for the masses is barely conceivable to us today. Today's stars tend to follow existing trends as they change their *looks* with every public appearance, whether a party in Versace, an opening in Gucci, or the Oscars in Dior. During the 1930s and 1940s, Hollywood's "Golden Age," movie stars set the trends: Marlene Dietrich as a female Don Juan in a made-to-measure suit and shirt with cufflinks; Jean Harlow as a fallen angel in white satin that flowed over her body like oil; Joan Crawford as a self-reliant woman in a broad-shouldered, tailored suit. These actresses, and others, became models for millions of women who, before *Vogue* and *Harper's Bazaar* were widely circulated, drew their fashion sense from the silver screen.

In 1932, within just a few days, the New York department store Macy's sold 500,000 copies of a white dress with gigantic, flounced sleeves worn by twenty-six-year-old Joan Crawford in *Letty Lynton* (1932). The designer of the original dress was Adrian, and his lavish yet refined creations had already established Greta Garbo and Jean Harlow as glamour goddesses. He understood the psychology of his trade: "You must never put costume jewelry or imitation lace on Garbo," he said. "Not that it would be noticed on the screen, but it would do something to Garbo and her performance."

As employees of MGM, Paramount Pictures, or Warner Brothers, designers such as Adrian, Travis Banton (1894–1958), Howard Greer (1886–1974), Walter Orry-Kelly (1897–1964), or Edith Head (1907–81) were not couturiers in the European sense; rather, they were art directors of femininity. Their designs illustrated the personas which the studio bosses and directors had created for their stars and to which the stars themselves, aided by cosmetic surgeons, diet gurus, and make-up specialists, actively contributed. "I dress for the image," Marlene Dietrich revealed to a reporter. "Not for myself, not for the public, not for fashion, not for men. The image? A conglomeration of all the parts I have ever played."

Regardless of Dietrich's past history in Berlin, Garbo's stubbornness, or Crawford's obsessive perfectionism, Hollywood's costume artists celebrated them in tweed or chiffon and with a precision of line or romantic opulence. Every detail was calculated, and physical imperfections were expertly disguised. In order to lengthen, optically, Norma Shearer's short legs, Adrian raised the waist of all her dresses. Turbans were prescribed for Gloria Swanson—whose private wardrobe included 300 dresses and suits as well as 100 pairs of shoes—in order to hide her oversized head and large ears.

The aim was more than mere beauty. Hollywood costumes enhanced a star's natural attributes—up to the point where she became her own image. The desired effect was a total fusion of person and look. "Her costumes always looked as though they really did belong to her," Edith Head wrote about Carole Lombard, whom she dressed at Paramount. Half a century later, fashion designers such as Giorgio Armani, Ralph Lauren, and Jil Sander adapted this principle for every woman and gave it a name: personal style.

Margit J. Mayer

02
03

COSTUME JEWELRY

01

From 1940 to 1950, American culture became the dominate influence in Europe. New York became the world's art center and Hollywood—with its movies and its stars—determined the direction of fashion, replacing Paris, which until then had been the capital of female elegance. Female viewers of Hollywood films wanted copies of the original clothing and jewelry worn by their favorite stars, believing that they would feel as fascinating and as sought after as their heroines. This desire for beauty and glamour was satisfied by the mass production of ready-to-wear clothing and accessories, available from the 1920s and continually expanding during the 1930s and 1940s. Mechanization allowed department stores to offer, year round, up-to-date clothing and accessories at affordable prices. Fashion, thus removed from the elitist world to which it had once belonged, was put within the reach of average women: they wore mass-produced styles taken, first, from the movies then, after 1939, from television. This interest in fashion was reinforced by the proliferation of major women's magazines and mail-order catalogues, which catered to the entire social spectrum. Finally, the thriving war industry that emerged with the outbreak of World War II employed female workers, who, in turn, became fashion consumers in a climate of unexpected, and of utterly new, prosperity.

During the war years, rationing of fabric compelled women to wear short dresses, which were often made from different materials; fabric saving strategies were evident in the cuffs and collars which were almost always white. Women also wore jackets and pants, which became the preferred uniform of many female factory workers. Precious metals were also rationed, and only costume jewelry was available on the market, for rich and poor alike. To embellish the severe, unadorned look of their clothing—and also to satisfy the desire for diversion that characterized these harsh times—women resorted to costume jewelry. It could be playful and ironic or gaudy and beaded, and could have rounded shapes or vivid gilding that, juxtaposed with brilliantly colored stones, could bring out the individual personality of the wearer. Costume jewelry during the war years thus had the double function of serving as a frivolous, amusing, new complement for clothing and also acting as a replacement to real jewels, which had always been a sign of wealth and prestige. It is no wonder then that during these years costume jewelry offered a heretofore unseen variety of designs, materials, and technical solutions, which were the highest expression of American style and culture. Patriotic pins (flags, "V" for victory signs, eagles as a symbol of American power, anchors) coexisted with sentimental designs of hearts, clasped hands, flowers in bloom, and arrows sending forth messages of love. After the war, costume jewelry's popularity continued to grow, and, in 1946, sales were estimated at approximately 200 million dollars. Women celebrated the return of peace and serenity by adorning themselves with cascades of costume jewelry. They were ready to resume their role as companions, mothers, and key figures in a world of luxury and elegance that, once again, came to New York via Paris in 1947—in the form of the "New Look."

Deanna Farneti Cera

02

03

"IN FACT COSTUME JEWELRY, AN EPHEMERAL AND AFFORDABLE ACCESSORY, RATHER THAN
A SYMBOL OF INTRINSIC VALUE, IS MORE CONSISTENT WITH THE AMERICAN LIFESTYLE.
NOT BY CHANCE IS COSTUME JEWELRY A TYPICAL EXPRESSION OF POPULAR CULTURE."
(DEANNA FARNETI CERA, 1991)

05
06

01

02

CLAIRE McCARDELL

One of the most revered names in American fashion is Claire McCardell. A native of rural Frederick, Maryland, McCardell moved to New York City, where she remained throughout her career, to study at Parsons School of Design. Her clothes quickly became synonymous with casualness in dress. Although her career began in the 1930s, many of McCardell's most famous designs answered the restrictions of wartime clothing production in such inventive ways that they became classics in fashion design.

A striking model of her own designs, neither McCardell nor her garments projected the image of New York sophistication, although her clothes came to be associated with the most sophisticated of New York's fashion elite. For her, the gingham and calico fabrics of the countryside were perfect for comfortable city clothing. Her collaboration with the manufacturer Townley in 1931 brought about a new interpretation of the "cotton frock." McCardellites—those who fill their wardrobes with her designs—are rarely willingly to part with these now vintage clothes. Age has nothing to do with it, only the memory of comfort in an age of formality.

Trained as a sportswear designer, McCardell, and her like-minded contemporaries, established New York City's Seventh Avenue as the epicenter of American fashion. Her materials of choice, many provided by the mills associated with Galey and Lord, were cotton calico and wool jersey. She liked simple, direct design. In the 1930s she created garments without traditional, structural elements. A particularly popular one, later known as the "Monastic" dress, took on form when simply belted at the waist. It was this, as well as other loosely fitted dress designs, that helped establish her as one of the initiators of the "American" look. Her garments were detailed with little brass hooks and other hardware closures, such as "spaghetti" or "shoestring" ties, double outline stitching, and big pockets. Many of these details are to be found in her famous "Popover" dress, which was introduced in 1942 and became a basic in all of her design collections. Interestingly, her inspiration for the Popover dress was the humble, American, cotton housedress.

Other McCardell icons are her diaper-draped bathing suits and nineteenth-century inspired "chemise" or "baby" dresses. Her designs could take any woman from the ski slopes to the seashore, from the supermarket to the star-studded gala. Witty prints, simple plaids, and sturdy things were what she favored, and to which she occasionally added a foray of exotic fabrics like Thai silk. With all of her designs, McCardell enjoyed experimenting with pattern, cut, and texture—but on a minimal level. Complicated cuts were not for her garments; she preferred to work with simple rectangles and triangles. If she felt that a button's front side was too shiny, she would have it sewn on backwards.

Elizabeth Ann Coleman

"CLAIRE COULD TAKE FIVE DOLLARS' WORTH OF COMMON COTTON CALICO AND TURN OUT A DRESS THAT A SMART WOMAN COULD WEAR ANYWHERE." (NORMAN NORELL)

CLAIRE McCARDELL

1905	Born on May 24 in Frederick, Maryland, United States
1926–29	Studies at Parson's School of Design in New York and in Paris
1929–32	Works as assistant to Robert Turk; becomes designer for the Townley Frocks company
1934	Designs combination fashions for Townley Frocks
1938	"Monastic" dress: an unlined, straight-cut dress; harem trousers; gymnastics outfits
1942	"Popover" dress; beach "Playsuit" with bloomer legs
1943	"Diaper" (wraparound) bathing and beach suit, a forerunner of the modern bodysuit; leotards: skintight, full-length, jersey bodysuits worn under long skirts; receives the Coty American Fashion Critics Award
1944	Makes Capezio ballet slippers fashionable under the name "Ballerinas"
1948	Receives the Neiman Marcus Award
1958	Dies on March 22 in New York

03
04

"I CANNOT DETERMINE WHAT TO DO ABOUT MY NEW GOWN; I WISH SUCH THINGS WERE TO BE BOUGHT READY-MADE." (JANE AUSTEN, 1798)

01

For millennia, clothing the human body had been an arduous and time-consuming process, involving not only innumerable hours of handwork but also numerous steps and decisions in the acquisition of the necessary materials, devising of the style, and overseeing the fit. Not everyone had the skill, inclination towards, or, most importantly, the time required for the creation of clothing. In 1798 the British writer Jane Austen wrote to a correspondent: "I cannot determine what to do about my new Gown; I wish such things were to be bought ready-made."

As the nineteenth century progressed, many elements conspired to make Jane Austen's wish come true. Faster than fashions could change came new machines for sewing, cutting, weaving, and embroidering. The first customers of ready-to-wear clothing were men whose wardrobes of separate pieces—such as a coat, vest, shirt, and pants—adapted far more easily to mass production than did the elaborate dresses affected by women. However, by the middle of the century, women could purchase, from a store or through mail order, items that did not require a close fit, such as cloaks and morning robes (housedresses). The quality of these first ready-to-wear items could be superb. By the end of the century, it was possible to obtain a catalogue from a New York department store, and elsewhere, and order ready-made clothing for men, women, and children—anything from dozens of different kinds of underwear to the most lavish or utilitarian wraps and coats. While these clothes could never be mistaken for custom-made or couture garments, they were marvels of the art of the machine age: rows of garments with crisp, uniform stitching, clean lines, and sturdy fabrics.

During the mid-nineteenth century, at the same time that New York City was developing into what would be the largest and most vital center for mass-manufactured, off-the-peg clothing, a new attitude towards how the most elite clothes were made was turning Paris into the center of haute couture. By the beginning of the twentieth century, it was commonly believed that fashion originated from the luxuriously artistic couture houses of Paris, and that ready-to-wear manufacturers watered down such creations. That an original, influential idea could come from a ready-to-wear designer, as happened in 1938 when Claire McCardell's "Monastic" dress became a runaway success, was a radical notion.

After World War II, Paris couturiers began to reconsider their former attitudes towards ready-to-wear. The first designers to experiment with prêt-à-porter looked to American manufacturers for machinery, instruction, and skilled labor. Such pioneer lines as Christian Dior–New York and Jacques Fath for Joseph Halpert, both from 1948, were based on the idea that there was a great appetite for cheaper versions of haute couture designs. The next wave of prêt-à-porter designs, aimed at a youthful market, meant avant-garde designs at affordable prices.

At the end of the twentieth century, the situation has come full circle: while the haute couture industry struggles to maintain an identity that is forward-looking, pertinent, and creative, the most influential designers are international, working within the confines of prêt-à-porter to push the boundaries of design. *Caroline Rennolds Milbank*

02

READY-TO-WEAR

04
05

"THEY STARVED FOR LUXURY. HE GAVE THEM PLENTY."
(DIANA VREELAND)

CHRISTIAN DIOR

01
02

The showpiece of Christian Dior's debut collection presented on February 12, 1947, was the Corolle line. The collection revealed an entirely new image for women, one that was slim-waisted with a pronounced, high bust, round, neat shoulders, and full-blown hips. "We are just coming out of a period of war, of uniforms and of military females as sturdily built as boxers.... I have designed flower-women," recorded Dior in his memoirs. Dior was to dress this new, curvaceous female body in luxurious finery and abundant fabrics. In a bold theatrical move, the hemlines of his skirts, whether full or straight, were dropped by nine inches. This dramatic gesture transformed the hemline into *the* barometer of fashion. Carmel Snow—the powerful editor-in-chief of *Harper's Bazaar*—was to exclaim: "Dear Christian, your dresses have such a new look." Thus a name was bestowed on this elegant, graceful, decorative, and ornamental femininity. In a matter of months, this fashion, dubbed the "New Look," had achieved worldwide popularity.

Inspired by the toilettes of the Second Empire, Dior used fabrics lined predominantly with percale, boned, bustier-style bodices, hip padding, wasp-waisted corsets, and petticoats that made his dresses flare out from the waist. He reverted to some of the structural tricks of the corset trade, which had fallen out of favor with the arrival of the century's foremost couturiers of free-and-easy women's wear, Paul Poiret and Coco Chanel. The renaissance had been underway well before Dior and could be seen in the "hourglass" figure acclaimed by American *Vogue* in 1939 and in Marcel Rochas's bustier dresses (1949) and waist-cincher, the *guêpière* (from 1945). In the postwar climate of frustrated desires and expectations, the New Look was as dazzling as a dream and made everyone forget the mundanity of their everyday lives. Dior's liberal use of material (twenty yards for the famous "Bar"-pleated skirt), choice of substantial close-weave fabrics (satins, taffetas, ottomans, and velvets, all of which were in marked contrast to the flimsy ersatz wartime materials), opulent embroidery, and unrestrained "couture detailing" (full drapery, gathers, bows, gores, and tucks) all freed the imagination from years of constraint and restriction.

Such overt lavishness did not go without opposition. A Dior model was harassed by housewives on the Rue Lepic in Paris, English tailors protested against the length of his skirts, and, in 1947, during Dior's visit to the United States, hostile banners were waved by the "Little Below the Knee Club." However, in 1948, as wartime shortages drew to an end, the New Look emerged victorious. The style history of the House of Dior ended in 1956 with the onset of the shirtwaisted *H*-line. Its influence, however, persisted well beyond the early 1950s, particularly in Brigitte Bardot's pink Vichy wedding dress of 1958. Dior's luxurious, elegant, and sculptured structures influenced decades of designers and secured the continuation of the House of Dior.   *Farid Chenoune*

CHRISTIAN DIOR

1905	Born on January 21 in Granville, France
1920–25	Studies at the École des Sciences Politiques, Paris
1928	Opens a small art gallery in Paris
1931	Produces hat sketches for the milliner Agnès and fashion illustrations for *Le Figaro Illustré*
1938	Designs with Robert Piguet
1942	Joins Lucien Lelong's design team
1945	Designs for Marcel Boussac's fashion house
1947	Presents first collection, Corolle line, which U.S. journalists hail as the "New Look"
1949	Founds Christian Dior New York Inc.; first license for nylon stockings
1950	Presents Vertical and Oblique lines
1951	Sets up diffusion department to market the Dior label internationally; presents "Oval" and "Longue" collections
1953	Founds Dior Delman for custom-made shoes after designs by Roger Vivier
1954	Lily-of-the-Valley line (with white as the preferred color)
1955	Founds Christian Dior London Ltd; Bijoux Dior fashion jewelry; A-line and Y-line designs
1956	Arrow, Aimant, and H lines
1957	Libre line based on the *vareuses* (fishermen-type smocks); dies on October 23 in Montecatini Terme, Italy; Yves Saint Laurent takes over as artistic director
1961	Marc Bohan made artistic director
1970–80	Christian Dior Monsieur line
1989	Gianfranco Ferré made artistic director
FROM 1997	John Galliano chief designer
PERFUMES	Miss Dior (1957), Diorling (1963), Eau Sauvage (1966), Dior Dior (1976), Jules (1980), Poison (1985), Dune, Fahrenheit, Dolce Vita (1995)

05

04

"THEY MAKE ROLLS ROYCES VERY CHIC YOU KNOW, BUT STABLE, UNMOVING ... HAUTE COUTURE CLOTHES ARE BEAUTIFUL, BUT YOU SEE THE BEAUTY OF THE CLOTHES, NOT THE BEAUTY OF THE BODY." (EMMANUELLE KHANH, 1964)

01
02

HAUTE COUTURE

In 1945 and 1946, the confederation of the French fashion industry, the Chambre syndicale de la couture parisienne, organized a traveling show, the "Theatre of Fashion," to be held in Paris, Barcelona, London, Copenhagen, Stockholm, Vienna, Rio de Janeiro, New York, and San Francisco. Its purpose was to draw back to Paris the international clientele that had so benefited haute couture prior to 1939 and World War II, thus returning it to its status as the capital of high fashion.

The decor was designed by Christian Bérard (1902–49) and Jean Cocteau, among others, and the most important houses presented their daywear collections on miniature wire dress models, a demonstration of fantasy and imagination which was to meet with notable success. With the triumph of Christian Dior's 1947 New Look, Paris' recovery was assured. By the early 1950s, two-thirds of the turnover of Parisian haute couture—a handcraft industry that guaranteed luxury, elegance, and exclusive creations—was generated abroad by dint of trade clients such as department stores and off-the-peg manufacturers, primarily in the United States. Though a number of prewar couturiers such as Marcel Rochas (1896–1971, House established in 1925), Maggy Rouff (1896–1971, House established in 1929), and Jacques Heim (1899–1967, House established in 1931) remained active, an upcoming generation was also on the horizon. The new group included Jean Dessès (1904–70), with his embroidered ball gowns (1937), Madeleine Vramant (1942), Carven (born Carven de Tommaso, c. 1909), the "little woman's" couturière (1944), Antonio Canovas del Castillo (1908–84) who worked as Lanvin's modelist (1950–62), and Hubert de Givenchy, who was to use Audrey Hepburn as his style muse.

Along with Dior, the supreme practitioners of the New Look generation were Jacques Fath and Pierre Balmain. Each was to develop his own style based on the hourglass vogue of the time: close-fitted bust, tucked-in waist, rounded hips, unpadded shoulders, and a tapered or full, elongated skirt. Partly inspired by Belle Époque models, Fath accentuated these swelling curves almost to the point of eccentricity (poufs, the hobble, Stylo line) and co-opted those male accessories that he found "rascally" (wing collars, ties, a carnation in the buttonhole, etc.), embodying this impish spirit in his star model, Bettina—who owed him both her name and her short "gamine" haircut, a fashion Fath had relaunched in 1949. By contrast, Balmain's more sober "New French Style"—as Gertrude Stein and Alice B. Toklas called it—is readily identified by outfits inspired by the world of sport (wool pea-jackets and ski pants in 1946) then, during the "Jolie Madame" years (1952–57), by city-wear costumes with discreet tennis stripes and "little" cocktail dresses or evening and ceremonial gowns decorated with embroidery by Lesage, Rébé, or Defour. The dazzling renaissance of Parisian high fashion, of which these celebrated embroiderers formed an integral part, should not conceal the fact that a slow decline was under way: there were 106 fashion houses in 1946, sixty in 1952, thirty-six in 1958, and by 1967 there were only nineteen. *Farid Chenoune*

04
05

CRISTOBAL BALENCIAGA

CRISTOBAL BALENCIAGA

1895	Born on January 21 in Guetaria, Spain
1915	Opens a couture salon in San Sebastian
1920	Opens a salon in Madrid
1937	Moves to France; opens an haute couture house in Paris
1947	Makes women's suits in a new "Barrel" style
1954	Develops a narrow, straight "*I*-shaped" line, which influences other designers; Balenciaga models are sold only to an exclusive private clientele
1957	Invents Trapeze line for dresses
1958	Introduces the Empire line; designs the "Pillbox" hat
1963	Shows his legendary cape-jackets for the first time
1968	Closes his salon and retires in Spain; manufacture of Balenciaga scarves, purses, and perfumes continues
1972	Dies on March 24 in Valencia, Spain
1978	Balenciaga retrospective, Metropolitan Museum of Art, New York
1987	Michel Goma designs a new ready-to-wear line under the name Balenciaga
1991–97	Melchior Thimister designs the Balenciaga collections
1996	Balenciaga-Hommage-Collection with trademark styles
SINCE 1997	Nicolas Ghesquière designs the Balenciaga collections
PERFUMES	Le Dix (1947), Quadrille (1955), Ho Hang (1971), Cialenga, Eau de Balenciaga, Lavande (1973), Prélude (1982), Rumba (1988), Balenciaga pour Homme (1990)

Creator of some of the most powerful styles of the twentieth century, Cristobal Balenciaga has frequently been described as a prophet. How he pictured the female form and how he used that shape as a jumping-off point resulted in some of the most dramatic shifts in silhouette to follow Christian Dior's postwar New Look. When Balenciaga showed his breathtakingly waistless chemise or "Sack" dress—shocking for those accustomed to the corseted look of the 1950s—he did so out of a sense of conviction about proportion. Seemingly simple, yet wildly controversial at the time, the dress, or rather its silhouette, would flavor the coming decade.

His most memorable dress and cloak designs, especially for evening wear, are defined by such striking forms as a tiered wedding cake, a lampshade, or a balloon (bifurcated or not) and backs billowing like spinnakers. Balenciaga was not only a genius of shape but also a master colorist—tempering matte black with nutmeg brown, enlivening robin's egg blue with the cheeriest cerise, choosing yolk yellow, grass green, or bubblegum pink for the grandest of ball gowns. For fabric he repeatedly chose to work with the lightest, paper taffeta and textured and upholstery-weight wools, like faille and mohair. A signature for him, as well as for his protégé Hubert de Givenchy, was gazar, a feather-light yet substantial silk that made even his most sculptural dresses seem ephemeral.

While his most renowned designs are ball gowns, his truly influential styles were those for daywear. Many designers, Coco Chanel foremost among them, have worked to give women a uniform in which they could live, i.e. a suit, but Balenciaga constantly played with the idea of what constitutes a suit. While nothing he designed ever had an air of "casual Friday" about it, there was an insouciance to a suit made with a straight coolie jacket, a tunic, a capelet, a shawl, or, perhaps most well known, a fisherman's smock. With coats and dresses he often had a soft touch, cutting the former with liquid folds and making easy little one- and two-piece dresses gently sashed with a band of glove leather, rope of thick piping, or heavy satin ribbon tied in a bow. His tailored clothes often reveal unusual erogenous zones: the bones of the wrist poking out from bracelet length sleeves, the base of the neck framed by a shallow, curved, stand-away collar.

Balenciaga's clientele was comprised of some of the most distinguished people of his day, from social arbiters Pauline de Rothschild, Bunny Mellon, Mrs. Arturo Lopez-Willshaw, and the Duchess of Windsor, to people in the arts like Clare Booth Luce, Rosamund Bernier, Diana Vreeland, Anita Loos, Inge Morath, and even Yul Brynner (photographed by *Vogue* in 1969 wearing pants made for him by Balenciaga). The fashion photographer Cecil Beaton, a friend of Balenciaga's, wrote in his diary (published as *Self-Portrait with Friends*, 1979) that Balenciaga's clothes were so particularly good because "they are the result of depth of thought, intense concentration, even physical suffering."

Caroline Rennolds Milbank

01
02

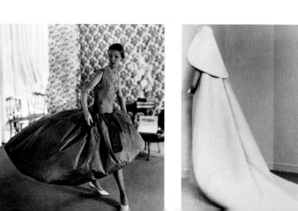

"ALMOST EVERY WOMAN, DIRECTLY OR INDIRECTLY, HAS WORN A BALENCIAGA."
(*HARPER'S BAZAAR*, 1940)

04

THE COCKTAIL DRESS

05

THE PERFECT DRESS FOR THE EVER POPULAR COCKTAIL PARTY.

No other garment is named after a drink; hardly any so closely related to a specific time of day nor, yet again, one so immediately associated with a particular sense of fashion history as the "cocktail dress." The thought of a cocktail dress instantly brings to mind a certain type of glass, a cherry or skewered olive, and a very specific social setting—and, from today's point of view, a very middle-class situation. The long years of deprivation during World War II brought forth a yearning for luxury and fashionable things, and women made a special effort to dress appropriately for every occasion; it was considered imperative that one's accessories matched perfectly.

The names of cocktail drinks such as "Shady Lady," "Pink Rose," or "Fallen Angel" evoke images of chiffon draped cleverly over the bosom, short bolero jackets, silk corsages, small feathered evening hats worn saucily over the face, and embroidered clutch bags that might hold, at the very most, a lipstick and handkerchief. Yet in the 1980s, when categories of clothing and their association with specific times of the day began to disappear, the concept of the cocktail dress became modern again. A jeans jacket worn with a Lurex skirt, or a metallic leather jacket worn with leggings, often took the place of conventional cocktail attire.

Mixed drinks—known as cocktails—were already popular in Europe in 1905, but the dress of the same name only came into existence around 1947. The elegant pajamas, formal dresses, and tea gowns of the 1930s may be regarded as its precursors, until an elegant, formal dress made from silk, velvet, or brocade, and about the same length as a day dress, started to be worn to cocktail parties as well as to festive occasions where a full, floor-length, evening gown was deemed inappropriate. The top was generally worked as a bodice hanging from thin spaghetti straps or, at the least, displayed a considerable décolleté. The youthful version had a bouncy, petticoat skirt, a tight bodice, and a wide bow of taffeta, sateen, *matelassé*, or, in summer, stiff cotton fabric such as piqué. Together with this attire, a young American woman would carry one of the newly manufactured, hard Lucite handbags.

In 1957 the cocktail dress was comprised of a balloon skirt with an accompanying short jacket or bolero. In general, women preferred a cocktail suit to a dress, made from either brocade or sophisticated black fabric embroidered with jet beading, and possibly trimmed in fur.

In the mid-1960s, this type of dress and the term were rejected as too conservative. But in the 1980s, it reemerged as an interim solution between sporty daywear and elegant evening fashions. In the mid-1990s, the cocktail dress underwent a revival with the rise of the nouveau riche. The dress was complemented by women's hair styled in French knots, dazzling brooches, small handbags, and sling-back pumps.

Gerda Buxbaum

06

"ELEGANCE IS FLUID. IT CONSISTS OF DESIRE AND KNOWLEDGE, GRACE, REFINEMENT, PERFECTION, AND DISTINCTION." (RENÉ GRUAU)

RENÉ GRUAU

RENÉ GRUAU

1909	Born Count Renato Zavagli-Ricciardelli delle Caminate on February 4 in Rimini, Italy
1923	Publishes first drawings at the age of fourteen
1924	Moves with his mother to Paris; decides to become a fashion designer
1935–39	Sells fashion drawings to the magazines *Fémina, Marie Claire, L'Officiel,* and *Le Magazine de Figaro*
1940	Settles in Lyon; works as a fashion designer for *Marie Claire*
1946	First collaborates with *International Textiles,* designs cover pages until 1984
1947	Meets Christian Dior; assumes artistic direction of advertising for Miss Dior perfume
1948–50	Moves to the United States; works initially as a fashion designer for *Vogue* and *Harper's Bazaar;* later works exclusively for *Flair*
1956–63	Designs costumes for various theaters; designs poster for the Moulin Rouge
1964–70	Works primarily in advertising
1980–97	Works as a fashion designer for various magazines and as an artistic consultant to major fashion houses such as Dior and Givenchy

René Gruau's name has been synonymous with exquisite refinement and seductive flair for the past fifty years. In the 1940s and 1950s he elevated the art of fashion illustration to a belle époque and became the favored artist of the haute couture world. Combining a free and expressive use of line with a classical sense of restraint, Gruau created subtle, sensual works of art that connoisseurs today compare to Toulouse-Lautrec (1864–1901) and Jules Chéret. His inkbrush drawing of a woman's face concealed by the flowing brim of a hat captivates the eye with its calligraphic simplicity—four brush-strokes—and most clearly exemplifies the distinctive characteristics of his work.

Gruau's life has been as glamorous as his art. He was born in Rimini in 1909 into a noble Italian family as Count Renato Zavagli-Ricciardelli delle Caminate. He began to sketch very early and published his first drawing when he was only fourteen years old. By the age of eighteen he was already publishing his fashion drawings in Italy, England, and Germany. In the early 1930s he and his French mother moved to her native Paris, where he took her family name, Gruau. For Gruau his mother would always remain the embodiment of social values: charm, elegance, and manners.

When Christian Dior opened his fashion house in 1947 and took the world by storm with his famous New Look, Gruau and Dior entered into a prolific working relationship. "I felt very close to the restless Christian Dior," the artist explains. "He used to discuss his ideas with me and I would show him my sketches. There was a bond between us that I have never encountered since." Gruau's classic style was a perfect complement to Dior's designs, and very soon Gruau became instrumental in developing the image not only for Dior's perfumes (notably Miss Dior) but also for many famous luxury products of the 1950s including "Rouge Baiser" and "Bas Scandale."

In 1948 the artist moved to the United States to work for *Harper's Bazaar*. Two years later he became the exclusive artist for *Flair*, the celebrated fashion, art, and society magazine published by Fleur Cowles. From the late 1940s onward, the "Gruau Style" blazed across the covers and pages of the world's leading fashion magazines: *Vogue, L'Officiel,* and *Le Magazine du Figaro* among them. Gruau's designs, ads, and illustrations characterize the graphic art of the 1950s like no other work. The widespread reproductions of these works as well as Gruau's productivity magnified their impact at the time. The era had found its true artist.

In 1982 the first exhibition of his work at the Bartsch and Chariau gallery in Munich marked the beginning of a Gruau renaissance, with major solo retrospectives in Paris, Rome, New York, Tokyo, and many other major fashion capitals around the world. With studios in Paris, Cannes, and Rome, René Gruau is, himself, an icon of the fashion and art worlds.

Joëlle Chariau

01

03

01 René Gruau, cover of *L'Officiel* depicting a Christian Dior design, October 1948, pastel, ink, and watercolor ••• 02 René Gruau, drawing advertising the Pierre Balmain Jolie Madame perfume, ink and watercolor, 1949 ••• 03 René Gruau, drawing of a Pierre Balmain design, *International Textiles*, March 1953, ink and gouache ••• 04 René Gruau, cover of *L'Officiel* depicting a Jacques Fath design, Summer 1947, ink and gouache ••• 05 René Gruau, drawing of a Christian Dior design, *Fémina*, April 1948, ink and gouache

04
05

JACQUES FATH

"I DID COLOR VARIATIONS, MIXED COLORS TOGETHER, AND IMAGINED COLORS TOGETHER. THE FIRST SCARF WAS A MAP OF CAPRI."
(EMILIO PUCCI)

ITALIAN HAUTE COUTURE

05

February 12, 1951, is the official birth date of Italian haute couture. However, this date is not significant unless it is seen within the historical and social context of Italy at that time and during the period immediately preceding it. Under Fascism, the bourgeoisie—which maintained its purchasing power—was dressed by well-established couturiers from Milan, Rome, Venice, Turin, and Florence (Biki, Fercioni, Caraceni). Most of these, however, were followers of, if not slaves to, the French fashion designers, whose designs they bought and copied. In 1935, the Italian Fashion Society (*Ente Italiano Moda*) was created, and, in keeping with Mussolini's specific wishes, agreed to use Italian ideas and materials. This, in turn, gave rise to a highly skilled and inventive artisan industry, although the quality of the work was hampered by wartime rationing.

In the immediate postwar period, Giovanni Battista Giorgini, a Florentine, was employed by American department stores to select and purchase Italian-made products. He came up with the idea of organizing a group fashion show in his own residence, the Villa Torrigiani. He decided to showcase the creations of a small group of Italian firms (some couturiers were also aristocrats) such as Simonetta Colonna Visconti di Cesarò, Carosa (Princess Giovanna Caracciolo), Maria Antonelli, Alberto Fabiani, Emilio Schubert, Noberasco, Vanna, the Fontana sisters, Germana Marucelli, and Jole Veneziani. A fashion boutique and knitwear section was also included, represented by Emilio Pucci, Avolio, Franco Bertoli, and Clarette Gallotti.

The most important American buyers were invited to Giorgini's first fashion show, held on February 12, 1951, in Florence. It proved to be a resounding success and drew the interest of both buyers and the international press. Indeed it was so successful that the next fashion show had to take place in a larger and more prestigious setting: the Pitti Palace. There, in 1952 in the Sala Bianca, the nineteen-year-old Roberto Capucci made his debut. Designers like Biki, Princess Irene Galitzine, Ken Scott, Mila Schön, Forquet, Renato Balestra, Sarli, Centinaro, Pino Lancetti, and André Laug also showed their designs at this venue. Valentino emerged and made his reputation, as did Krizia and Missoni, two rising stars in the fashion world of the early 1960s. Men's fashion followed suit, and it too was a perfect fusion of sartorial ability and original creativity, visible in the work of Angelo Litrico, Brioni, Bruno Piattelli, Carlo Palazzi, Testa, and Nino Cerruti. However, in the 1960s there were some "defectors"— Capucci, Fabiani, and Simonetta all chose to present their collections in Paris—and these, combined with the growing success of ready-to-wear fashion, signaled the decline of the Pitti show.

The theaters of Cinecittà had made Rome the capital of "La Dolce Vita," and movie stars from all over the world flocked to the ateliers of the grand couturiers. Thus the capital city naturally evolved into the official heart of Italian haute couture. In the 1970s Krizia, Missoni, and Ken Scott discovered that they could mass-produce their creations in the factories of the North and resumed showing their work in Milan. Walter Albini, who designed five collections, also joined their ranks, as did Jean-Baptiste Caumont: the new energy center of "made in Italy," ready-to-wear fashion was born.

Anna Gloria Forti

04

FASHION SALON OR BOUTIQUE, PAJAMAS OR BABY-DOLL NIGHTIE,
SHIFT DRESS OR PETTICOAT, STILETTOS OR BALLERINAS, MINK STOLE
OR NIKI SCARF, BATHING
SUIT OR BIKINI ... **WOMAN OR TEENAGER?**

01

Historically, clothes for girls were always simpler, smaller, cheaper versions of what their mothers wore. Although the fashion designers of the early twentieth century occasionally directed their attention to the *jeune fille,* there was never any possibility of buying anything styled specifically for girls. Boutiques evolved from the street shops that were initially attached to couture salons. Lucien Lelong and Elsa Schiaparelli were the first to open these new-style shops in the Paris of the 1930s, selling mainly accessories. In 1948, Jacques Fath created special designs for a department store for the first time. The boutique increasingly became devoted to inexpensive and less elaborate models from the couture collection, and it was this idea of the "boutique collection" that formed the basis of prêt-à-porter (ready-to-wear).

For the first time in the history of fashion, clothes for girls were designed differently from women's wear. Fashion was no longer produced solely for the mature woman, but also in response to the different needs of young people; their economic importance as an additional, new consumer market was slowly being recognized. The so-called separates—uncomplicated and versatile clothes made from inexpensive materials—were seen on the small-waisted young women at dances and sporting activities. Broad bodices emphasized the waist and starkly broke up the silhouette of short pleated skirts, wide skirts, "Capri" pants, and jeans.

This type of fashion could be bought in the new boutiques, which were provisionally established within big department stores as places to sell small series of items; these later evolved into the teen's department. Matching jewelry was light, made from unconventional and inexpensive materials such as synthetics (soft plastic), glass, straw, flowers, or wood. A range of casual fashions, derived from the campus attire at American universities, was offered under the label "College Style."

Adult women continued to wear ensembles, and in general their attire was conceived of as sets in which everything matched: gloves, bag, hat, shoes, stockings, nail polish, hair color. Even dogs were chosen in matching shades. A slender line was achieved by means of pencil skirts, elegant princess or shift dresses, lengthwise seams that made one look taller and slimmer, and beltless dresses that gently skimmed the waist. The result was a certain fixed, overall look. Women slipped back into their conventional roles, even visually; for example, a gray flannel suit or a sweater dress was always correct and ladylike attire. Women had their clothes made by a dressmaker or would buy models from a large fashion salon. They generally wore a pearl choker (sometimes made of faux pearls), button-shaped earrings, or else heavy, pretentious, paste jewelry, the development of which was later revived by Christian Dior and American film stars.

Gerda Buxbaum

02
03

"JEANS WERE THE INSIGNIA OF RESISTANCE FOR ONLY A SHORT TIME.
THEN THEY BECAME THE UNIVERSAL, UNISEX APPAREL WORN BY MOST
OF THE WORLD'S POPULATION." (ULF POSCHARDT, 1998)

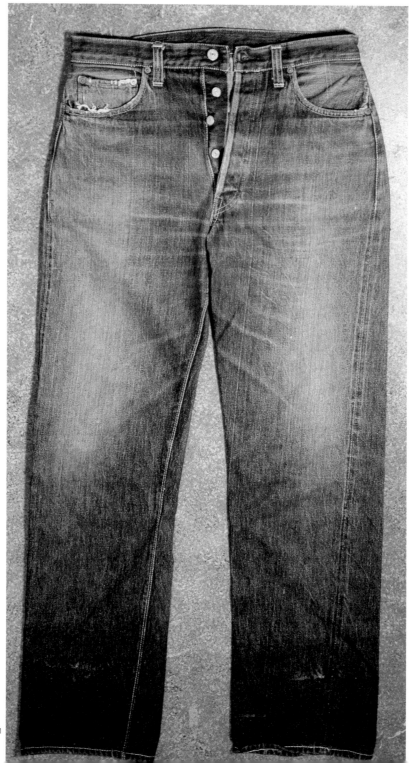

01

T-SHIRT, JEANS, AND LEATHER JACKET

During the 1950s, for the first time in history, the term "youth culture" emerged, signaling that a new generation of young people wanted to differentiate themselves from their parents in both their ideas and external appearances. The source of this development was not Europe, still shaken by the after-effects of war, but the United States. The young Hollywood actors Marlon Brando and James Dean, together with the rock 'n' roll superstar Elvis Presley, became icons of the younger generation. Their characters in such films as *A Streetcar Named Desire* (1951), *East of Eden* (1955), and *Jailhouse Rock* (1957) embodied the image of the rebellious teenager, and their clothing reflected a shared attitude: a rejection of the Establishment and of the clothing mandated by their parents' generation.

This younger generation began to wear clothing that was in opposition to their parents' socio-economic values: the garments of laborers, farmers, and soldiers—in other words, the social "under-class." For the first time, denim jeans, until then frowned upon as working pants for gold diggers and cowboys, were shown on young, sexy stars—and these youthful film idols wore them tight and dirty! When the King of Rock 'n' Roll, Elvis Presley, the cult star of a generation of teenage girls, gyrated his hips clad in skintight jeans, the rise of denim jeans as *the* prime article of teen dress was unstoppable.

Marlon Brando's attire in *A Streetcar Named Desire* triggered the start of another cult garment— the wrestlers' training, or muscle, T-shirt—which he wore tight, exposing his biceps. Following this film, a range of white T-shirts, previously made only as undergarments, could be purchased as outer-wear at many American department stores. With Brando's film *The Wild One* (1955) the teen en-semble expanded to include the black "Perfecto," a waist-length, leather jacket originally worn by American fighter pilots. Through its association with bike-riding outlaws, it held a very special attrac-tion for teenagers. The combination of T-shirt, jeans (especially Levi's), and leather jacket, became the uniform of the American youth, sometimes referred to as young hooligans by their parents.

This outfit also appealed to European teenagers, who eagerly copied the *look* of the jean-clad American GIs in Europe, Elvis Presley, and Hollywood and European film stars. However, the European teenagers of the early 1960s, dressed in their jeans and T-shirts, were somewhat subdued in comparison to their American counterparts.

Today, T-shirts and jeans, elements of this formerly rebellious look, are treasured articles of clothing worn around the world—a uniform for the masses, from babies to senior citizens. The black Perfecto, on the other hand, still retains an association with the outsider: in the 1970s it was the preferred garb of fringe groups such as Punks, Skinheads, and Bikers.   *Beate Dorothea Schmid*

04
05

03

"ACCESSORIES ARE WHAT, IN MY OPINION, PULL THE WHOLE LOOK TOGETHER AND MAKE IT UNIQUE." (YVES SAINT LAURENT, 1982)

ACCESSORIES

01

Accessories, carefully coordinated—even in everyday wear—had enormous fashion status in the 1950s. "Ladies wear hats" was the successful advertising slogan used by milliners at that time, and it was taken for granted that a lady kept her hat on when in society or at the theater. Delicate hatpins, which looked so elegant on Audrey Hepburn or Grace Kelly, had a fresh, youthful appeal, while big cartwheel hats had an interesting, seductive allure. The 1950s saw the appearance of close-fitting cloche hats with satin ribbons around the brim tied into a bow in the front.

During this time it was also important to have handbags or purses that matched one's gloves and footwear in both color and style. The fashionable handbag was one typified by small handles that could be elegantly draped over the forearm. The *non plus ultra* was a Hermès handbag fastened with a leather strap. The American actress Grace Kelly (who became Princess Grace of Monaco in 1956) used to carry one, making it a symbol of distinction as the "Kelly" bag. Travel baggage and other high-quality leather goods from Gucci or Louis Vuitton became symbols of luxury and wealth. For women who could not afford such exclusive wares, bags made from imitation leather were fashionable, as were homemade crocheted bags made from raffia and fastened with metal clips. In the United States the arrival of transparent plastic bags caused a sensation. These bags with their diverse, box-like shapes were made from hardened, colored plastic (often in combination with metal) which produced a highly extravagant effect. They were made by famous manufacturers such as Llewellyn, Patricia of Miami, and Rialto.

Gloves were an important part of a fashionable ensemble and a Lady always wore them, even in summer. These could be made from nylon or could also be crocheted. Evening wear included gloves made from the finest glacé leather—the longer the glove, the shorter the sleeve—and a broad mink stole to warm one's bare shoulders.

In terms of footwear, the once fashionable pump, with its round toe and thick block heel, was transformed in the 1950s into a pointed toe with a stiletto heel. This made for a considerably more slender-looking foot, but the stiletto's destructive effects on parquet flooring and linoleum often caused annoyance. Haute couture demanded extravagant footwear and Charles Jourdan (1883–1976) and Roger Vivier (b. 1913), who worked, among others, for the House of Dior, provided it. However, sporty young girls demonstrated their independence from the restraints of haute couture with a look that was personified by flat ballerina slippers and a small Nicki scarf slung cheekily around the neck.

Ingrid Loschek

02

03   04

05   06

01

02
03

"THE HIPPIE REVOLUTION KILLED THE SWINGING LONDON IMAGE, THE POP
DANDY AND DOLLY 'FRUGGING' IN AN *IN* DISCOTHEQUE, STONE DEAD."
(GEORGE MELLY, *REVOLT INTO STYLE*, 1970)

SWINGING LONDON

In April 1966 *Time Magazine* ran a twelve-page cover story under the headline: "London: The Swinging City." As is the case with many media discoveries, uncovering a trend announces its demise. While
American magazines, such as *Esquire* and *Life*, followed the lead with further articles on London's
position as the new world capital of fashion and style, British designers and entrepreneurs found their
profits and sense of optimism shrinking as the decade of youth moved towards old age. The label
"Swinging London," however, proved to be popular and described an extraordinary revolution in
attitudes and cultural life.

After World War II British teenagers found that they had twice as much disposable income as their
parents had when they were teenagers. The new spending power of the young was channeled into
leisure, particularly music and fashion. New London-based radio stations and record companies
catered to an increasingly diversified market of youthful consumers who identified their allegiance to
style and pleasure through the adoption of subcultural looks—ranging from the sharp, Italian chic of
the Mod to the Americanized denim and leather machismo of the Rocker. Immigration from Britain's
former colonies in the late 1950s led to further diversification in terms of musical and sartorial taste,
introducing West Indian styles to London's cultural fabric. In comparison to the stately traditions of
Paris and the relative conservatism of American fashions, the situation in London offered a radical
slant on the production and consumption of clothing.

New teenage markets also encouraged the opening of specialized retail boutiques catering to
consumers who were defining new trends as they shopped. In 1955 in Chelsea's Kings Road, Mary
Quant opened her first shop, Bazaar. Frustrated by the antiquated women's wear styles, she produced
her own modern, monochromatic designs that captured the forward-looking spirit of the time: by
1963 her mass-produced Mod look was exporting London taste to New York. In 1957, John Stephen, a
young Scotsman with training in the retail industry, opened a shop off of the depressed Carnaby Street
that specialized in young men's fashion. Already in 1954, Bill Green's shop, Vince, had established the
underground fashion credentials of the area, though his initial stock of tightly tailored and brightly
colored clothes was taken up by only a few brave style-leaders. By 1961, Stephen managed to popularize and modify the look so sufficiently that Carnaby Street became a national focus for cutting-edge
men's fashion.

From these small beginnings, London's fashion scene expanded, re-formed, and attracted international attention. By the end of the 1960s, its personalities and styles had been captured on film in
Michelangelo Antonioni's *Blow-Up* (1966) and Nicolas Roeg's *Performance* (1970), as well as promoted in magazines such as *Queen* and *Town*. Through an ever-changing succession of shops that
by 1970 included Barbara Hulanicki's Biba and Tommy Roberts's Kleptomania, these purveyors
defined the hippie, retro-chic clothing of the London look. Since then the world's fashion press regularly returns to London's streets in search of new directions.   *Christopher Breward*

01

One of the greatest fashion revolutions of this century is based on a traditional garment originally worn by ancient Greeks and Romans—the tunic. For centuries men wore this together with leggings or tights as their working garb. In the 1950s, however, when it appeared as women's wear—in the exciting shape of the miniskirt—it was seen as an outrage because it exposed the female thigh.

The British designer Mary Quant started sewing clothes out of frustration over the stuffy teenage fashions of the 1950s. She created comfortable, loose smocks without bodices, petticoats, or frills. In 1958 she designed her first super-short shift dresses, which seemed more like children's clothes than for adults. *Vogue* first took note of her in 1963, long after many of her designs had been successfully sold: the straight, sleeveless tunic with an attached, tiny, pleated skirt (only thirty centimeters in length); the mini-length "Tent" dress (1960); and the short "Rex Harrison" cardigan dress made of Shetland tweed (1962).

The "Lolita," "Schoolgirl," and "Good Girl" looks created by Quant necessitated new materials and accessories. To achieve a "wet" look for her raincoats, she used PVC, and she created many new decorative patterns, such as her childlike daisy design which still remains the logo for Mary Quant cosmetics. She devised satchels with long straps (instead of relying on the customary ladylike handbags) and even promoted a new hairstyle—not one set in rigid waves, but a novel, flexible, and geometrical cut that could be blown-dry—Vidal Sassoon's "Wedge." Her super-short miniskirt also called for new underwear: bodystockings, pantie girdles, tights, and pantyhose—the push-up bra and suspender belt did not stand a chance.

This English "child's" dress was adopted in a very different manner in France. Pierre Cardin, one of the most avant-garde fashion designers at that time, created mini-length, angularly cut shift dresses that, instead, had something robot-like about them. They were made from stiff, heavy materials that transformed them into hard-edged contemporary sculptures. His miniskirts—still by no means generally accepted—sometimes resembled medieval surcoats, held up in the center front by straps. He produced bodysuits to be worn with tiny loincloth skirts and introduced the use of vinyl and plastic as well as silver-dyed leather. All this experimentation occurred within the realm of haute couture, which Cardin continues to use as his laboratory for invention.

The most famous outfit by André Courrèges, who had trained with Balenciaga, consisted of a double-breasted jacket in broad stripes and a slightly flared skirt; it was copied around the world and in all price ranges. Indispensable accessories included a helmet with a chinstrap, a hat which looked like a baby's bonnet, or a cowboy hat, together with flat-heeled, mid-calf boots of white plastic. According to Courrèges, these boots restored the correct proportions and helped the wearer to remain "in contact with the earth and reality."

Gerda Buxbaum

02

"ELEGANCE IS NO LONGER SIGNIFICANT; CLOTHES HAVE TO BE FUN."
(YVES SAINT LAURENT)

03

04

01

"I BELIEVE THE BODYSTOCKING OR A FORM OF IT WILL BE THE MAIN ELEMENT OF FASHIONS OF THE FUTURE." (JACQUES FONTERAY, ONE OF THE COSTUME DESIGNERS FOR *BARBARELLA*, 1968)

SECOND SKINS

03

The typical contemporary street scene, teeming with people of all ages dressed in post- or pre-sport variations of bodysuits, bike shorts, and jog bras, owes much to the pioneering work of a handful of prescient designers: Claire McCardell, Rudi Gernreich, and Giorgio di Sant' Angelo (1936–89). In careers that spanned seven decades and were influenced by the clothes worn for active wear—the dancer's and trapeze artist's leotard, the swimmer's maillot, and the wool knit one-piece suits first worn by skiers—these designers devised new ways to clothe the body.

Efforts to reduce the body's coverings to their barest essentials have typically involved stretch fabrics. Although Charles Frederick Worth (1825–95) had worked with jersey, and Coco Chanel had served to popularize it, McCardell was the first to design, in 1934, a modern system of dress that could, in various combinations of the "basics," serve as an entire wardrobe. Made of black wool knit, the five easy pieces included bare and covered-up tops, along with several choices of bottoms, that could be used in various ways to go from bicycling on the beach to dancing at dinner. Five and six decades later, designers would continue to experiment with similar ideas.

During the early 1940s, McCardell turned to the leotard as the basis for a new look; there was something indelibly modern about basing an ensemble on a black turtleneck and tights. Gernreich, whose background included modern dance, expanded this concept even further. Although he is most remembered for his 1963 topless bathing suit, his greatest impact came from such lively turnouts as minidresses, tunics, shorts, and one-piece jumpsuits shown with patterned or brightly colored tights that were an integral part of the look—all made in springy knits.

The next major development came from the test tube. The designer most often associated with experimental new fibers is Sant' Angelo. While McCardell and Gernreich were instrumental in introducing such concepts as the leotard, Sant' Angelo worked together with the company Dupont to devise not only suitable replacements for wool or acrylic knit, but fantastic ones: silk that could stretch in any direction and new fabrics that were transparent, took color beautifully, and could be painted, tie-dyed, or embroidered. From the 1960s to the 1990s, he worked with Lycra-enhanced materials of all kinds to devise ensembles based on such versatile elements as bodysuits that could double as bathing suits or evening tops, and tubes that could be worn as tops, skirts, cummerbunds, or shrugs.

These were not just successful designs that launched a thousand copies; they were concepts that infiltrated every aspect of how we dress—from Olympic sports to glamorous awards ceremonies. Stretch fabrics provide freedom and comfort. Obsolete are the many layers of the past, the need for separate underclothes, and the idea that any garment serves a single purpose. Perhaps most importantly, these second skins showcase bodies that are now far more designed—by athletic trainers and surgeons—than the clothes. *Caroline Rennolds Milbank*

02

04

01

STREET STYLE

"Street Style" gives self-expression to youth. It is a powerful language with which the young can define their passions and identify the like-minded, their gang. Thriving in the generation gap that broke open in the late 1950s, it is a look created by the young, the dispossessed, and the outsider and paraded on the streets. The street context is important, otherwise the look risks loosing its vitality and authenticity—its magic.

The do-it-yourself approach is another distinctive trait of street style: contemporary mainstream clothing or secondhand garments are altered, decorated, and customized with "tribal" insignia. It is a style that also defies gravity: it moves up the generations—from daughters to mothers, sons to fathers, and amateurs to professionals. 1962 to 1968 were crucial years in which the allure and originality of street style challenged, and finally broke, the hegemony of high fashion.

At the heart of any street style fashion is popular culture—popular art, music, and politics. During the 1960s, different looks, reacting to these things, evolved on the heels of one another: "Beatnik," "Mod," "Rocker," and "Hippie." The progression was precise, though diehards could always be found once a look had moved on. The decade commenced with the Mods or Moderns. In opposition to the old-fashioned, acutely class-conscious, and xenophobic attitudes of the Teddy Boys, the Mods celebrated the look of things monochromatic, black-and-white, unpatterned, sharp, tight, urban, foreign (especially French and Italian), and mechanized. The Mods favored pop music and Modern jazz over rock 'n' roll, expensive Continental casual clothes, and close-fitting suits. They were undecorated, lean, and slick. Amphetamines heightened their almost kinetic sense of frenzied motion.

By 1967 the Hippies were the most articulate and extreme outsiders of the decade. They not only took issue with the lifestyle of the older generation but also its politics and its fundamental socio-economic structure. Their protest took on an international dimension linking the baby-boomer generations on both sides of the Atlantic. Protest was at the heart of this street style and the most passionate focus of protest was the Vietnam War. Hippie dress proclaimed an allegiance to a shifting melee of beliefs: internationalism, multiculturalism, peace, and experimentation with free love and drugs. The peace symbol, Marijuana leaves, psychedelic patterns and colors, ethnic decorative devices, and the interlocked yin-yang symbol embellished cheap, customized, and secondhand clothes in a sartorial celebration of the counterculture.

The Hippie aesthetic ousted the sharp, the slick, and the urban. Fashion went limp, and backbones were out. In 1967 the hemline dropped two feet and wispy, whimsical, mawkish, "period" dress outdated the strict and the short. Dressed in widows' weeds and under the influence of psychedelic drugs, there was a sense of langor and indolence among those in the forefront of youth culture. After the high-water mark of idealism, reached in the "Summer of Love" in 1967, disillusionment characterized the close of the 1960s. The energetic optimism that opened the decade gave way to introspection.
Jane Mulvagh

02

03

"HAUTE COUTURE IS DEAD; I WANT TO DESIGN FOR THE STREET ...
A SOCIALIST KIND OF FASHION FOR THE MASSES ..."
(EMMANUELLE KHANH, 1964)

01 André Courrèges, 1968 ••• 02 Paco Rabanne, 1970 ••• 03 Paco Rabanne, dress made of aluminum discs, 1967 ••• 04 André Courrèges, Autumn/Winter 1968/69
05 Pierre Cardin, 1966

01

02

03

> "THE FUNCTIONAL MUST BE THE SOUL OF A DRESS, ITS COMPOSITION,
> ITS INTERIOR RHYTHM ... AESTHETICS IS THE ENVELOPE."
> (ANDRÉ COURRÈGES, 1967)

The drama of the space race was heightened by the fact that television had, by the early 1960s, become widely available. It was impossible not to be moved and inspired by live, action footage of hero-astronauts; their closely cropped heads, five-o'-clock shadows, and silver suits became every bit as emblematic of their daring as the leather blouson and aviator glasses donned by Lindbergh. Fashion tuned in right away.

In 1961 the Russian Yury Gagarin became the first man to orbit the earth and André Courrèges opened his Paris fashion house. Within a few years, Courrèges designs would epitomize the glamour of space exploration. In lieu of moon boots, his aficionadas wore go-go boots; his tennis ball-like sunglasses had eye slits that looked like what an alien might sport, and module-colored sequins sparkled on his laboratory-white frocks.

Space-age fashions did not so much reject traditional materials like wool, silk, and cotton as they emphasized the man-made—particularly plastic. From the Lucite heels of Beth Levine's stocking shoes to the clear bubble helmets worn by Pucci-clad Quantas stewardesses, plastic was the wave of the future. Biodegradability not yet being a concern, part of plastic's appeal was that it was disposable. What a lark to buy one of Betsey Johnson's clear vinyl minidresses, decorate it with the decals provided, wear it once, and then toss it aside. See-through plastic was also a way of flirting with nudity, part and parcel of a utopian, gender-free future. Rudi Gernreich featured clear vinyl panels down the fronts and sides of his minidresses and used them to hold his bathing suits together.

Shiny Mylar, reminiscent of astronauts' suits, was a boutique favorite. Even better than metallic fabric was metal itself, used for the harness halters of Pierre Cardin dresses and the spring coils that held Gernreich's necklines together. There was an armor aspect to all this metal, and no one brought chain mail more up to date than Paco Rabanne, who pieced together mini dresses and body coverings out of metallic discs and circlets.

Most intriguing about space-age fashion was the idea of unisex—lack of gravity seemed to level the playing field. In futuristic movies and television shows, as well as on the runways, both sexes wore versions of unitards, jumpsuits, tunics, and leggings. Cardin dressed men and women alike in rounded helmets, flat, plastic eye shields, sturdy ribbed unitards, and jumpsuits with industrial zippers. Many of his designs featured the abstract motif of a band ending in a circle. Often trapunto stitched, this futuristic decorative element had no gender background (like flowers for women or pinstripes for men).

In space, clothing needed to perform and was not intentionally decorative—it solved problems. Man's ingenuity coped with tight quarters, temperature extremities, and troublesome blast-offs and re-entries. If man could walk on the moon while snacking on freeze-dried ice cream, anything was possible. Space-age fashions greeted the future with open arms.   *Caroline Rennolds Milbank*

05

04

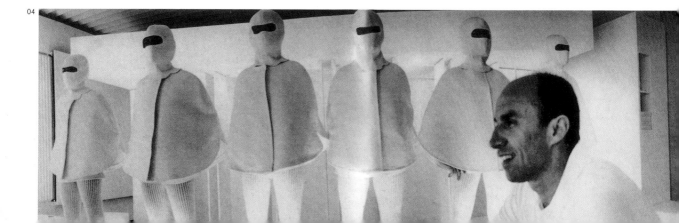

"BLACK-AND-WHITE SIGNS ARE LIKE FAMILIAR ANTIPATHIES OF THE PAST—DAY AND NIGHT, ANGEL AND DEVIL, GOOD AND EVIL—IN REALITY COMPLEMENTARY PARAMETERS, FRUITFUL ANDROGYNY."
(VICTOR VASARELY)

OP ART CLOTHING

01
02

In 1955, the exhibition *Le Mouvement* was held at the Paris art gallery of Denise René. Its theme was various artists' approaches to kinetics. Among the artists included was Victor Vasarely (1908–97), whose pieces were based on the effects of light and the contrast between black and white. This exhibition established his reputation as a leading figure of Op Art, a term coined in 1964 to describe art that explored human perceptual processes through optical effects.

The works of Op Art's practitioners were perceptually ambiguous and often suggested dizzying movement, either through subtle shifts in color or black-and-white patterns and lines. The graphic simplicity of these optical illusions made it possible to adapt Op Art to textile and fashion design—and the fashion world did so. Particularly in the years between 1963 and 1966, fashion makers reduced the art movement to its boldly attractive patterns, which were translated into textile designs and accessories. One American dress manufacturer, Larry Aldrich, featured dresses in fabrics that were based on paintings by the Op artist Bridget Riley (b. 1931).

In 1966, the magazine *Neue Mode* declared: "The new wave in printed patterns is called Op-Art. Modern painting and architecture stood godfather to their design—in other words, no trace of romanticism! Strictly geometric patterns—optically distorted—are the typical characteristics of this striking and eye-catching design. The cut must be simple. Whether spirals or distorted checks, stylized circles or rectangles—everything is 'black on white,' the great hit for fashion-loving teenagers and those in their twenties."

Another art movement entered the fashion scene in 1965 in the form of Yves Saint Laurent's "Mondrian" dresses. In 1966, a German women's magazine reported: "The Mondrian style in fashion has existed precisely since August 2, 1965. On this day, Yves Saint Laurent showed his winter collection in Paris for the first time.... In the meantime, fashion has further developed all the modern-art themes, and is offering thousands of accessories—from scarves to sunglasses, jewelry to shoes—part chic, part crazy, which are presented as Op Art, Mondrian, geometric fashion, Courrèges style. They can be recognized by the combination of color contrasts, whereby black and white will be absolutely tops for spring 1966."

The crossover between art and other genres such as fashion, architecture, music, and design has reached an unprecedented degree in the 1990s. Cultural hybrids, such as those formerly found in subcultural contexts since the advent of Pop Art and Punk, continue to enter the established art business. This is not surprising in light of our postmodern sensitivity to the mutability of the body, beauty, and gender and the idea that identities are contradictory and unstable. *Gerda Buxbaum*

03

04

01

"SHE [PEGGY MOFFITT] TAUGHT ME HOW MUCH MORE
A MODEL PUTS IN HER WORK THAN JUST A PRETTY FACE."
(TWIGGY)

FASHION MODELS

02

The youth-oriented pop culture and English fashion scene, which flourished in Swinging London in the 1960s, produced a new type of woman—one that was quite contrary to the 1950s ladylike mannequins that had served as models for a generation of young, married housewives. Rebelling against middle-class values and prescribed lifestyles, teenagers, especially young women, rediscovered themselves in an androgynous ideal of beauty which blurred previously set markers identifying the sexes, rejecting them as constricting and clichéd roles. Thus, the Beatles appeared with unmanly, long hair, while young women cut their hair mannishly short. Androgyny was associated with extreme youthfulness, almost childishness—a refusal to become adult and sensible (like the previous generation). This trend attempted to reverse the stereotyped ideal of the female body propagated from the 1930s to the late 1950s. The fashions of the British designer Mary Quant, the significant elements of which were miniskirts and short, straight shifts emphasized in her "Schoolgirl" look, called for young women with boyish figures and long, slender legs. The mature, childbearing woman with her curvaceous, hourglass silhouette was no longer considered attractive; instead it was the apparently sexless child-woman.

No one embodied this ideal more than Leslie Hornby, known as Twiggy, who was discovered in London at the tender age of seventeen. With no detectable bosom, endlessly long, stork's legs, a high, pale forehead, and innocent Bambi eyes, Twiggy—dressed in Quant's shifts and minis—was the antithesis of the worldly types preferred in the 1950s, such as the American models Dovima and Lisa Fonssagrives. Twiggy's measurements became both dream and trauma for an entire generation of female teenagers who attempted to emulate their idol, sometimes with the aid of radical starvation diets. Twiggy was also the first fashion model to achieve international fame, a preliminary step toward the supermodel cult of the late 1980s. Since her look was so different from previously held notions of beauty, Twiggy and the "Twiggy ideal" came up against many opponents. The press referred to her as a "pale, starved clothes hanger," and parents blamed her for their daughters' eating disorders. Never really relishing her part in the international fashion jetset, Twiggy retired from the modeling business at the early age of nineteen and made more or less successful attempts at acting. In 1976 she published her autobiography, *Twiggy*. Despite her extremely brief career, she was the very symbol and incarnation of the zeitgeist of the 1960s, as Veroushka was for the 1970s and Claudia Schiffer for the 1980s.

A more feminine notion of beauty returned in the 1970s and 1980s, but the Twiggy type and the ideal of the childlike or sexless woman have experienced a revival since the early 1990s. The ethereal Kate Moss, who has often been compared to Twiggy, introduced this new decade of skinny models or "waifs" that reached a peak in the mid-1990s. Its culmination may be seen in the ultra-thinness of the contemporary fashion model Jodie Kidd (beside whom Twiggy would have looked like a well-nourished farm girl) and "Heroin Chic."

Beate Dorothea Schmid

03
04

"I FELT THE CUSTOMERS AT PARAPHERNALIA WERE LOOKING TO OUR CLOTHES AS PASSPORTS TO A NEW AGE, A NEW BIRTH." (BETSEY JOHNSON)

ACID COLORS, PAPER, AND PVC

Paper clothing and domestic products made from paper were a short-lived but widespread phenomenon from 1966 to 1968. The first paper clothes were produced in the United States in 1966 by the Scott Paper Company in conjunction with a promotion for paper napkins, toilet paper, and paper towels called "Colorful Explosions." Two types of A-line dresses, "Paper Caper," were issued. These were produced in four sizes using two different prints: one was a black-and-white Op Art design, the other a bandanna design on a red background with a yellow-and-black Paisley pattern. The dresses could be worn about five times; all that was needed for alterations was a pair of scissors, and for repairs, a piece of tape. Special boutiques opened, the first of which was the Waste Paper Boutique. A promotional "Happening" helped this idea become a success and gave a particular boost to paper fashion by claiming to be modern and artistic.

This inexpensive fashion survived for only a short time. Designer paper clothes were quickly established, with prices comparable to those for textile fashions. Elisa Dabbs became a recognized paper couturier and Harry Gordon produced "Poster" dresses which sold for three dollars. Paper clothes were financially, socially, and aesthetically successful, and indeed, they were the ultimate ready-to-wear.

The fact that Andy Warhol (1928–87) was involved gives us an indication of the milieu in which the frenzy for paper raged. The boutique Paraphernalia opened in September 1965 on New York's Madison Avenue and was both a laboratory and a showcase for undiscovered design talent. "Anyone who takes fashion seriously is dreadful. I think it's just clothes. It should be fun, and nothing about it should be taken seriously," stated Paul Young, the founder of Paraphernalia. He also started the company Puritan, which sold clothing that embodied the look of the 1960s "flower power" youth.

Research into materials brought about changes in clothing; and the synthetic revolution introduced technical fibers—which had actually been designed for the army, space travel, and sport—into everyday wear. André Courrèges, Paco Rabanne, and Pierre Cardin acted as mediators between fashion and cutting-edge technology. They developed methods of producing clothes by means of a casting process which was used, for example, in Cardin's "Giffo" raincoat and "Cardine" dress. Paraphernalia's clothes made from PVC, vinyl, and Dacron—materials originally intended for utilitarian purposes—were easier to clean using window-cleaning fluid than by sending them to the dry-cleaner. "Hey, your dress looks like my shower curtain!" The crazier and more novel it was, the better.

Gerda Buxbaum

01

02
03

05

06

"F EVERYBODY'S NOT A BEAUTY, THEN NOBODY IS."
(ANDY WARHOL, 1975)

POP ART FASHION

03

Pop Art, drawing its inspiration from the imagery of consumer marketing and popular culture, was destined to connect with the world of fashion. Pop Art emerged around 1960, primarily in New York and London, where artists were painting bold and colorful images of everyday objects, often distorting their appearances through enlargement, repetition, or isolation. Many of these artists became famous, and their paintings became icons of the 1960s: Andy Warhol and his Campbell's soup cans, Coca-Cola bottles, and portraits of Marilyn Monroe; Roy Lichtenstein (1923–97) and his comic-strip paintings; Jasper Johns (b. 1930) and his American flags; and Robert Indiana (b. 1928) and his huge *LOVE* painting.

It was not long before some of the Pop artists began to produce "wearable" art. Warhol was the most closely connected to fashion. He had begun his career as a commercial artist, designing window displays and drawing shoes for fashion companies and magazines. After he achieved Pop Art fame, he began to design clothes based on his paintings—the "Fragile" dress (1963), the "Brillo Box" dress (1964), the "S & H Green Stamps" blouse (1965), and the "Campbell's Soup Can" T-shirt (1980). Warhol took a real interest in fashion: he collected clothes, hung out with fashion designers, and his style magazine, *Interview,* featured exposés on celebrities such as Elizabeth Taylor, Yves Saint Laurent, Calvin Klein, Halston (1932–90), and Diana Vreeland (1906–89), as well as the work of fashion photographers Cecil Beaton (1904–80) and Helmut Newton (b. 1920).

The best "Pop Art" fashion, however, was that produced by designers who copied Pop Art's bold, iconographic look. This often meant a "Warhol" look. In 1965 the American designer Betsey Johnson (b. 1942), a friend of Warhol's, helped to launch the hip New York City boutique Paraphernalia, where clients could buy transparent plastic, noisy metallic, or throwaway paper minidresses and suits which featured silk-screened Pop images, electric lights, or Day-Glo colors. The French designer Yves Saint Laurent invented his own images that mimicked the Pop Art look, while the American designer Halston created dresses with large floral prints directly borrowed from Warhol's *Flowers* series (c. 1972).

In the 1990s there continues to be a place in the fashion world for Pop Art's way of poking fun at glamour. Stephen Sprouse (b. 1953), given exclusive rights to use Warhol's famous images, has designed several lines based on Warhol's work, including the *Camouflage* series (1988). Sleek cocktail dresses, printed with repetitive images of Chairman Mao Zedong, by Vivienne Tam (b. 1962) are a *hommage à Warhol,* as are the designs of Jean-Charles de Castelbajac (b. 1949) which feature Campbell's soup cans, garish reproductions of famous Old Master paintings, or TV cartoon characters. The most luxurious, over-the-top Pop garments are those of Gianni Versace. His—Warhol again—"Marilyn Monroe" dress (1991) and Roy Lichtenstein-inspired "Whaam!" dress (1996) best capture Pop Art's mélange of kitsch, irony, and beauty.   *Jane C. Milosch*

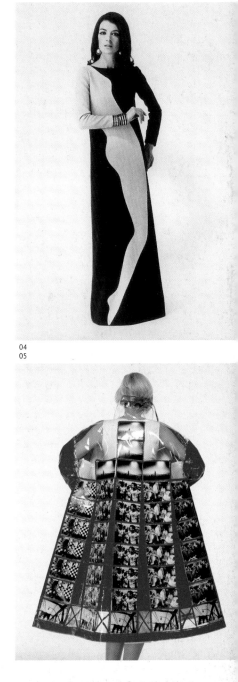

04
05

02

"I LOVE OLD THINGS. MODERN THINGS ARE SO COLD. I NEED THINGS THAT HAVE LIVED." (BARBARA HULANICKI OF BIBA)

"I LOVE OLD THINGS. MODERN THINGS ARE SO COLD. I NEED THINGS THAT HAVE LIVED." (BARBARA HULANICKI OF BIBA)

DRUGS, DREAMS, AND DUSTY COLORS

01

When people talk about "the Sixties" they often mean the years from 1967 to 1975, and, in any case, there were different events that characterized the 1960s. Fashion marked a fundamental cultural change between the early and late 1960s. Between 1965 and 1967, the uncluttered, futuristic designs of André Courrèges and Mary Quant—featuring short skirts, childish pinafores, and boxy shapes—were superceded by a return to the styles of Art Nouveau, Hollywood, and William Morris (1834–96). Perhaps this mirrored the changing mood of the period, from that of optimism and scientific discovery to that of pessimistic radicalism, revolutionary slogans, and environmental concerns. The shift away from Quant's chirpy Mod girls and Swinging London's miniskirted chicks, reflected a growing nostalgia for the past and, to some extent, a loss of belief in the future, as the long boom began to mutate into its opposite.

That is not to say that fashion designers consciously expressed such a mood, but fashion was beginning to be influenced, more than ever before, by youth movements and street styles. Quant successfully interpreted the Mod style for mass-produced fashion, but the Hippie style was not so easily adapted for the high street; the Hippies' ecologically based reliance on secondhand clothes, and their creation of a picturesque aesthetic required a new approach. It was cleverly achieved by British designers Barbara Hulanicki, the creator of Biba, and Laura Ashley (1925–85) (though later and less inventively), as well as through the Bus Stop boutiques of the early 1970s. Rock bands, John Lennon and Yoko Ono, and singers such as Janis Joplin and Jimi Hendrix gave the strange collage of the hippie-ethnic style a currency throughout mass culture. For young women, who lacked the time or confidence to hunt through market stalls and thrift shops (of which there were few in the 1960s), Biba, and those who came afterwards, provided a unique style.

The essence of the Biba style was an etiolated Pre-Raphaelite silhouette. Ragamuffin curls fell round dreamy, druggy faces onto tiny shoulders and arms dressed in tight sleeves that belled out at the wrists. There were long-sleeved granny vests under short-sleeved droopy cardigans over bell-bottom pants or long, floaty skirts. Sometimes these were made from flashy, Jean Harlow satin or Victorian, embossed velvet, sometimes from jersey or "old-fashioned," 1940s floral prints, and there was an occasional hint of fake leopard and the World War II turban. The dirty, muted colors were a revival of William Morris's palette and the 1870s Aesthetic movement: sludge brown, brick dust, airforce blue, sage green, cream, or dusty pink.

Above all, Biba was more than a trend. She anticipated postmodern fashion bricolage and was the first to draw so openly on street fashions and mass culture for her look. Therefore, although her designs seemed to look to the past, she was actually a designer of the future. While her shops looked like fin-de-siècle caverns, she pioneered open-plan dressing rooms and engineered the shift from fashion to designer lifestyle. Henceforward, fashion would no longer be a matter of changing styles; it would always be about a total *look*.

Elizabeth Wilson

02

01 Antonio, *Fashion Study*, 1964 ••• 02 "Rainbow Room," Biba Boutique ••• 03 Sonia Rykiel, 1976 ••• 04 Jean Cacharel, 1977

03
04

RADICAL CHIC

01

Poor people dress up; only rich people can afford to dress down. To the poor, secondhand dress bears the stigma of poverty and thrift, and the look of impoverishment is one to be avoided. In the twentieth century, secondhand dress only became fashionable in the affluent postwar period, when teenagers of affluent families and Bohemians used it to make a statement. In the 1950s Beat girls perused rummage sales in New York City and wore satin dresses and silk blouses from the 1930s and 1940s—challenging middle-class American respectability.

In the late 1960s and 1970s, secondhand dress became associated with the counterculture and its aspirations towards an alternative society. It signaled a refusal of materialism and a utopian desire to escape the trammels of consumer capitalism. Yet this resistance to material wealth often produced stylized images of poverty which seemed to mock the fact of real poverty, as well as the very real exploitation rife in the garment trade. In 1974 the American writer Tom Wolfe called it "radical chic" and jeered at the affluent young people who played at revolution, slumming it in "poor" clothes.

Yet its connections to Hippies and the counterculture did mean that retro-chic, or "Vintage" dress as it came to be known, offered a genuine alternative to those who either did not want, or could not afford, expensive designer clothes. For men, it signaled hedonism as opposed to the rigid conformity of the tailored suit. In 1967, the British Pop artist Peter Blake designed a sleeve for the Beatles' *Sergeant Pepper* album, and it marked a key moment in the development of an eclectic hippie style. The Beatles' lurid military uniforms, like the army surplus clothing that followed in the 1970s, mocked militarism and implied a critique of the Vietnam War.

Retro dress differentiated its wearers from mainstream society, and its colorful motley allowed young people of limited means to participate on equal terms in the fashion system. Similar to nineteenth-century dandyism, getting it right depended more on originality and talent than on money. The clothes were found in jumble sales and rag markets, which enjoyed a revival across Europe beginning in the late 1960s. In London small shops with secondhand merchandise opened with such names as Serendipity and Granny Takes A Trip. The look was nostalgic and romantic, in contrast to the high-tech modernity of the 1960s. The natural fabrics of vintage clothing were valued over and above the synthetics that dominated the mass market. Old fur coats were worn over printed crêpe dresses from the 1930s and 1940s. Antique lace petticoats, Victorian shawls, army greatcoats, and tailored woolen jackets from the 1940s were anachronistically mixed to produce an individual look which could never be replicated by the big stores. Designers did, of course, try to imitate these countercultural styles (as did Yves Saint Laurent with his luxurious "Ethnic" look), but they never quite got it right. Fashion itself was out of fashion within the counterculture.

Caroline Evans

02

03

04

01

"A SEARCH FOR NEW VALUES LED TO 'FLOWER POWER' AND THE HIPPIE MOVEMENT, AS WELL AS AN INTEREST IN THE OCCULT, ASTROLOGY, ORIENTAL PHILOSOPHY, MUSIC, AND RELIGION." (GERDA BUXBAUM, 1999)

THE FOLKLORIC LOOK

04

"An avalanche of folklore, hippie dressing, in short, everything you can get from a rag seller," so lamented André Courrèges about the decline of functional clothing. But function appealed to young people only when it could be used as a path away from the ladylike and stiff formal outfits of the 1950s.

The Hippies, or "flower children," were the center of a movement that emerged in the United States in the mid-1960s. With their flowers, clothing, and music, they protested against the Establishment and drew attention to their pacifistic, back-to-nature attitudes towards life. They primarily opted for garments from remote geographical areas that had barely come into contact with the industrial age: South American ponchos, Eskimo ear-warming caps, Afghan sheepskin jackets, and, most of all, cheesecloth blouses and shirts from India. Colorful, lavishly embroidered clothes in Persian patterns were worn together with Indian silver jewelry draped around the waist and hips as well as the ankles. Jeans were embroidered, painted, or decorated with floral appliqués.

The "Czar" look, which featured Eastern Orthodox crosses, and the 1967 "Zhivago" look, which included rough sheepskin coats laced with passementerie, were superseded by the "Khaki Safari" look, off-the-shoulder "Carmen" blouses, African-inspired, highly polished, metal necklaces, and simple suits with stand-up collars inspired by Nehru's jackets. In 1968, the German fashion magazine *Neue Mode* observed: "Apart from the return to Romantic and Art Nouveau styles, the rustic country look, the sporty club style, and colorful Mexican fashions are all the rage."

The "Ninotchka" look was everywhere in 1970—the year in which long-haired fur coats and Yeti jackets, Turkish harem pants, the brightly colored fabrics of the "Gypsy" look, ankle-length patchwork skirts, and gaucho pants, along with Indian embroidered empire yokes, were in fashion.

In 1969 an article in the fashion magazine *Madame* entitled, "Indian Look between Charlatanism and Snobbery," raised a cautiously critical voice: "Observant watchers have noted that an Indian wave has flooded the European and American continents. The exotically colorful, irrationally magical, is trumps. And it is not just the Hippies who are to blame, but also the representatives of a new philosophy of non-violence who are to be taken more seriously. Even fashion ... has adopted a romantic Indian look as its model. The currently popular trouser suit, with its long coat-jacket, is clearly reminiscent of Indian Punjabi dress. Long silk shawls, colorful smocks with wide silk sleeves, embroidered little blouses, jewelry, and, in menswear, the long Gandhi skirt, reveal Indian influence."

In 1975 China was the *in* country. Peasant smocks characterized the "Noble Peasant" look in 1976 and Zouave pants the "Bedouin" look. A year later, the "Mongol" look made its début, featuring cossack outfits. *Gerda Buxbaum*

02

01

YVES SAINT LAURENT

1936	Born on August 1 in Oran, Algeria
1955	Begins as assistant to Christian Dior
1957	Becomes chief designer for the House of Dior, following Dior's death.
1958	First collection; Trapeze line attains international recognition
1960	Creates the "Beat" look for Dior
1962	Presents first collection under his own name
1963	"Op Art" look
1965	"Mondrian" and minidresses
1966	Opens first Rive Gauche boutique for ready-to-wear fashions; creates smoking jackets and tuxedos for women; first "Pop Art" dress; "Zhivago" and "See-Through" looks
1967	Spring/Summer "African" collection
1968	"Safari" and "Carmen" looks; transparent evening dresses made from black chiffon
1971	Poses nude for an advertisement of his YSL pour Homme perfume; Autumn/Winter: "Nostalgic" look
1976	"Russian" collection: "Peasant" look with babushka
1979	"Hommage à Picasso" collection; "Scottish" look; clothes inspired by the Ballet Russes
1983	*Yves Saint Laurent: 25 Years of Design*, exhibition, Metropolitan Museum of Art, New York
1987	Mini-length balloon skirt
1988	"Homage to Cubism" collection
1996	Made Chevalier de l'Ordre des Arts et des Lettres
1998	Fashion show with 300 models at the Soccer World Cup; Alber Elbaz becomes artistic director of Women's Fashions and Heidi Slimane of Men's Fashions
PERFUMES	Y (1963), Rive Gauche (1970), YSL pour Homme (1971), Kouros (1981), Paris (1983), Champagne (1990)

"The latest at Dior is the 'Beat Look': pale zombie faces, leather suits and coats; knitted caps and high rollneck pullovers; endless black...." This was how British *Vogue* described Yves Saint Laurent's 1960 Autumn/Winter collection; it would prove to be his last work for the House of Dior. The sacrosanct loftiness of haute couture was not to be destroyed so easily by the street fashion of a twenty-year-old man. When Christian Dior died in 1957, Saint Laurent became the chief designer for the House of Dior. With his first collection, a year later, he created the Trapeze line, which produced frenzied enthusiasm and even street demonstrations.

In 1962, Saint Laurent presented the first collection under his own name, and it required the work of eighty dressmakers and tailors in three workshops to produce. The double-breasted blazer with gold buttons worn together with white Shantung silk pants was like a beacon to a long series of revolutionary creations; it was followed later by the smoking jacket, or tuxedo, for women, the see-through blouse, bermudas for evening wear (1967), and the gold leather trenchcoat (1980).

Most impressive is Saint Laurent's extraordinary, innate sense for color, which he employs with great virtuosity like no other couturier. He reduces *ad absurdum* all prevailing conceptions and rules about acceptable color combinations. Radiant orange together with pink and deep red become something matter-of-fact and easy, while violet combined with yellow and petrol blue, black with brown, or light blue with olive green and orange, become provocative accent colors.

His "Zhivago," "See-Through," "Safari," and "Carmen" looks, the vivacious, embroidered miniskirts of the "Gypsy" look (1969), the ravishing silk shawls of the "Slinky" look (1970), the "Noble Peasant" look of the "Russian" collection (1976), and the fur-trimmed coats of the "Mongolian" look (1977) made his career into a tour de force. And, in 1971, when he appeared nude in an ad promoting his perfume, that caused a sensation too!

Saint Laurent's interest in the fine arts is revealed in various designs: works inspired by Op Art (1963), a Pop Art dress inspired by Andy Warhol (1966), gowns with Braque motifs (1984), harlequin dresses from the "Hommage à Picasso" collection (1979), a lavish "Matisse" evening gown (1981), and his "Homage to Cubism" collection (1988). The master of haute couture embroidery, François Lesage, reproduced images of Van Gogh's irises and sunflowers on Saint Laurent's legendary jackets, which required more than 600 hours of laborious work. *Gerda Buxbaum*

02

Yves Saint Laurent advertising his first perfume for men, 1971 ••• 02 Yves Saint Laurent, Collection Russe, Autumn/Winter 1976/77 ••• 03 Yves Saint Laurent, pink evening dress with sash and yellow
ket, Autumn/Winter 1992/93 ••• 04 Yves Saint Laurent, see-through black silk chiffon evening dress with ostrich feathers and gold snake belt, Autumn/Winter 1968/69 ••• 05 Yves Saint Laurent, beige
ton safari jacket with bermuda shorts, July 1968

YVES SAINT LAURENT

"IT WAS SAINT LAURENT'S ACHIEVEMENT
TO MAKE FASHION UNFASHIONABLE. HE
TRANSFORMED THE FASHION DIKTAT INTO
A FASHION YEARNING."
(LAURENCE BENAÏM)

03

04
05

"THE 'SOLDIERS' DRESSED BY FASHION ARE ONLY IN UNIFORM INSOFAR AS THEY WEAR ALL THE ELEMENTS OF A UNIFORM. HOWEVER, THESE UNIFORMS DESIGNATE THEM AS WARRIORS OF A DIFFERENT ARMY." (ULF POSCHARDT, 1998)

MILITARY STYLE

01

Young people often wear military clothing for the same reasons that work clothes are worn, out of practical and financial concerns as well as for durability. Conventional military attire became popular in the late 1960s, when fashion shifted away from a psychedelic, decorative look to a simple, army surplus one.

Many youth cultures express their confrontational attitudes towards society through accessories and alterations to their clothing. By means of tears, sewn-on patches, and jarring combinations of exposed undergarments, military clothes are often deprived of their threatening status—they become civilianized. (Military clothing worn by young people rarely mimics a high-ranking officer's uniform or complete combat attire.) Hippie pacifists drew peace symbols on their military parkas, counter-symbols to the supposed authoritarianism and militarism of the state.

A further aim is to make military clothing unsuitable for its original purpose. In using the entire color palette to produce the camouflage pattern (including pink and orange), and by applying it to all types of clothing, from shoes to skirts, the visual impact is completely altered. Camouflaged clothing appears in various forms and designs in youth or subcultures such as Punk, Skinhead, Techno, Hip-Hop, and Rastafarian. As worn by these groups, the camouflage pattern actually draws attention to the wearer and shouts: "Don't hide, be visible!"

In the 1960s British Mods favored oversized parkas with U.S. Air Force emblems, while their Rocker opponents wore steel helmets and emblems and medals of the German *Wehrmacht*. Peace-loving Hippies in the 1970s revived the wearing of *Bundeswehr* parkas. The world of high fashion and design experimented with the "Military" look by adopting the typical olive-green color known as khaki. During the mid-1970s, Punks wore the entire range of military garb: dyed and torn combat pants with lots of pockets, army boots or Doc Martens' work shoes, camouflage gear, cartridge belts, and long dark-green leather "Gestapo" coats. Low cost and durability were important prerequisites for street style clothing and for those who lived on the streets. In addition, altered military clothing created a menacing look so that people kept their distance.

Military style clothing continues to play an important role in regards to sexual identity. In some subcultures, certain military-looking uniforms function as a statement about the wearer, often to satisfy or exaggerate a heterosexual image of masculinity. Some women wear military garments as a vehicle for breaking down traditional roles. In the case of female Punks, Doc Martens' and military pants expressed an aggressive demand for equal rights—a look seen in the comic-strip figure Tank Girl and the Punk rock band, riot grrrls.

Birgit Richard

02 03 04

05

06

01
02

FASHION GETS PHYSICAL

04

In the April 1977 issue of *Vogue*, the American television star Farrah Fawcett appeared skateboarding in her favorite sneakers. These were not childish Keds or goofy Converses, but good-looking Nike "Senorita Cortez" running shoes—and they looked as chic as anything the magazine's readers had ever seen. By 1981 another blond with dazzling teeth, Olivia Newton-John, had a hit single that explained the Nikes' appeal: "I Wanna Get Physical," she sang—and fashion did too.

In previous decades, every athletic pursuit (bicycling, cricket, tennis) had its corresponding costume. Even spectators at Ivy League college football games in the 1920s had theirs: the fur stadium coat. But by the late 1970s, spectators had become participants. Aerobics and jogging were more than just that decade's popular workouts; they were sexy. And fashion was the point at which sport met sex.

Racing to keep pace with fashion's "jogger-naut," manufacturers devised new wardrobe applications for performance fabrics and trims once reserved for the ice rink, the ski slope, and the pool: acrylic fleece, Lycra, terrycloth, polyurethane, parachute cloth, coated zippers. Visors were worn not as functional shields to combat the sun's ultraviolet rays, but as *cool* fashion accessories. Even a famous cigarette company got physical: a 1977 advertisement for Virginia Slims featured a model wearing a hooded top and pants made of scarlet fleece called the "Ginny Jogger." The *look* of fitness was chic. Athletic style was the name of the game, whether or not one actually broke a sweat. Part of the breathless advertising copy for the Ginny Jogger actually read: "play in it or just sit around looking smashing in it."

In 1993, Ralph Lauren opened the Polo Sport emporium in the glossiest of shopping districts, New York's Madison Avenue. The store sells everything from ski boots and hiking apparel to fragrances with the Polo imprimatur, raising active wear to high fashion.

The athletic look was born in America, but international designers would quickly get a piece of the action. Today, high-tech garments by The North Face and Marmot are worn by would-be alpinists who never see a mountain. Nike's "swoosh" logo is as coveted as that of Coco Chanel (whose head designer, Karl Lagerfeld, has toyed with scuba *tailleurs* and Lycra leggings). In fashion terms, the stripes down the side of an Adidas track pant are as valid as the satin stripe down the leg of a tuxedo trouser by Helmut Lang—who once outfitted his runway models in scuba footwear.

More than two decades after fashion first got physical, the demand for designer sporting goods shows no sign of slowing down. Following Polo's lead, Miuccia Prada recently introduced a collection called "Prada Sport"; Tse Cashmere and Marc Jacobs make deluxe, multi-ply, hooded sweatshirts; and every label from Donna Karan to Hermès has left its mark on the sneaker. The athletic style has become a lifestyle.

Julia Szabo

05

01

GEOFFREY BEENE

02

"MY CLOTHES EMBRACE THE BODY." (GEOFFREY BEENE, c. 1985)

What is a dress but cloth, seams, closure, and, once on, the body? Geoffrey Beene continuously investigates these basic elements that comprise the very essence of fashion. He starts with intriguing fabrics that may be as Old World as chine taffetas paired with brushed lace or as new as the airiest of weightless jerseys tied with a filament of plastic tubing. Next, but hardly secondary, he experiments with the seams. Beene makes them do his bidding by turning them this way and that, or by disciplining them to stand up straight. Hardly incidental to the whole of the dress, they might be three-dimensional, padded to emphasize the curve of a ribcage or the jut of a hipbone, or march across the ridge of the shoulder, drawing the eye beyond the silhouette and its boundaries. Finally, Beene adds the closure. Something most designs aim to conceal, it can be glorified in Beene's dresses, entwined by fourteen-foot-long industrial zippers in eye-popping colors.

Although any single dress by Beene stands as a microcosm of his artistry, one must look at his work as a whole to discover just how strong the threads are that wind their way from design to design. Going back decades, one finds consistent leitmotifs in his work: a bib panel gently evoking the starched front of an old-fashioned men's dress shirt; a curved band encircling the waist, suggestive of a fencer's jacket, a corselet, or a waistcoat; a trompe l'oeil shirt collar, sometimes complete with necktie. There are some fabrics which Beene can practically call his own: men's shirting, matte jerseys, *point d'esprit*, lace, and horsehair—all used with modern legerdemain. In lieu of traditional couture embroidery, Beene repeatedly chooses to work with trapunto, lines of channel stitching, and forms of appliqué. When used together, these elements of stitchery comprise a sophisticated patchwork whose homey American origins are rendered unrecognizable through superb contemporary craftsmanship.

Described as the most inventive designer working in America today, Beene's clothes are a marvel of contrasts: as beautifully and intricately constructed as any couture garments can be, yet designed to be revolutionarily light and free. Some dresses or jumpsuits are almost monastically covered up; others make use of slivers of sheer fabrics curving from one erogenous zone to the next. Like Madeleine Vionnet, to whom he is often compared, Beene tames, reveals, and highlights the curves of the female body by means of triangles; these can take the form of shard-like cutouts, inserts, or panels in varying degrees of transparency. Lest we take fashion too seriously, Beene often adds an element of humor to his work: the amusing translation of a football jersey into a floor-length evening dress or the surprising taffeta and lace underskirt—only seen while kicking up one's heels—under an otherwise sober black dress. *Caroline Rennolds Milbank*

GEOFFREY BEENE

1927	Born on August 30 in Haynesville, Louisiana, United States
1946	Briefly studies medicine and works as a window dresser for a department store in Los Angeles
1947	Studies at the Traphagen School of Fashion, New York
1948	Studies at the Ecole de Chambre Syndicale de la Couture Parisienne
1954	Works as a freelance designer for various New York fashion houses
1963	Becomes self-employed and presents collection under his own name
1964	Designs small "Empire" style dresses for clients such as Jackie Kennedy and Pat Nixon; receives the Coty Award for the first time
1965	Designs flannel and wool jersey evening dresses and lace, satin, and chiffon day dresses
1968	Designs sequined evening gowns inspired by American football jerseys
1969	Introduces a menswear line, the sporty Beenebag line, and the Bridge line of accessories and interior décor
1972–73	Has a stylistic turning point and abandons classic pattern construction in favor of a softer, more modern structure; designs jersey dresses that are spontaneously draped around the body
1986	Receives the CFDA Designer of the Year Award for the first time
1993	Becomes the first designer to use female dancers instead of supermodels to present his creations
1994	*Geoffrey Beene Unbound*, retrospective, Fashion Institute of Technology, New York
1999	Presents the first curved zipper in his Spring/Summer collection
PERFUMES	Grey Flannel (1970), Bowling Green (1987)

03

01

A FALLEN BLOSSOM
RETURNS TO ITS BRANCH
A BUTTERFLY.
(ARAKIDA MORITAKE)

KENZO: EAST MEETS WEST

KENZO TAKADA

1939	Born on February 27 in Himeji, Japan
1958	Studies at the Bunka Gakuen School of Fashion in Tokyo
1965	Moves to Paris; sells fashion sketches to Louis Féraud; designs prêt-à-porter models with the help of the textile firm Pisanti; designs for Rodier and the magazines *Elle* and *Jardin des Modes*
1970	Opens Jungle Jap boutique in Paris
1972	Awarded prize by the Fashion Editors Club of Japan
1976	Establishes Kenzo label; first collection inspired by the kimono
1977	Gives fashion show for the opening of Studio 54, New York
1978	Introduces influential "Egyptian" collection
1980	Directs the film *Dream after Dream*
1983	Initiates colorful menswear collection; establishes first Kenzo boutique in New York
1984	Made Chevalier de l'Ordre des Arts et des Lettres
1985	Receives Mainichi Fashion Prize
1986–88	Introduces new lines: Kenzo Jeans, Kenzo Junior, Kenzo Bed Linen, Kenzo Enfant, Kenzo Bébé, Kenzo City
1989	Opens boutiques in Brussels and Stockholm; Seibu exhibition in Tokyo
1990	Opens shop in Hong Kong
1991	First show in the Cour Carrée, Louvre; opens shop in Singapore
1995	Opens shop in Sydney, Australia
1998	Opens menswear shop in London
PERFUMES	Kenzo (1988), Kenzo pour Homme (1991), Parfum d'été (1992), Kashaya de Kenzo (1994), L'Eau par Kenzo, Kenzo Jungle (1996)

In the spring of 1970, in one of the salons that line the large boulevards of Paris, a new collection—with dresses as fresh as flower petals—was presented. In 1971 *Elle* magazine wrote the following about Kenzo: "His daring blend of colors and patterns have the light touch of an engraving. He knows how to take three meters of cotton, and a piece of trim, and make them blossom into a dress—the likes of which have never before been seen in Paris—in the same manner as people in his homeland assemble cherry-tree branches into a bouquet while meditating in an hour-long prayer."

Kenzo's 1973/74 collection, which he named the "Romania" look (and which he felt to be one of his best) was comprised of short, fitted jackets worn over heavily ruffled dresses and skirts with volants. Skirts were layered on top of each other and worn with rustic sweaters, tied with belts. His 1975/76 collection cannot be described as truly Japanese in spirit. There was a hint of Chinese in his use of rich colors and shimmering satins, a hint of gypsy in the layers of floral printed skirts, and even something Egyptian in his use of the flat hipline, reminiscent of those seen in Pharaonic tomb paintings.

When designing, Kenzo always starts by sketching the head, which highlights his preference for folklore and tradition. In all cultures, the headdress is the most important piece in any traditional costume, the distinguishing characteristic—and tradition plays an important role in Kenzo's designs.

His Military look of 1978/79 contained a number of new elements: quarter- or semi-circles inserted into skirts, dresses that hung from the neckline like soutanes, diagonal lines of buttons on raglan sleeves, wide pants, full pants pleated at the waist, and blossom-like or majorette-like miniskirts.

Price increases in 1980 nearly tempted Kenzo to throw in the towel. His concept of fashion for amusement no longer seemed viable. However, he persevered and tried to present affordable designs in each collection, like his flower-print ensembles made of fine, soft, cotton jersey—a fabric hitherto reserved for use in T-shirts. His method of first creating a single, original piece of clothing, inspired by his travels, and using it as the departure point for other designs, is an important part of his philosophy. Over the years he has combined these individual pieces into a kind of imaginary folklore, and he has become the recognized expert of the so-called small pieces—separates—that are ideal for mixing and matching. To Kenzo these designs are "a little bit like a mixed salad, which one eats without spending a lot of time or a lot of money."

Gerda Buxbaum

02

01 Kenzo, "Ethnic" collection, Autumn/Winter 1982/83 ••• 02 Kenzo, advertising campaign for 1985 Spring/Summer collection ••• 03 Kenzo, Iman in red, Spring/Summer 1983 ••• 04 Kenzo, wraparound, pleated skirt over trousers, Spring/Summer 1979 ••• 05 Kenzo, wide-legged, jersey trousers, Spring/Summer 1979

04
05

"THESE ARE THE FACES OF OUR TIME, AFFIRMING EVERYTHING DENIED BY THE USUAL CLICHÉS AND INVITING US TO SEEK BEAUTY IN ALL RACES AND DARING US TO BE DIFFERENT."
(OLIVIERO TOSCANI)

UNITED COLORS OF BENETTON

01

In 1985 in Paris, Mikhail Gorbachev and his presidential retinue were traversing the Champs Elysées, when Gorbachev's attention was caught by an image on advertising billboards that flanked the street. These depicted two black children kissing—one with the flag of the United States, and the other with that of the Soviet Union—and above them the phrase: "United Colors of Benetton." The advertising campaign was the work of the Italian photographer Oliviero Toscani. Twenty years had passed since 1965, when Luciano, Giuliana, Gilberto, and Carlo Benetton, four siblings in Belluno, Italy had opened their first shop. In the intervening years they had invaded the world with eight thousand points of sale, created a new lifestyle, and revolutionized retail sales. Their shops' sweaters and casual clothes, range of colors, and reasonable prices—aimed towards a young clientele—created a new alternative to traditional boutiques.

The initial idea belonged to Luciano, the eldest of the four. During the 1950s, when Italy's economic boom was slowly beginning, he started working as a clothing store clerk in Treviso. He noticed that people had money to spend, but that stores' merchandise was out of step with the fashions of the time. Thus, in 1955, the "Très Jolie" design collection was launched, the first homemade collection by the Benettons. Years later Luciano summarized his instinct in this way: "It is always the customer who chooses what we sell. Production always follows public demand." This approach, which led to two seasonal collections, Autumn/Winter and Spring/Summer, was accompanied by a revolutionary system of franchising. Benetton shops were characterized by original and, above all, unconventional design. When customers entered their shops they were meant to be inspired by the rich display of sales articles.

Thus, Benetton shops around the world, from Scandinavia to South Africa, Japan to Eastern Europe to the United States, became cult sites. Their merchandise became a "must" for entire generations that, with every change of season, waited in line to purchase new models in new color ranges. Some items even created sensations: the 1982 blue-and-white rugby shirt became a basic necessity for every Ivy League college student, while Lady Diana's patronage of Benetton led to the slogan: "Benetton dresses queens as well as the masses." While the fiancée of Prince Charles and later as a mother, Diana was a Benetton habitué and bought the young princes' clothes at the Benetton 012 shops.

The billboards that had captured Gorbachev's attention were part of Toscani's second large-scale advertising campaign for the company. Over the years other scandalous campaigns followed, including those featuring two young people dressed as a priest and nun, kissing, and a young man who had died from AIDS. These ads aimed to reaffirm the concept that had first animated Toscani's image of Benetton in 1984: "All the Colors of the World."
Andrea Affaticati

BENETTON

1935	Luciano Benetton born on May 13 in Treviso, Italy
1965	Founds the Benetton company together with his brothers Gilberto and Carlo and his sister Giuliana
1972	Introduces 012 shops with childrens' fashions
1974	Benetton takes over the Sisley company (founded in 1968 to manufacture denim fabrics)
1982	Advertising campaigns in collaboration with the photographer Oliviero Toscani create a sensation; development of an international corporate image
1988	Introduces Zerotondo infants' wear
1993	Founds Fabrica, a testing laboratory for new forms of communication
1997	Benetton Sportsystem-Playlife merges with the groups Nordica, Prince, Rollerblade, and Killerloop

PERFUME United Colors of Benetton (1985)

02

03

04

01

"IN SETTINGS THAT RESEMBLE EACH OTHER, A 'UNIFORMED' MASS DANCES A LINE DANCE THAT IS THE SAME FROM CONTINENT TO CONTINENT." (W. MEZGER, 1980)

DISCO

The disco fashion of the 1970s is now seen as an aesthetic faux pas, a fashion characterized by superficiality. Disco was the first club and dance fashion, and it highlighted the inseparable relationship between youth culture and consumer products. Disco's dress code, as with every youth "scene," served to differentiate the movement from other styles. Door screening policies, with their exclusive criteria, were used to assess the style of those attempting to enter clubs, and as such they shaped their world according to the dictates of fashion.

Disco style was fashion for the weekend because that was when the *action* took place. Films such as *Saturday Night Fever* (1977) and *Thank God It's Friday* (1978) make this abundantly clear. The glamorous styling typical of disco was intended exclusively for this self-contained universe. Removed from this environment disco fashion looked banal and was unsuitable for daywear. The atmosphere of large discotheques—revolving spheres, stroboscopes, black light, dry ice, and dance floors illuminated from beneath—determined the evolution of a specific type of clothing. The fact that the dancers' legs were lit up indicated a nascent awareness of the potential for presentation of the body in dance. Apart from erotic display, disco fashion also allowed androgynous posing in skintight garments such as catsuits and see-through suits (similar to those worn by gymnasts) made from synthetic elastic fibers.

These figure-hugging suits with their wide flares made the wearer look out of proportion. However, worn with platform shoes they made the wearer look taller and created the impression of the dancer being simultaneously suspended above, and rooted to, the dance floor by the weight of shoes and fabrics. The motto was "Dress for effect," so shimmering, reflecting materials such as satin, Lurex, velvet, and PVC were favored. Silver was a frequently used color, and it helped to elevate the situation, to take it out of the ordinary, to make it seem as if one were dancing on a planet far removed from earth.

The entire body became a reflective surface; even shiny lip gloss followed this principle: it acted as a counterpart to the glittering disco sphere by refracting light and producing its own light effects. While the body underwent this dissolution into a light-form, it was also accentuated through dance movements, a combination that has again become important in the disco revival of the 1990s.

Birgit Richard

03

02

04

01 and 04 Vivienne Westwood, "Vive la Cocotte" collection, Autumn/Winter 1995/96 ••• 02 Vivienne Westwood, "Five Centuries Ago" collection, Autumn/Winter 1997/98 ••• 03 Vivienne Westwood, "Five Centuries Ago – Men" collection, Autumn/Winter 1997/98 ••• 05 Vivienne Westwood, "Pirate" collection, 1981

"IN THIS SEA OF BANALITY, DISTINCTION AND ELEGANCE OF DRESS IS OF MORE VALUE TODAY THAN IT EVER WAS BEFORE." (VIVIENNE WESTWOOD)

VIVIENNE WESTWOOD

04

The start of Vivienne Westwood's fashion career is legendary. Today, this self-taught designer and businesswoman belongs to the exclusive circle of creative people who set the tone in the world of fashion. In the mid-1970s, Westwood, together with Malcolm McLaren, made newspaper headlines with their S&M clothing and pornographic, aggressive-looking accessories designed for the London "scene" and punk music group, the Sex Pistols. Since 1971, Westwood's secondhand boutique, Let It Rock, on King's Road, in London, was an insider's source for Teddy Boy suits, then Rockers' gear, and later African fashion. The shop, successively named Too Fast To Live, Too Young To Die (1972) and Sex (1974), became Seditionaries in 1977 and "the place" for Punkers and punk fashion. Westwood, trained as an elementary school teacher, metamorphosed into the Queen of Punk.

In the early 1980s, when punk fashion had already been commercialized, Westood and McLaren presented their first catwalk shows, premiering with the "Pirates" collection (1981). In the following years they presented their "Savages" (1982), "Buffalo Girls" (1982/83), and "Punkature" collections—all were extremely successful and copied. Westwood's sensational solo career began in Paris with her "Witches" collection (1983), and, within a few years, she was catapulted to the top of the fashion world. Today, Westwood presents her lines in Paris (Gold Label), Milan (MAN), and New York (Red Label), owns several shops, and sells her own brand of perfume.

Westwood's success is rooted in her unconventionality and readiness to take risks, coupled with a high degree of personal ambition and self-discipline. To be able to look back, to master the techniques of the tailor's craft, and to be knowledgeable of history in order to move forward forms the basis of her artistic creation. As Westwood states: "Creativity comes from technique." Her knowledge of the history of clothing and her fascination for different cultures—their sense of elegance, liveliness, potency, eroticism, or sauciness—fuels her ingenious designs for men and women. She invites wearers to expand their horizons, develop their personalities, and adopt playful attitudes towards dress—to experiment with erotic or sexually-charged looks instead of becoming conformist, "neutralized" by the average range of consumer products. (Westwood is particularly suspect of the shabby, comfortable look.) Her credo is: "Fashion is about sex." Modes of expression from the eighteenth-century Rococo period to the culture of the *demimonde* are her favored models, to which she adds wit and irony.

Westwood's fashion is theatrical and volatile, often teetering on the edge of bad taste. Her designs skillfully and intentionally push the boundaries between traditional, vulgar, and middle-class taste. Anyone aspiring to wear the Fashion Queen's label must be prepared to stand out.

Gundula Wolter

VIVIENNE WESTWOOD

1941	Born Vivienne Isabel Swire on April 8 in Glossop, Derbyshire, Great Britain
1971-80	Opens Let it Rock boutique, King's Road, London, together with partner Malcolm McLaren, founder of the punk rock group, the Sex Pistols; name of boutique changes periodically: Too Fast Too Live, Too Young Too Die (1972), Sex (1974), Seditionaries (1977), and World's End (1980)
1981	Presents first collection, "Pirates," inspired by the seventeenth century; introduces the Gold Label line for demi-couture
1982	Shows collection in Paris for the first time; "Buffalo Girls" collection in muddy colors and camouflage anticipates the "Grunge" look of the 1990s
1983	Starts her solo career with the "Witches" collection
1984	"Mini Crini" collection: hooped skirts inspired by Victorian crinolines, tailored jackets, platform shoes
1990	Receives CFDA Designer of the Year Award; first menswear collection during Florentine fashion fair Pitti Uomo
1992	Awarded Order of the British Empire by Queen Elizabeth
1993	"Anglomania" collection in the English style: multicolored tartan evening gowns, platform shoes with 25cm-high heels; introduces Red Label prêt-à-porter line; professor at the Hochschule der Künste, Berlin
1995	Costumes for the film *Leaving Las Vegas*
1997	Has her "Five Centuries Ago" collection photographed in the style of famous paintings
1998	Introduces Anglomania line for jeans and casual wear
PERFUME	Boudoir (1998)

05

NO FUTURE/NO FUTURE/NO FUTURE FOR YOU/NO FUTURE/NO FU-
TURE/NO FUTURE/FOR ME (*GOD SAVE THE QUEEN*, SEX PISTOLS, 1977)

PUNK

01

02

Punk is a state of mind and was a fashion. It had greater impact on Western popular culture—from music to fashion, from graphic design to politics—than any other youth movement since the Hippies in the 1960s. Yet the hardcore of the cult lasted a mere thirty months, from the summer of 1975 to January 1978. Centered in London, it focused on, at most, 200 teenagers. Punk was spawned in a small, highly stylized shop, Seditionaries, in West London, which was owned by Vivienne Westwood and Malcolm McLaren.

"Do it yourself!" was Punk's clarion call, referring to both the making of music and clothes. The originators, the most inventive "doers," were three teenagers: Johnny Rotten and Sid Vicious of the seminal punk band, the Sex Pistols, and Jordan, a shop assistant at Seditionaries who became the female punk icon celebrated in Derek Jarman's film *Jubilee* (1978). These creative youths achieved a look which instantly communicated all the pain and anguish of lost adolescence. This look centered upon self-mutilation, damaged and asexual clothing, a violent rejection of prettiness or naturalness, and a cacophony of visual references wrenched from their familiar settings and fused together in a new and shocking amalgam. Drainpipe pants (a rejection of hippie flares) were teamed with slashed school blazers worn inside out and held together with safety pins. Decorative devices were seized upon that smacked of political bad taste (the swastika), sexual bad taste (the "used" tampon or condom), filth (the lavatory chain), cheapness (the black bin-bag, safety pins), the macabre (razor blades) or the morbid (the skinny black tie worn as a hangman's noose). Anything that would annoy adults—Nazism, Marxism, treason, blasphemy, and sexual perversion—was deployed. To a greater extent than former youth cults, women determined the style and activities of Punk as much as men did. Women combined elements of militaristic and sado-sexual or bondage dress with brazenly artificial make-up and hair. The look yelled "Loveless!"

Inspired by the teenagers that flocked to Seditionaries, Westwood, a self-taught seamstress, harnessed this unbridled creativity and explored the possibilities of Marcel Duchamp's "ready-mades" by taking everyday, mass-produced objects out of their contexts and tailoring them into a punk uniform—the Bondage Suit. (Initially this suit was black cotton; only later did Westwood cut it from tartan wool). It consisted of bondage pants, which hobbled the legs together with a knee strap and covered the bottom with a toweling bum-flap, a parachute shirt hung with four straps attached with D-rings and a large plastic Hoover ring, a T-shirt or muslin shirt sloganed with an obscenity, a mohair jumper, and multi-buckled bondage boots. McLaren, drawing upon his art training and flirtation with French Situationism, deployed the blank white T-shirt as a canvas, onto which he scrawled statements intended to confront and shock the general public.

Punk was the birth of a powerful partnership between music and fashion. Westwood and McLaren successfully brought these two markets together, meeting the youths' demand for a look modeled on their pop idols and music.

Jane Mulvagh

03

04

01

THE OVERSIZED LOOK

Christian Dior's New Look demolished the wartime silhouette in one stroke. To fashion-conscious women frustrated by the monotony of prevailing fashions, this came with the force of a new, personal liberation. As women became increasingly aware of equal rights and career recognition, fashions changed. Women "denied" their bodies by artificially broadening their shoulders with shoulder pads and wide sleeves and by wearing oversized garments.

In his essay "Starkes Geschlecht" (The Strong Sex), the philosopher Walter Seitter describes the body as a store of raw materials, an experimental field and parade ground for fashion. The silhouette as a graphic outline and form of demarcation or expansion is one of clothing's most striking features. Tightness and looseness alternate, and the richness of shapes fluctuates between opposite extremes. The aesthetics of the silhouette of clothing can be traced back to certain basic geometric figures (circles, squares, triangles, lines) as well as to appropriate size or symmetry ratios. Alterations in the body shape or contours can be brought about by gymnastics, bodybuilding, slimming diets, plastic surgery, or distorting clothing.

The objectivization of women was caused by the emphasis placed on the fitted waist (corset), characteristic of European dress. Length and height were achieved through hairstyles, hats, and shoes, while width was produced by crinolines, collars, sleeves, and ruffs as well as by artificially broadening the shoulders. As early as 1581, a roll of linen, padded with cotton, was bound around the armpit and shoulder in order to broaden the effect of the shoulder. In 1833 epaulettes—shoulder pieces which developed from armor and which were used to attach a shoulder strap and military rank badges—were added to emphasize enormous sleeves. In 1897 shoulder wings were used, around 1905 shoulder supports, and in the 1930s shoulder pads—all of which gave the torso a triangular shape.

At the end of the 1970s, Claude Montana and Thierry Mugler created extra-wide shoulders, and Pierre Cardin called his 1979 line "Superman." These extreme bodily emphases led to an overall enlargement in the appearance of the female body so that even petite women "swam" in X-large or XX-large coats, men's shirts, or T-shirts—all of which could be worn as dresses.   *Gerda Buxbaum*

02

"JUST AS THE TOPIARY TREES OF A GARDEN ARE PRUNED, SO WE ARE SHAPED ONE YEAR INTO A BALL AND THE NEXT INTO A SPINDLE ..."
(ANNA MUTHESIUS, 1903)

03
04

"HOW THE DELIBERATELY ANTI-FASHION LOOK OF CORPORATE AMERICA WAS GIVEN A DESIGNER MAKEOVER." (JULIA SZABO, 1999)

01

Upon its publication in 1975, a groundbreaking book entitled *Dress for Success* caused a furor in the fashion industry. Its author, John T. Molloy, set forth a system of dressing for the ambitious professional male that would assist him in his ascent up the corporate ladder. What scandalized Seventh Avenue? Molloy's characterization of it as an evil empire out to separate a man from his earnings. In 1977 Malloy produced the sequel *The Woman's Dress for Success Book*. Legions of ambitious women adopted the deliberately anti-fashion uniform promoted in this book: comically feminized business suits with shawl collars and demure knee-length skirts, high-necked blouses with jabots and vests, and men's-style shirts with bow ties. Validating Molloy's assessment of the fashion industry as one based on greed, enterprises such as the women's outfitter Alcott & Andrews quickly cropped up to cash in on the demand for what was arguably the nadir of twentieth-century women's fashion: corporate drag.

By the 1980s, young, upwardly mobile professionals of both sexes had earned themselves an acronymous nickname: yuppies. The "go-getter" decade made millionaires of those who had dressed for success (as well as a few who had not, such as the resolutely shleppy, Microsoft mogul Bill Gates). Fashion was no longer the enemy; it was an ally, but it came at a price. Flashy clothes and accessories rigged with instantly recognized logos, such as Ralph Lauren's polo player and Chanel's interlocked Cs, had the power to convey life-altering status of the sort Molloy's book had described. The goal of dressing rich, however, was not to look like you were on the way up, but to give the impression you had already arrived.

For men, the uniform was a power suit à la Michael Douglas, as seen in the movie *Wall Street* (1987), together with an Hermès necktie. For women, it was a sexy, big-shouldered skirt-suit designed by Donna Karan conveying, as Melanie Griffith states in the 1988 film *Working Girl*: "a head for business and a bod for sin." As re-invigorated by Karl Lagerfeld, the iconic Chanel suit now conveyed that its wearers not only belonged to the upper crust, but that they were also confident and high-spirited enough to break the rules, pairing a decorative *tailleur* with jeans.

In the 1990s the look of success is subtler. It is still sexy, especially as interpreted by Gucci designer Tom Ford, whose recent office-babe collection featured pinstripe trouser suits worn with halter-tops and aggressively high heels. When compared with a 1980s power suit, a 1990s business ensemble by Jil Sander, Calvin Klein, or Helmut Lang is so quiet it is practically invisible. Yet each conveys the twin images of competence and sophistication, important for survival in the modern corporate milieu. As the late 1990s revival of interest in classic tailoring suggests, the fashion aesthetic and the dress-for-success ethic can play together and win.　*Julia Szabo*

03

DRESS FOR $UCCESS

04
05

01 Comme des Garçons, "lace" sweater, Autumn/Winter 1982/83 ••• 02 Comme des Garçons, fine layered cotton dress, "Clustering Beauty" collection, Spring/Summer 1998 ••• 03 and 04 Comme des Garçons, daytime wear with exterior seams, 1981 ••• 05 Comme des Garçons, an unusually colorful Spring/Summer 1996 collection

"I PREFER PEOPLE TO LOOK AT MY WORK AS A STRONG EXPRESSION OF BEAUTY. UNDERSTANDING IT IS UNIMPORTANT. SUPERFICIAL BEAUTY IS NOT ENOUGH."
(REI KAWAKUBO)

COMME DES GARÇONS

01
02

03

REI KAWAKUBO

1942	Born in Tokyo, Japan
	Studies fine arts in Tokyo
1964	Works in the advertising department of the Japanese textile firm Asahi Kasei
FROM 1967	Freelance stylist
1969	Founds the Comme des Garçons label for women's wear
1973	Comme des Garçons Co. Ltd. in Tokyo
1975	Establishes first collection and boutique in Tokyo
1978	Comme des Garçons Homme menswear line
1981	Presents prêt-à-porter collections biannually in Paris; introduces Comme des Garçons Tricot and Comme des Garçons Robe de Chambre lines; "lace" knitwear: sweaters purposely knitted to incorporate holes, rips, and tears
1983	Presents furniture line; wins Mainichi Newspaper Award, Tokyo; opens boutique in SoHo, New York
1984–88	Comme des Garçons Homme Plus, Comme des Garçons Homme Deux, Comme des Garçons Noir, and Comme des Garçons shirt range; publishes Comme des Garçons magazine Six biannually
1989	Opens flagship store in Tokyo
1991	Made Chevalier de l'Ordre des Arts et des Lettres
1993	Essence of Quality, exhibition by Comme des Garçons Noir, Kyoto Costume Institute, Tokyo
1996	Participates in the Florence Art & Fashion Biennale
1997	Awarded honorary doctorate by the Royal College of Art, London
PERFUMES	Comme des Garçons (1994), Odeur 53 (1998)

The Japanese call her designer label "Garçons," the French "Comme de," and English speakers simply say "Comme." Comme des Garçons—the NASA of the fashion world—is one of the new design laboratories operated by Rei Kawakubo. "I don't want or need to explain. I don't talk too much. Clothes are my statements. That is an old Japanese way of thinking. What matters is what you create .... Comfort, a home, hold back the energy that drives innovation. You need to be hungry, to lack comfort. Possessions make you smug. You always see the same things." Her different and innovative way of seeing things provokes varied reactions. Her "hunchbacked" clothes have been laughed at, but she accepts laughter as long as it is not cruel but open and honest.

The shriek of outrage that resounded through the international press in 1981—when Rei Kawakubo first showed her fashions in Paris—was the loudest ever heard in the fashion industry. Beauty, charm, eroticism, sex appeal—all the ideals of Western womanhood—seemed to be gravely imperilled by this Japanese provocateur. The press had a field day with the so-called post-Hiroshima look, with its aesthetic of destruction, poverty, and hunger and with its depressing mood engendered by the use of the color black. Controversial black—it is the color symbolic of anarchy, of the intelligentsia and artists, of elegance and distinction (the little black dress), of inflexibility and ascetic austerity (Spanish fashion), a symbol of the bourgeois work ethic (seventeenth-century Netherlands), and a firm component of uniforms and folk dress. But it is also the color of power, violence, and sadism, of mourning, and of the clergy (Luther's cassock).

Comme des Garçons, which means "like boys"—what women in the early 1980s were least supposed to be—expressed criticism of the prevailing social construct of women and, importantly, of the very concept of fashion. Instead of the dialectics of concealing and exposing, and the dependent conventions of sexuality and sensuousness, the designs result in a different sensuousness, one of changing silhouettes that are graded in the depth of the fabric. Comme des Garçons was one of the first firms to radically eliminate the merchandise character of the clothes in its shops, and great emphasis is placed on making the shops look like something other than trading centers. Unlike the fashion press, the magazine Six (published by Rei Kawakubo) avoids the aesthetic of a mail-order catalog; its contents are stamped with Kawakubo's principles, not her clothes. "It is very important to preserve traditions and culture. The idea is not to be iconoclastic, to make sweeping changes, but to be careful not to do things in the same way."

Gerda Buxbaum

04

05

KARL LAGERFELD

1938	Born on September 10 in Hamburg, Germany
1952	Moves to Paris and attends the Lycée Montaigne
1955	Receives first prize in a coat design competition sponsored by the International Wool Secretariat
1955–58	Works as assistant to Pierre Balmain, Paris
1959–63	Artistic director at Jean Patou
FROM 1964	Active as freelance designer for the houses of Krizia, Fendi, and others
1963–84	Chief designer for the house of Chloé (also 1992–97)
1974	Founds own line, Karl Lagerfeld Impression
1979–81	Guest professor at the Hochschule für angewandte Kunst, Vienna
FROM 1983	Artistic director of the House of Chanel
1984	Designs prêt-à-porter for Chanel; founds KL and KL by Karl Lagerfeld lines
1987–95	Active as a designer for the large German clothing manufacturer Klaus Steilmann
FROM 1987	Active as a photographer; publishes various books
1993	Receives Lucky Strike Designer Award
1996	Receives the *Kulturpreis* of the Deutsche Gesellschaft für Fotografie
1998	Opens Lagerfeld Gallery in Paris
PERFUMES	Chloe (1975), KL (1982), KL pour Homme (1986), Lagerfeld Photo (1990), Sun Moon Stars (1994), Jako (1997)

KARL LAGERFELD

Superlatives do not nearly suffice to describe the diverse activities and richly faceted personality of Karl Lagerfeld. "Karl the Great," "Emperor Karl," and "Jack-of-all-Trades"—as the press call him—are some of the titles given to this talented designer. Apart from his main occupation as chief designer for major fashion houses such as Fendi, Chloé, and currently Chanel, he has also established his own commercial labels: Lagerfeld and KL by Karl Lagerfeld. He has launched a number of perfumes under his name, has been active as a costume designer, and is professor of fashion at the Hochschule für angewandte Kunst in Vienna. He surprised the fashion world with a delightful children's book, *The Emperor's New Clothes*, which he illustrated, and he is also a fashion photographer whose work has appeared in countless books. He is known for his aura of unapproachability and is feared for his cutting critiques.

Apart from his great passion, photography, Lagerfeld believes that his greatest talent is "to bring things that others have started to a better conclusion"—a talent which in 1983 gained him the position, after decades of activity as the creative head of various leading fashion firms, of chief designer for the House of Chanel. Lagerfeld, with his immense energy and creative ideas, has rejuvenated the Chanel image, brushing away the cobwebs that had gathered after Coco Chanel's death in 1971. He has always stayed true to the Chanel style and its unmistakable elements, but he has catapulted it into the immediate present by means of new materials and cheeky tailoring. Traditional Chanel admirers were shocked when Lagerfeld produced Chanel suits in the "Jeans" look in 1991. Yet the suits, piped with blue and pink, with a provocative mixture of luxurious tweed and street fashion, sold well.

Every season Lagerfeld plays with the classic Chanel suit, coaxing novel and unexpected aspects out of it. In autumn 1992 he integrated the "Biker" look into the updated Chanel collection, photographing his discovery and style muse, the German model Claudia Schiffer, in a leather Chanel suit. The classic cut of the suit and the typical gold costume jewelry accessories were his homage to Coco Chanel. Further coups by "Karl the Uninhibited," as fashion journalists have occasionally called him, include the Chanel jacket worn in combination with men's underwear (1995) or with short hot pants instead of the original modest knee-length suit skirt (1998), and having his models wear open jackets revealing flashes of naked bosom. Every season Lagerfeld produces not only creative excesses on the catwalk but also brings forth a ready-to-wear line of classic Chanel—wearable clothes in the style of Mademoiselle herself but refined and updated by Lagerfeld. *Beate Dorothea Schmid*

01

"THE ESSENCE OF FASHION IS ITS CHANGEABILITY. IT SATISFIES THE CURIOSITY, THE HUMAN DRIVE TOWARDS WHAT IS NEW." (KARL LAGERFELD)

05

03
04

"JUST LIKE THE SILHOUETTE OF A CAR NEEDS TO BE CHANGED PERIODICALLY SO AS NOT TO LOSE ITS POWER OF ATTRACTION, IN THE WESTERN WORLD THE FEMALE BODY IS ALSO RESHAPED FROM TIME TO TIME." (BERNARD RUDOFSKY, 1978)

01

POUF, BUSTLE, TUTU, AND CRINOLINE

Right in the middle of "power dressing," with its exaggeratedly broad, padded shoulders and pinstriped suits for working women, in the midst of the "rags and holes" look derived from British subcultures and the fashion scene's preference for artificially creased fabrics, another aesthetic emerged that recalled the seventeenth-century Baroque era and the splendor of its courtly festivities and status-obsessed French aristocracy.

This was sparked in 1982 by the tutu (the little, tulle ballet skirt), a stiff, mini petticoat. Teenage girls wore these to discotheques in the form of a miniskirt that stood out stiffly in multiple layers of brightly colored, or garishly neon, tulle flounces. Young women wore them not only in the evening but also during the day as a balloon skirt gathered at the hem. In the calf-length version, they resembled stiff, elegant Dior models from the 1950s. A more decadent version designed for cocktail parties (which were once again in vogue) took its cue from Hollywood glamour, especially the blockbuster film *Amadeus* (1984). Jean-Paul Gaultier's designs—with underwear as outerwear styling, exposing lace bodies and under-wire bras—set this look.

The definition of a petticoat, as used here, refers to a wide, stiff underskirt of nylon or starched cotton, often with lace flounces, to which a bodice or bustier was sometimes attached. In 1985 Vivienne Westwood brought out a collection entitled "Mini Crinolines." It featured tight corsets whose cuts and construction were based on her painstaking research of original, eighteenth-century crinolines.

Designs by the Japanese couturier Yamamoto made reference to the "cul de Paris," which had swollen to extremes precisely 100 years before. This so-called Parisian bottom, with more or less lavish bunching up of the dress, first became popular in ladies' fashion under the term "bouffant" in the late Baroque period, around 1690–1700. Roughly a century later, it became fashionable again as a *tournure* or bustle, a roll-like device worn over the bottom in order to give a dress volume, which, in turn, originally derived from the polonaise flounce.

Nearly every designer drew on the history of the female skirt, quoting various phases of its development and commenting on it with a certain irony. Not even Helmut Lang could completely avoid fullness at the back of his designs, attaching a train to a short skirt in reduced black-and-white combinations. Karl Lagerfeld brought the eighteenth century—his favorite historical period—to life with coatdresses of pastel satin, the skirts of which were not, as formerly, floor-length, but rather mini and skintight and to be worn with thigh-high boots. In the same collection, there were pageboy suits with knee breeches made of velvet, brocade, and silk with gold thread worn under jerkin-like jackets. Gianfranco Ferré accented simple black bodysuits with extravagantly wide gold belts, fastened around narrow waists like Baroque picture frames. Several designers reduced the crinoline to a skeleton and made it transparent. Often the supportive frame—the construction—was all that remained visible.

Gerda Buxbaum

03 04 05

01

"I'M NOT JUST SELLING CLOTHES. I'M OFFERING A WORLD, A PHILOSOPHY
OF LIFE." (RALPH LAUREN)

U.S. LIFESTYLE

Whereas European fashion in the 1980s, from Paris-based, Japanese designers to Christian Lacroix, celebrated cutting-edge originality, the two dominant U.S. designers of the decade were developing a different vision. Ralph Lauren and Calvin Klein did not see fashion as an avant-garde art form only for the initiated. In a typically American, democratic way, and with an eye on production turnover, their aim was to conquer everyone's closets: rich or poor, old or young, fashion-conscious or not. Yet fashion, in the form of clothing, was not enough for Lauren and Klein. To them, clothes were, and are, just one piece in a jigsaw puzzle of style that covers the whole of everyday life—from jeans to tableware, underwear to hand towels, sunglasses to furniture.

Lauren designed his first collection in 1967, unusually wide neckties that he personally presented to store buyers. Encouraged by his success, he launched a line of menswear in 1968 under the prestigious logo of a polo player. His shirts and suits broke with the conventions of that time: no polyester, no hippie influence. Rather, they were dandified versions of Ivy League classicism, mixed with elements of cowboy and safari clothing. In 1971 he turned to women's wear, and his tailored shirts made from "masculine" fabrics became his first big sellers. Lauren's adaptations of the signature styles of Katharine Hepburn, Jackie Kennedy, and the women in Hemingway's circle turned out to be almost frighteningly timeless. In the 1990s he reacted to the increasing casualness of fashion with his Polo Sport line in which he applied his power-through-style principle to futuristic materials; the parkas and baggy pants of this label became status garments on the hip-hop scene.

Klein also started out with a narrowly focused collection: women's coats. Five years later he launched Calvin Klein Jeans, using billboards depicting Brooke Shields—photographed by Richard Avedon (b. 1923)—to establish himself as a pioneer of erotically suggestive advertising. Unlike Lauren, whose lifestyle universe permits conspicuous decoration (as long as it sports a pedigree), Klein adheres strictly to the modern dictum of "form follows function." "I've never been one to see women in ruffles," he told *Time* magazine in 1996. "To me it's just silly."

During the 1980s and 1990s the two designers turned their businesses into global licensing empires. Season after season, both of them drew inspiration from the treasure trove of American glamour: Lauren from the "Golden Age" of Hollywood, Klein from a jet-set ideal of sexy modernity. Their influence on the generation of designers who followed them—for example, Michael Kors (b. 1959), Isaac Mizrahi (b. 1961), and Marc Jacobs (b. 1960)—and on mass labels such as GAP or Banana Republic cannot be underestimated.

Advocates of the European ideal of fashion-as-art may accuse these two large-scale entrepreneurs of being uncreative. Yet the coherence and dynamism of their style worlds, visualized through perfect, stage-like shops and masterly advertising campaigns, mark them as creative forces of the first rank. With them, fashion has become a philosophy of life.

Margit J. Mayer

02

03

Ralph Lauren with his dog wearing a tweed jacket ••• 02 Polo Ralph Lauren, 1920s-style resort wear ••• 03 Banana Republic, from the catalogue of the Spring 1999 collection ••• 04 Polo Ralph Lauren, nd-knitted sweater with jeans shorts

"WHY CAN'T A WOMAN GO OUT IN A T-SHIRT? THE BODYSUIT THAT I DID
IS BASICALLY A T-SHIRT. IT WAS ABOUT GIVING WOMEN BACK THEIR BODIES
AND GIVING THEM BACK THE COMFORT OF THEIR BODIES."
(DONNA KARAN, 1996)

01

02
03

05

DONNA KARAN

Confident, streamlined, and quietly luxurious, Donna Karan's designs are the epitome of late twentieth-century urban style. Since Karan's debut in 1985, her signature women's wear collections have demonstrated a soft, sculptural awareness of the female form through severely tailored citywear. In the 1980s this was represented in her integrated wardrobes of smoothly cut, monochrome separates that addressed a generation of women seeking to juggle busy careers and social lives. Her designs provided wearable solutions for women who wanted their clothing to portray an image of authority and yet retain an intrinsic femininity. They drew upon the practical, body conscious forms of sportswear to produce outfits for the office, which were constructed from supple, stretchy fabrics which swathed the body in the sensuous folds of luxury fabrics like cashmere.

Karan's advertisements reinforced this vision of dynamic femininity, in aspirational scenes of successfully balanced careers, social, and domestic lives. Seemingly diverse roles were given a sense of unity through her simple but sophisticated designs. This ideal culminated in her campaign of 1992, which depicted a female candidate running for the U.S. presidency under the slogan: "In women we trust." This brought together not only Karan's desire to address women directly, promoting a sense of strength, confidence, and ambition, but also the essentially American ideal that her designs represent. They draw upon the pared-down modernity of earlier designers such as Claire McCardell, whose sporty and dance-inspired designs dressed the proto-career woman of the 1940s and 1950s, freeing her of the molded forms of Parisian couture and creating an ideal of functional, multipurpose clothing stripped of unnecessary detail. Karan could be said to have inherited and built upon this dictum, adding a sense of luxury and glamour while retaining the idea that clothing should be designed to make women feel in control rather than controlled and restricted.

Karan's own image is closely identified with that of her label, emphasizing her intimate knowledge of her customers' lifestyle and needs as well as their anxieties about their bodies. Her clothes are cut to emphasize the vertical, creating long, lean silhouettes that streamline any figure. Her pioneering of the "body," a leotard-like garment that eliminates excess fabric, has been instrumental in smoothing out unnecessary bulges and lines. The designer's reliance upon black as a base color for most of her collections is also a tactic used to elongate and flatter the figure.

She has sought to apply this philosophy to both her menswear and her sportier diffusion line, DKNY, once again providing solutions for busy, urban lives. Her complementary accessories and home line extend her themes further, proposing the construction of whole living environments: calm, controlled, and uncluttered spaces amid the chaos of the city. It is no accident, though, that her own brand identity is closely linked to New York. Both epitomize a sense of dynamic internationalism while remaining intrinsically American in character.
Rebecca Arnold

DONNA KARAN

1948	Born on October 2 in New York, United States
1968–69	Studies at Parson's School of Design, New York
1968–74	Works as assistant to Anne Klein
1974–82	Responsible for Anne Klein's collections
1982	Launches secondary line Anne Klein II
1984	Founds company, Donna Karan New York; invents a new basic garment for women's wear—the bodysuit
1988	Introduces less expensive DKNY line
1997	Introduces D Karan line for the underthirties, Donna Karan Underwear, accessories, fashion jewelery, and two menswear lines
PERFUME	Donna Karan New York (1992)

04

"IF YOU CAN'T BE ELEGANT, AT LEAST BE EXTRAVAGANT!"
(MOSCHINO)

02

FRANCO MOSCHINO

1950	Born on February 27 in Abbiategrasso near Milan, Italy
1968–71	Studies fine arts at the Accademia delle Belle Arti, Milan
1970–80	Works as an illustrator for various fashion magazines; also works periodically for Gianni Versace and as a stylist and freelance designer for various Italian fashion companies; becomes known for his provocative and irreverent style
1983	Presents first collection, "Couture!"
1986	Introduces first menswear collection
1985–89	Introduces the secondary lines Cheap and Chic and Moschino Jeans
1994	Dies on September 18 in Milan; Rossella Iardini assumes leadership of the Moschino design team
PERFUMES	Moschino (1990), Cheap and Chic by Moschino, Oh! De Moschino (1996), Moschino Uomo (1997)

Franco Moschino was endowed with a strong sense of fantasy. His artistic sensibility and talent for design led him to study at the Accademia di Brera in Milan, where he devoted himself to various activities, including freelance illustration work. He found this type of work to be most rewarding and in the 1970s worked as a fashion illustrator and designer for various fashion houses and magazines, including *Gap Italia* and the up-and-coming designer, Gianni Versace.

In 1978 he began designing for the Cadette collection, which, as Moschino himself wrote in a press release, "presented various 'anomalies' with regard to the canonical molds of fashion, particularly Italian fashion." He summarized the basic concept of the Moschino style as "leaving"—again, these are his own words—"the utmost freedom of choice to those who want to dress themselves." He refuted the traditional definition of a couturier as a "creator of fashion," almost reducing his work to that of a stylist. He once said: "My models are classic ones which have always existed in people's closets, only I put them together in an unusual way." Moschino's design and fashion sense, coupled with irony and strong communication skills, were the characteristic prerogatives of his style. This is evident in his "Couture!" collection of 1983, presented in Milan, the first under his own label.

International recognition was immediate, and nearly two decades of success followed. Moschino's first menswear collection (1986) addressed fashion stereotypes, but in an ironic and unconventional way. His presentations were always surprising events that created a stir, and his irreverent approach led him to conceive of new formulas for invitations, stagings, and advertising campaigns. He created some of his most surrealistic accessories by appropriating the tri-color bands of the Italian flag as well as other Italian symbols. From safety pins to artificial gems, these things became cult items. In 1987 he launched his first perfume, and in the following year he presented his "Cheap and Chic" collection as well as "Fur for Fun," which featured the first ecological furs. During the late 1980s Moschino began to distance himself from the world of fashion shows, and by the early 1990s he rebelled against the fashion system. A committed pacifist with interests in social and ecological issues, he launched a campaign against drugs, animal abuse, and violence in 1992. In 1994, he premiered his ecological collection "Ecouture!"

This enfant terrible of fashion died in 1994. Yet his message lives on through his family and co-workers: Moschino's brother, Angelo, is president of the company and heads the foundation that raises money for children with AIDS, while Rossella Iardini, who was Moschino's close collaborator until 1981, is responsible for the brand's image and style. Today, the Moschino line of perfumes has expanded, and new stores have opened around the world.   *Anna Gloria Forti*

01

MOSCHINO

03

STOP
THE
FASHION
SYSTEM
!

04
05

MOSCHINO

JEAN-PAUL GAULTIER

1952	Born on April 24 in Arcueil near Paris, France
1970	Works as design assistant to Pierre Cardin
1971	Joins the House of Jean Patou
1974–75	Returns to work for Cardin's manufacturing operations in the Philippines; designs Cardin's collection for the United States
1976	Debuts with his first collection, featuring clothes made from woven placemats, which is ridiculed by the press
1978	Forms partnership with Japanese textile manufacturer Kashiyama
1979	"James Bond" collection receives much attention
1980–81	Presents "High-Tech" collection featuring trash containers
1982	"Paris Gaultier" collection: reminiscent of existentialist fashion of the 1950s
1984	First menswear collection, "L'Homme Objet," focuses on the male décolletage
1985	Opens studio in the Galerie Vivienne, Paris; creates the skirt for men for his collection "Et Dieu Créa L'Homme"
1988	Secondary line Junior Gaultier
1989	Designs costumes for Peter Greenaway's film The Cook, The Thief, His Wife and Her Lover
1990	Designs costumes for pop star Madonna's Blonde Ambition tour; his designs spark the trend of underwear as outerwear
1993	Launches Gaultier Jeans line
1996	Designs costumes for Luc Besson's film The Fifth Element; "Cyber" collection and men as "Pin-Up Boys"
1997	First haute couture collection
1998	"The Charms of Frida Kahlo" collection for women; "Sevillanas" collection for for men
1998–99	"Saint Germain des Prés" collection for women; "Italian Style" collection for men
PERFUMES	Jean-Paul Gaultier (1993), Le Mâle (1995)

JEAN-PAUL GAULTIER

Jean-Paul Gaultier is an aesthetic provocateur. He launched his debut collection in 1976 and his first menswear collection in 1984, but his designs and fashion shows are still directional and even controversial. He is best known for his gender-bending styles—putting women in pinstriped suits and men in skirts. He is also notorious for emphasizing sexuality through the use of fetishized garments, such as the corset.

Gaultier subverts the clichés of masculinity and femininity. Responding to the feminist concept that fashion objectifies women, his first menswear collection, "L'homme objet" (1984), focused on the male décolletage. "Et Dieu créa l'homme" (1985) featured skirts for men, while "Joli Monsieur" (1985/86) put men in dresses. Gaultier also explored the theme of androgyny in collections such as "Une Garde robe pour deux" (1985). In place of the bland unisex ensembles that signified androgyny in the 1970s, Gaultier boldly juxtaposed sexually dimorphic garments such as the bustier and the tuxedo. He dressed both men and women in impeccably tailored suits and jackets, underwear-as-outerwear, and a multicultural mix of ethnic-inspired garments.

Sexual fetishism is a recurrent theme in Gaultier's work. As a child he was fascinated by his grandmother's pink lace-up corset, which seemed to epitomize the mystery of femininity. He has designed many corset-inspired clothes for both sexes—probably the most famous is the corset that he created for Madonna's Blonde Ambition tour (1990)—and even his perfume is packaged in a corset-shaped bottle. He has also designed a number of fetishistic shoes, including a pair with multiple high heels. Although some journalists claim that Gaultier's customers look like "fetishistic whores," others praise his use of humor and irony.

Heavily influenced by the punk subculture, Gaultier often uses "bad taste" in an effort to break taboos. His 1993 "Hasidic" collection was particularly controversial because it irreverently played with the traditional clothing of a religious minority. That same year, Gaultier also produced his homage to body art, a collection that combined the punk aesthetic with the new subcultural movement toward neo-primitivist tattoos and body piercing. The runway show—which featured heavily tattooed and pierced models—shocked many viewers.

Gaultier has unconventional ideas about beauty and ugliness. He often selects "real people" as models (such as fat women), who challenge the culture's dominant ideas about beauty. In 1988 he launched his diffusion line Junior Gaultier with an advertising campaign that featured elderly people. His fashion shows are highly theatrical, featuring, for example, a vampire climbing out of a coffin. Gaultier has also produced an album of house music, How To Do That (1989) and hosted the British television show Eurotrash. Long known as the "enfant terrible" of French fashion," Gaultier is today recognized as one of the world's most important fashion designers. *Valerie Steele*

01
02

03

an-Paul Gaultier, "Mad Max" collection, Autumn/Winter 1995/96 ••• 02 Jean-Paul Gaultier, "Les Tatouages" collection, Spring/Summer 1994 ••• 03 François Berthoud, linocut of Gaultier design, e, 1987 ••• 04 Jean-Paul Gaultier, bustier for Madonna's Blond Ambition World Tour, 1990 ••• 05 Jean-Paul Gaultier, "French Cancan" collection, Autumn/Winter 1991/92 ••• 06 Jean-Paul Gaultier, rtising campaign, women's perfume, 1993 ••• 07 Jean-Paul Gaultier, advertising campaign, "The Charms of Frida Kahlo" collection, Spring/Summer 1998

"GAULTIER ... ONCE DREAMT OF CREATING THE COLLECTION TO END ALL COLLECTIONS—A GENDER-CROSSING, RELIGION-MARRYING, RACE-DEFYING, BORDER-ERASING HODGEPODGE FROM WHICH MEN AND WOMEN WOULD BE FREE TO CHOOSE." (*VISIONAIRE'S FASHION 2000*, 1997)

"IT WAS THE SHAPE UNDERNEATH THAT COUNTED, AND IF YOU DIDN'T HAVE IT YOU WERE BETTER OFF LEAVING LYCRA AND LATEX ALONE."
(VICKY CARNEGY)

STRETCHED

Stretch materials have a long history: elastic and woven textiles were known in ancient Egypt (circa BC 1500) and the Copts were masters in a special knitting technique. In the fifteenth century, berets, caps, and gloves were knitted by men and women, and in the sixteenth century, Queen Elizabeth I of England wore hand-knitted underwear. Shortly before the French Revolution there were knitted (elastic) gilets and riding breeches. In the 1800s men wore extremely tight-fitting, knit pants, and women began wearing a flesh-colored, tricot knit under their transparent chemise dresses. The Biedermeier period, in the early nineteenth century, introduced corsets made from resin fibers and elasticized finery. The invention of jersey in 1882 opened up new possibilities.

In 1900 cotton jersey was introduced into riding breeches and sports legwear; in 1912 it was used for the first bathing costumes, and shortly thereafter the first artificial silk stocking appeared in England. During the 1930s, three new fabrics came onto the market: Bleyle (manufactured by a German company of the same name), wool charmeuse, and Lastex—woven from rubber fibers. The 1940s and 1950s saw the appearance of nylon fabrics, underwear, and stockings (1941), the pullover dress (1952), and jersey cowl dresses (1955). From 1965 on, artificial silk knitwear, tops in gym-shirt or tank-top style, rib-knit pullovers, and jeans made from stretchable synthetic materials became popular. 1966 saw the start of the "stretch" era, resulting in the introduction of the revolutionary bodystocking and the molded bra. In the 1980s gymnasts' suits made their way into daywear in the form of leggings, and the bodysuit replaced the classic blouse.

The foremost designer of wearably sexy fashions, the Tunisian Azzedine Alaïa—who studied at the Ecole des Beaux-Arts in Paris—opened his workshop in Paris in 1970, after having worked for a few months with Guy Laroche (1923–89) and Thierry Mugler. He first caused a stir in 1980 with an oversized patent leather coat decorated with metal studs. In 1985 he created the stretch cult object *par excellence:* a Latex dress laced up at the sides which he made for singer Grace Jones to wear to the Fashion Oscars.

At the end of the twentieth century, stretch fabrics—which make it almost impossible to wear underwear and which reduce the weight of the garment to a minimum—have become what jersey was for Coco Chanel: a gentle but lasting revolution. Using the elastic-band technique of Alaïa, garments now stretch like rubber, following every gesture, movement, or slightest bend of the body but always revert to their original form. A woman wearing such a garment, as a living, free-moving sculpture, embodies the synthesis of sculptural art and fashion.

Robes à bandés is what Hervé Léger calls his body-hugging garments made from bands of elasticized fabric. Léger started his career by designing accessories for Swarovski, then becoming Karl Lagerfeld's assistant at Fendi and Chanel before finding success with his own collection in 1992. He introduced cocktail dresses made entirely from elasticized bands in rainbow colors in 1994, and later added stretch lace to his collections.
Gerda Buxbaum

01
02

03

04
05

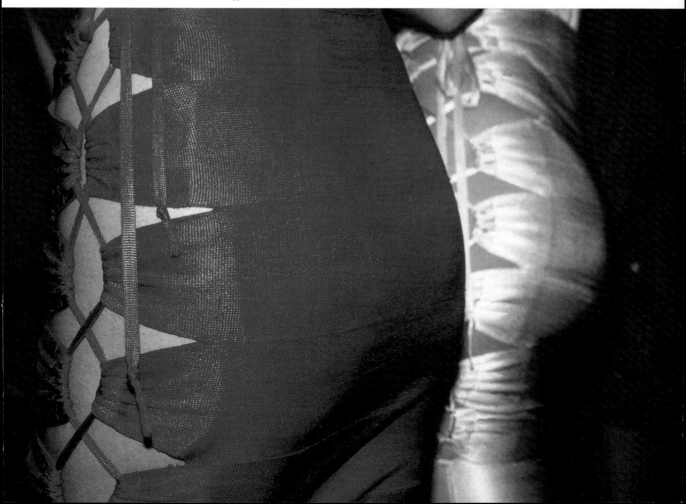

"I HAVE NO DESIRE TO GIVE LECTURES ON THE SUBJECT OF FASHION. I PUT MY MONEY ON FEELINGS: WEAR IT AND ENJOY IT." (GIANNI VERSACE)

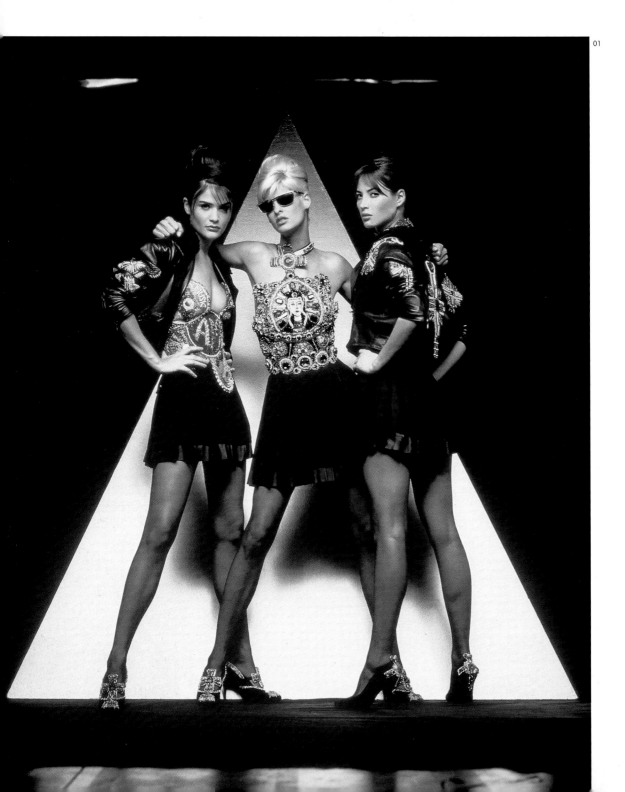

01

GIANNI VERSACE

Gianni Versace's talent was immediately evident with the presentation of his first two collections, one designed for Florentine Flowers in 1972 and the other for Callaghan in the following year. Versace, then twenty-five years old, had been breathing fashion since his childhood, which he spent partly in his mother's dressmaking workshop. As a young designer, he advocated an expressive freedom which set his work apart and which would make his name synonymous with daring, provocation, and the aesthetic sublimation of desire. It has been said that he rewrote the logic of appearances.

Versace's importance to the history of fashion lies mainly in his having carried the seduction of the unusual to extremes. He did so by audaciously introducing stereotypes of vulgarity into the world of haute bourgeoisie—plunging necklines and miniskirts, sheath dresses, and gaudy accessories—and by using apparently improbable combinations of fabrics, colors, and prints. Throughout the 1980s, Versace's style created a new fashion-media relationship, helping to establish an icon of a lifestyle, and reinforcing the importance of clothing in the social imagination. Asymmetrical cuts, layering, draping, optical designs, metallic mesh, and the use of studs and lace are some of Versace's aesthetic "inventions" that have become his trademark. He was also one of the first designers to totally reinvent certain materials. In his winter collections of 1983/84, he replaced the weave in his tweeds, creating a striped effect, and in his 1994 collections he experimented with printing on polyurethane and the use of rubber. His desire to reinvent materials led him to explore previously unthinkable combinations such as leather and silk, jute and gold, metallic mesh and faux gems—working always in the service of a feminine aesthetic.

After his death, the stylistic control of his company passed into the hands of his sister, Donatella, who had been his collaborator for years and worked with him on some of his collections. His brother, Santo, is also involved in the administrative and business management of the company. This transition of leadership has only minimally modified the Versace approach to fashion. Donatella has undoubtedly contributed her own personal vision to the "Versace" look, but she has moved forward in the spirit of aesthetic research that has always distinguished the company. She has been particularly successful in her efforts to appeal to the young client, with collections that increasingly reflect the spirit of the times and which reinterpret and "upgrade" the canons of street fashion. The consolidation of the relationship between fashion and rock music has also had a significant influence on the Versace look. Rock was a great source of inspiration for Gianni, but it has become a true leitmotif for Donatella. Her collections abound with musical references and icons, and she has also become involved with the growth of young rock groups who act as authoritative spokespersons for youth styles. "Thinking about tomorrow" and "daring to be" are the two fundamental guidelines that have marked the success of the Versace collections, past and present.

Carlo Ducci

03

04

02

ISSEY MIYAKE

1938	Born on April 22 in Hiroshima, Japan
1963	First fashion collection, "A Poem of Cloth and Stone," Tokyo
1964	Receives diploma in graphic design from the Tama Art University, Japan
1965–69	Studies at the École de la Chambre Syndicale de la Couture Parisienne
1966	Works as design assistant to Guy Laroche; from 1968 to Hubert de Givenchy
1969	Designs ready-to-wear for Geoffrey Beene, New York
1970	Establishes Miyake Design Studio (MDS) in Tokyo
1971	Establishes Issey Miyake International Inc. (IMI)
1972	"What is Bodywear?" fashion show in Tokyo
1973	Presents collection for the first time in Paris, and subsequently twice yearly
1976	"Issey Miyake and Twelve Black Girls" fashion show in Tokyo/Osaka (one of the models being Grace Jones); opens flagship boutique—designed by Shiro Kuramata—in Tokyo; introduces the Issey Miyake men's collection
1977	Receives the Mainichi Design Award
1979	"East Meets West" show in Aspen, Colorado; first fashion collection shown in Milan
1981	Introduces the Plantation line
1982	Presents Spring/Summer 1983 collection on the aircraft carrier Intrepid, New York
1983	Issey Miyake Spectacle: Bodyworks, exhibition, Tokyo, Los Angeles and San Francisco
1984	Receives Neiman Marcus Award, Dallas and Best Foreign Designer Award from the Council of Fashion Design, New York
1985	Receives the Oscar de la Mode award in Paris; introduces the Issey Miyake Permanente line
1986	Begins collaborating with photographer Irving Penn
1988	Issey Miyake: A-Un exhibition, Paris
1991	Made Commandeur de l'Ordre des Arts et des Lettres by the French government
1992	Receives the 1991 Asahi Prize
1993	Introduces the Pleats Please Issey Miyake line; receives Chevalier de l'Ordre National de la Légion d'Honneur
1995	Autumn/Winter 1995–96 collection featuring "Beautiful Ladies"
1996	Participates in the premiere fashion and art biennale in Florence, Italy
1998	Issey Miyake: Making Things, exhibition, Paris
PERFUMES	L'Eau d'Issey (1992), Le Feu d'Issey (1998)

"I AM ALWAYS RETURNING TO ONE PIECE OF CLOTH—A RECTANGLE—BECAUSE IT IS THE ELEMENTARY FORM IN CLOTHING."
(ISSEY MIYAKE)

It was predicted that Miyake would "snip up" the weighty terms of fashion, architecture, and design and make light, airy garments from the remnants. His clothes dance around a woman's body as lightly as cobwebs and create something like pupation in an insect: they can transform the body with bizarre additions, or sheath it in a bulky mask of fabric. Miyake's ultra-fine, delicate architectural pleating is just one of his attempts to provide the wearer with new elements of creativity. John Forsythe, with whom Miyake designed a number of dance productions, notes with astonishment that the designs from the Pleats Please Issey Miyake line "create an echo in harmony with the body rhythms." One dancer compared these costumes—made from finely folded gauze with a matte sheen in metallic shades—to bundled seaweed.

Miyake takes the colors and shapes of shells, algae, and stones as his inspiration and uses modern technologies to transform silk, cotton, paper, bamboo, and plastic into new and surprising materials. The results are hooded coats made from densely woven, synthetic fibers which replicate the structure of paper, dresses made from mosquito nets, hats made from Bromelia-fiber gauze, shell-shaped pullovers made from fishing line encased in cotton, oil-impregnated coats made from the hand-made Japanese paper abura gami (traditionally used only for umbrellas), and silicon bodices for pants made from polyurethane-coated polyester jersey.

In his 1982 "Bodyworks" designs, Miyake demonstrated how he brings the ideas of fashion and architecture closer together: his cast breastplates of laminated polyester, as well as his sculpted shapes of wire and cage-like rattan forms, function like housing for the body. The 1988 A-Un exhibition presented an astonishing overview of Miyake's materials and garments from the preceding decade. His fabrics—folded, twisted, bleached, quilted, knitted, crumpled, recycled, or pressed together in two or three layers—seem to reproduce the waves of the earth, and his translucent coats are like skins of golden paper.

Already in 1978, Miyake started with the idea of linking East with West in his fashion designs. He wanted to create completely novel clothes that would assimilate the traditions and cultures of the entire world. Towards this end, he took as his central concept "one piece of cloth." Today he is still working with this same concept. His clothing designs give the body total freedom and movement and fulfill his own demands for beauty and practicability.

Gerda Buxbaum

01

1 Issey Miyake, "Flying Saucer" dress, Spring/Summer 1994 ••• 02 Issey Miyake, "Plastic Body," Autumn/Winter 1980/81 ••• 03 Issey Miyake, "Paradise Lost," Spring/Summer 1977 ••• 04 Issey Miyake,
Body Works: Fashion without Taboos, exhibition, Victoria & Albert Museum, London, 1985 ••• 05 Issey Miyake, *Making Things*, exhibition, Fondation Cartier pour l'art contemporain, Paris, 1998
•6 Issey Miyake, *abura-gami* dresses from *A-UN*, exhibition, Musée des Arts Décoratifs, Paris, 1988

ISSEY MIYAKE

04

03

05
06

> "IN THE ACT OF DECONSTRUCTING, FASHION SUCCEEDS FROM TIME TO TIME
> IN SHEDDING LIGHT ON THE CONSTRUCTION PLANS OF BOURGEOIS SOCIETY."
> (ULF POSCHARDT, 1998)

THE DECONSTRUCTIONISTS

01

Deconstructionism, in fashion, rejects customary rules and breaks all conventions. It questions aesthetic norms about bodily proportions and the criteria of beauty, emphasizes the adding on, or discovery of, an irrational moment, and reveals the processes of tailoring in clothing. The shape and the construction of the garment is more important than the color.

In fashion the deconstructionism trend was started by the Japanese designers Rei Kawakubo (Comme des Garçons) and Yohji Yamamoto, who were slowly establishing themselves in Paris in the 1980s. In the 1990s the Belgians Ann Demeulemeester and Martin Margiela emerged as its main representatives.

In 1992 Demeulemeester showed her designs for the first time in Paris: her deliberately scruffy, laddered, and askew nylon stockings shocked the audience. Her work intentionally makes the broken and the dilapidated visible and gives it the status of a desirable consumer product: outlaw and establishment, provocation and pleasure are merged. In her creations the unfinished and the accidental, soft and rigid, naked and clothed (regardless of erogenous zones) collide and find a new harmony.

Margiela highlights the fragmentary aspects of Deconstructionism by putting things together that do not necessarily belong together; for example, setting too wide a sleeve into too narrow an armhole. In this way it is not the body as a whole that is emphasized, but rather its discrete parts. Margiela recycles old fashion, tears it apart, reverses it, and puts seams and zippers on the outside. He thereby exhibits the origin and the artificiality of the tailor's art as well as the soul, or rather the soullessness, of fashion. His recycling is based not on ecological but rather aesthetic motivation. In 1997 in a Rotterdam exhibition, Margiela smeared his clothes with bacteria which destroyed them within a very short span of time. In so doing he compared the natural cycle of creation and decay to the consumer cycle of buying and discarding.

The manner in which Yamamoto succeeds in making the creative process and the history of a garment visible is very different. In his clothing—he does not like to talk about "fashion"—seams do not simply have the function of holding the fabric together, they also give a dynamic force to the fabric and allow the emergence of apparently arbitrary indentations, of asymmetrical points of fabric and patterns. Kawakubo's mission has been from the outset to create forms that no one has ever seen before and to produce optical stimuli that are completely contrary to our normal modes of perception. For her 1996/97 collection, she created clothes with asymmetrical bulges and bumps which created a fictitious body and presented themselves as sculptures in motion.

The London-based designer Hussein Chalayan is considered the most logical of these conceptual designer-artists. His designs deny limbs (in part as a deconstruction of the Muslim understanding of being veiled) or have arbitrary openings in the garment—but it is the fabric that is important and which makes movement possible.

Ingrid Loschek

02

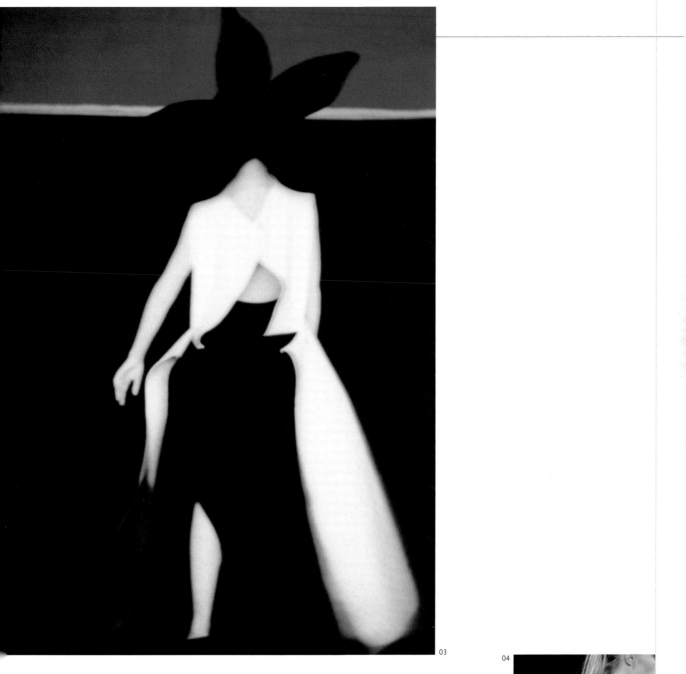

03

04

"GRUNGE IS SYNONYMOUS WITH THE CONDITION OF YOUTH AND STANDS FOR FEAR OF THE FUTURE AS WELL AS ECOLOGICAL AWARENESS, A FEELING OF HELPLESSNESS, AND THE DESPERATE SEARCH FOR NEW VALUES." (GERDA BUXBAUM, 1999)

03

For spring 1993 Marc Jacobs (b. 1960), who was designing ready-to-wear for Perry Ellis, introduced a collection of clothes inspired by music, the street, and youth culture. The casual, rumpled attitude of the clothes was fashion's interpretation of the guitar heavy, rock 'n' roll music popularized by a host of bands coming out of Seattle, Washington—most significantly Nirvana and Pearl Jam. The look of the clothes was based on the uniform of youth in the Pacific Northwest: "Grunge" was born. And the veteran fashion editor Andre Leon Talley was quoted as saying that this could portend the death of fashion.

Grunge, arguably more than any other trend of its day, was a puzzle to consumers. This style promoted silk blouses that looked like worn, old flannel shirts and sweaters purposely woven to be oversized, to hang slightly askew. This was not an American brand of the intellectual Deconstruction-ism made famous by Japanese designers such as Rei Kawakubo of Comme des Garçons. Instead, this was a far more serendipitous look that had been born in the streets and appropriated by high fashion. The point of Grunge was to look disheveled, to look as if one had simply rolled out of bed and gathered up the first handful of clothes within reach. Ironing be damned.

Jacobs, an afficionado of contemporary pop music and youth culture, sanitized the style with fine fabrics and expensive craftsmanship, but he did not attempt to soften the overall visual impact, nor did designer Anna Sui, another proponent of Grunge. Other designers, more typically associated with the "ladies who lunch crowd," also took up the Grunge banner. Even Christian Lacroix and Karl Lager-feld at Chanel offered their well-heeled customers frocks that were created to look rumpled and ill-kept.

In many ways, the thinking was that Grunge represented a liberation of sorts. This freewheeling style would release fashion from the constraints of protocol and would breathe life into a stuffy milieu. But critics judged Grunge harshly because it was unattractive and impractical for most women over the age of twenty-five. And designers realized that they could not maintain their high-toned image while peddling clothes that looked as if they had been plucked from the dirty laundry basket. In less than a year, Grunge died at the hands of unimpressed consumers.

While the initial reaction to Grunge was negative from both critics and consumers, and the trend itself short-lived, the style ultimately helped to expand the definition of what could be considered fashion. It continued a tradition begun decades earlier of allowing music and youth styles to influence the ateliers. In its wake, Grunge left fashion more comfortable, accommodating, and relaxed.

Robin Givhan

01

02

GRUNGE

FINE AS A SPIDER'S WEB, DELICATE AS CRYSTAL—CLOTHES
FOR WOODLAND FAIRIES, WATER NYMPHS, GODDESSES,
AND ANGELS ...

03

FAIRY-TALE COUTURE

Interfacing is the no-nonsense face—or rather mask—which confronts us through the electronic, computerized, and automated world of today, and there is a hint of fairy-tale magic about it. At the touch of a button, we have information about things taking place around the world "live" on screen—odysseys into cyberspace via the Internet. Fashion has countered this high-tech functionalism by emphasizing the magical and designing clothes fit for fairies or elves. Clothing elaborately embroidered with glittering flowers of crystal and jet beads transforms the working woman into a creature of luxury whose body seems to be sewn into a wisp of transparent chiffon.

Layers of imperceptible delicacy blur the boundaries between skin and fabric. Silk muslin shimmers as though embroidered for a goddess, while cascades of lace give the effect of having been blown onto the body. During the daytime, however, it is back to basics; transparent, dreamlike clothing is not for the office world. Couture at the end of this century presents itself as a journey across continents, as a fantasy trip through cultures and mythologies. Mermaids' dresses of crepe mousse are paired with sandals embroidered with beads, a feathered choker, silk netting, and organza orchids around the décolletage.

Marlene Dietrich herself took great trouble over the artistic finesse and magic of her stage costumes made from flesh-colored fabric: "The material is called 'Soufflé'; which means breath.... It was a breath, that's true.... I looked naked, although I wasn't. For hours we sat in the room where the girls were embroidering on a large frame. Every bead, every sequin was important. Jean Louis and I decided where every diamond, piece of mirror, or glass bead should be placed."

Figures like water nymphs appear as visions of inescapable charm, their bodies covered, as though with fish scales, by a skin consisting of innumerable, greenish, gleaming beads and iridescent sequins. Their garments look as if they were drenched by glittering, silver droplets. Branches of glass beads—like aquatic plants—wind around their arms which seem to entice one into the abyss of tiny magic mirrors. The marmoreal body of an angel-like fairy, or an oriental princess, appears draped in panels of golden plissé and filigree-like lace.

The Symbolist poet Stéphane Mallarmé's literary image of a swan frozen in a lake is interpreted in crystal-white "Ice Princess" dresses: crystal beads, like frozen drops of dew, cover white "plumage" of cool, transparent organza. The contemporary British designer John Galliano states: "My vision: a nymph who, in her heart of hearts, is a leopardess." *Gerda Buxbaum*

04

02

"SIMPLICITY IS THE SOUL OF MODERN ELEGANCE." (BILL BLASS, 1992)

PURISM: CLEAN CHIC

01

They are often called the new classics, and they represent the principle of clarity. Giorgio Armani, Calvin Klein, and Jil Sander propagate a quiet, unobtrusive look which should not be confused with minimalism. "Purism" makes use of neutral tones like gray, white, and beige.

Purism—striving for stylistic purity based on architectural and geometric forms—is a style that looks noble and makes enormous demands on the creativity of the designer. It requires the greatest possible degree of creative strength, the courage to omit everything that is superfluously decorative, a limited use of accessories (such as jewelry), and a fine sense of fabric and fit. This is a restrained, understated style which makes the facade recede in favor of the personality and underlines the essence of the wearer in the most sophisticated manner. Clarity emphasizes individuality and brings decency, dignity, relaxation, and peace into a beneficial association. Perfection lies in the art of omission, and it makes this quality visible. Simplicity today is a refined and carefully calculated approach; nothing is as difficult to achieve as meaningful simplicity.

Pure style builds on clear lines and on the symbolic power of the color white. The antiseptic, clean aesthetic is emphasized by using white, which stands for light, abstraction, and innocence. This style, which has also been labeled emancipatory and futuristic, is related to the 1960s and brings back some important basics from that time: the polo dress, the cardigan, and the shirt-blouse. Simple, unpretentious, pragmatic, and uncomplicated are its catch words, and for years it has been aiming toward an ever-greater perfection—clothes that function.

Reduction, restriction, and the reversion of the complicated to the simple; this is not a cluttered effect. This return to the basics has been repeated time and again throughout the history of fashion. It is part of the historical evolution. The source of Armani's creativity is the functionalism that is traditionally inherent in his field: menswear. While the American designers—Calvin Klein, Donna Karan, and Bill Blass (b. 1922) (who coined the significant phrase "Simplicity is the soul of modern elegance" for a Neiman Marcus promotion)—are representatives of a style which is based on the American tradition of functional clothing.

Gerda Buxbaum

02

03
04

TRANSPARENT LOOKS

Crystal-clear transparency in fashion has only become possible through the development of new technologies in synthetics. In previous decades, transparent fabrics swathed the body in gossamer layers, but the "youthquake" of the 1960s laid the body bare due to its penchant for exposure and its craving for the naked truth. Rudi Gernreich scored a major success with his "topless fashion" which exposed the youthful body in unveiled perfection.

Today, however, designers and architects alike are experimenting with a new infra-transparency which no longer exposes but, instead, veils. New powder and make-up products (often called "naked" and "nude") and flesh-colored, diaphanous fabrics introduce this new, erotic dimension to fashion. The boundaries between body and fashion disappear as body and fashion merge into one, diminishing the aggression that characterizes the brashness of the "Bare" look. A simultaneous view of different, spatial layers transforms illusion into allusion. A return to layered dressing has made underwear an increasingly important, visible, "inner" component in multi-layered apparel—inverting the traditional clothing concept which reigned from the Middle Ages through the eighteenth century—although these layering methods continue in the Japanese tradition of discretion and distance.

Net and mesh fabrics are used to create a partial transparency, to divide the body into different optic fields, and to evoke an aura of diffusion when used for stockings or gloves. Madeleine Vionnet used many transparent fabrics for her evening gowns in the 1930s. Her expert diagonal seaming and faggotting, in combination with the bias cut, draped the garment over the body with a fluidity that was sculptural. In the 1960s Paco Rabanne made dresses of chain mail or plastic discs which looked like magnified webs. Similarly, André Courrèges designed utopian chain mail tunics and worked with delicate organza, cut into grids, which he tailored into white suits, chemise dresses, overalls, and skirts.

Lace—ornamental motifs on an open ground—is the only material that suggests intimacy and formality, bedroom and ballroom; it has become an expression of exquisite femininity and is used in an endless variety of applications. Luxury items, such as the lace fan or exclusive lace insets in evening gowns, are a thing of the past. However, luxury material lace has become a contemporary favorite; it is draped over or beneath other transparent, textile layers to create a new aesthetic in clothing.

Gerda Buxbaum

02

01

SHE WAS AN ENCHANTING WILD THING, A SENSUAL, BARBARIC CHILD, BARELY CLOAKED IN A WHITE HAZY CLOUD, A SWATH OF MIST, IN WHICH HER WHOLE FORM WAS JUST VISIBLE."
(ÉMILE ZOLA, *LA CURÉE*, 1871)

04

03

05

"WHAT I DO IS ABOUT NOW. IT'S ABOUT THE LIVES WE LEAD."
(HELMUT LANG)

HELMUT LANG

01

02

Whether masculine-cut or futuristically transparent women's suits, whether utilitarian, rebelliously elegant, Day-Glo striped, or cuffed jeans, Helmut Lang's clothes set the tone for the 1990s. He is among the true fashion inventors of the twentieth century, and his designs provoke irritation because they are very often ahead of their time. Lang's fashions frequently point to major social changes before their initial tremors can be felt: the nomadic image of globalization, the scars and triumphs of women's liberation, the fusion of American and European culture, the yearning for simplicity, and the desire for luxury. All of these are evoked for us, sharply and beautifully, in Lang's clothes. "I don't believe that fashion evolves on its own," he once said. "There are more radical social changes behind it."

Although Lang was born in Vienna, he spent his childhood in a mountain village in Austria. He never attended fashion school, never assisted a designer, and never wooed the press to gain attention. At his first show in Paris in 1986, in the midst of Jean-Paul Gaultier's and Azzedine Alaïa's era of sexy extravagance, Lang presented severe, Loden jackets and tailored, white shirts. Yet his subsequent rise to cult designer did little to alter his tendency toward being a loner. In fact, his style retained a strange, even brusque manner. In the spring of 1999, for example, the journalists who attended his New York fashion show were expecting clean, turn-of-the-century, 2000 purism. Lang showed them mean black, shabby silver, and expedition parkas. Shortly afterwards war broke out in Kosovo.

Like Coco Chanel before him, Lang draws on memories of his poor childhood as the basis for his style. Accordingly, he has transformed the fabrics and details of the Austrian national costume, the dark, single-breasted suits of Balkan emigrants, and the vests and anoraks that he wore for sports as a schoolboy, into clothes that have earned him a reputation for being avant-garde. Over the years, he has become a master in balancing sexual provocation and self-protection, restraint and aggression, romanticism and realism. In creating on his own terms, Lang has succeeded in something that not all artisans of the catwalk can boast of: replacing money and compulsive innovation with sincerity.

Lang has never made things easy for himself—nor, consequently, for his clients. He has always understood, instinctively, that fashion is a battle between the new and the old and that, in a battle, there is no room for sentimentality. It is perhaps no coincidence, then, that his name incorporates the German word for courage, *Mut*.

Margit J. Mayer

HELMUT LANG

1956	Born on March 10 in Vienna, Austria
1978	Introduces first women's wear collection
1979	Opens Bou Bou Lang boutique in Vienna, where he sells his own designs
1984	Presents women's wear collection inspired by Austrian folk costumes
1986	Presents collection for the Paris/Vienne exhibition at the Centre Pompidou, Paris
1987	Introduces first menswear collection
1988	Holds first show in New York
1990	Introduces first collection of men's shoes
1993–96	Guest professor at the Hochschule für angewandte Kunst, Vienna
1994	"Trash and Elegance" collection: narrow shift dresses of polyester and patent leather overlaid with a layer of lace or organza, pink rubber dress with lace fused onto it
1995	"Radical Couture" collection: superimposed, transparent layers, trains, embroidered shirts, luminous prints, capes with bra straps
1996	Works jointly with the artist Jenny Holzer for the Florence Biennale; introduces less expensive jeans collection
1997	"New Aristocrats" collection: contemporary interpretation of romanticism with diagonal sashes and neo-tuxedos
1998	Moves to New York; receives Pitti Immagine Award, Best Designer of the Nineties
1999	"NASA Nomads" collection; creates joint venture with Prada

03

04

"NOWADAYS THE HOUSE OF CHANEL SELLS NOTHING MORE THAN ITS LOGO AS THE ULTIMATE SYMBOL FOR FASHION ... IT SELLS ITS HISTORY BETTER THAN FASHION COULD."
(BARBARA VINKEN, 1993)

DESIGNER LABELS

01

Georges Vuitton could never have guessed what kind of a trend he had initiated when, in the 1880s, he designed a geometric flower pattern to accompany his luggage company's initials, identifying his suitcases as brand articles. Vuitton's bold move allowed the bourgeoisie of the industrial age to signal their affluence when arriving at foreign shores, thus bolstering their self-confidence and reflecting the new order in the era of capitalism: money, not breeding, was henceforth the dominant signifier of class.

A few years later, Jean Patou, a gentleman's couturier of the 1920s and 1930s, embroidered his monogram onto the beach sweaters he sold in Biarritz and Deauville, France. Likewise, Coco Chanel's logo of two, interlocked Cs was instantly recognizable. Similarly, the snaffle bar on Gucci loafers gave every self-respecting man of the 1970s the feeling that he, too, had a foot in the good life.

Yet these early attempts at product differentiation were merely a preamble to what happened in the last two decades of the twentieth century when fashion became a universe of labels, a language of initials and logos: Hermès' H as a belt buckle, Gucci's G stitched onto pants and shirts, the letters of the word "DIOR" jingling from the handle of a bag like a bunch of keys. Nothing was spared from designers' voracious appetites for signature hieroglyphs. Gianni Versace took the Medusa-shield of the goddess of wisdom and turned it into a button. Ralph Lauren appropriated the image of the polo player from the recreational pastimes of the ultra-rich and sewed it onto the fronts of his shirts. The process has since trickled down to all levels of society. Money is no longer required for membership in a global community whose Nike footwear says, "We are the winners."

The roots of this phenomenon may be found in the fashion industry's changing role in society. As it became more democratic, the fashion world maintained its advertising of a heraldic system that supported an aristocracy of buying. This advertising eventually turned into a global language and its vocabulary became simpler—since shoes or handbags, for example, are easier to recognize and copy than the cut of a shoulder. As a result, international consumers now leaf through magazines, select products, and let the brand names speak for who they are and who they want to be.

What will happen next? It appears that, recently, trendsetting fashion houses have become tired of their winning formulas. In 1999 Vuitton's creative director Marc Jacobs (b. 1960) interpreted the company's monogram design in kitschy, lilac-and-red patent leather, thereby giving it an ironic twist. Chanel's "2005" handbag omits any references to the House's past, replacing its former conservative image with fast-forward futurism. And the countless variations of Fendi's "Baguette bag"—so-called because it is often jammed under the arm like a long loaf of French bread—launched in 1997, are proof that it is indeed possible to combine status gain with playful individuality. *Margit J. Mayer*

02

03
04

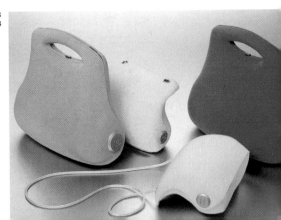

Gianni Versace, printed blouses and leggings, 1991/92 ••• 02 Louis Vuitton, "Bisten" suitcase, Centenaire Monogram line ••• 03 Gucci, patent leather boots, advertising campaign, 1995
Chanel Le 2005 d'été, cult bags, Spring/Summer 1999 ••• 05 Ralph Lauren, advertising campaign for Polo Sport Ralph Lauren

05

"I MAKE UGLY CLOTHES FROM UGLY MATERIALS: SIMPLY BAD TASTE. BUT THE
END UP LOOKING GOOD ANYWAY." (MIUCCIA PRADA, 1995)

02

The Prada label made its appearance in Milan in 1913. Mario Prada manufactured high-quality leather handbags, luggage, shoes, and accessories; all of his designs maintained a stylistic distance and were fashionable, yet classic enough to survive beyond a single season. The Milan shop, located in the Galleria Vittorio Emanuele, became an international point of reference in fashion. However, the remarkable transformation of the label came with the arrival of Mario's granddaughter, Miuccia, who took over the company in 1978, and who is responsible for its designs. Her husband, Patrizio Bertelli, is Prada's business manager.

In 1983 Prada opened its second shop in Milan, on the Via della Spiga, an event that coincided with the boom in sales of Prada's black, nylon handbags and backpacks, which carried the unmistakable triangular label that soon became not only a status symbol but also the trademark of the "Prada" style. Miuccia's grandfather had previously used the black, nylon fabric—which had originally been developed for military items—as wrapping for his luggage range. 1983 also saw the first line of Prada footwear; Prada women's wear was introduced in 1989; a menswear line and the moderately priced Miu Miu label was created to attract a younger clientele in 1992; and 1998 saw the introduction of Prada Sport. The growth and commercial successes of Prada have been exponential: four shops in the mid-1980s, eleven in the mid-1990s, and seventy-eight by late 1998 as well as 118 shops within department stores. All of these are managed by I Pellettieri d'Italia, the parent company of the group. The company philosophy is based on maintaining complete control of the product, from the manufacturing phases through to distribution and marketing.

Miuccia Prada has developed a unique style that skillfully mixes intellectual purity and eccentric elegance, futuristic minimalism and multicultural inspiration. Perhaps better than any other designer, she represents the global aesthetic of the 1990s. Visionary, instinctive, curious, and attuned to rapid changes in dress and society, Prada bases her decisions on a number of clear and basic rules. First of all, she believes in experimentation—in materials, lines, mixes of influences, and inspirations. Second, she believes in creating fashion for a clientele without using age as a criterion: "age is a non-criterion because it would be limiting." Third, her designs respond to the concept of "conscious modernity," without adhering to any aesthetic preconceptions, and take risks when the mood strikes—as they are the result of imagination and rationality.

According to Miuccia Prada, being in the forefront is not a choice: "I follow my instinct; and even if I question whether what I am doing makes perfect sense to me or others, in reality the important thing is that I thoroughly believe in it."

Carlo Ducci

05

03
04

01 Rifat Ozbek, Spring/Summer 1991 ••• 02 Jean-Paul Gaultier, "Les Tatouages" collection, Spring/Summer 1994 ••• 03 Dries van Noten, haute couture, 1997 ••• 04 John Galliano for Dior Couture, Autumn/Winter 1998/99 ••• 05 John Galliano for Dior Couture, inspired by the Massai, Spring/Summer 1997

GLOBAL VILLAGE

As fashion pushes towards the twenty-first century, a style has emerged that reflects the globalization of the design industry and offers an optimistic vision of the future. Designers such as Dries Van Noten (b. 1958), Jean-Paul Gaultier, and Vivienne Tam were among the most adept at incorporating a host of complementary and even contradictory cultures into their work.

In 1997, Gaultier presented a collection in Paris that he described as a reaction against the antagonistic relationship that France had with its African immigrants. "I have a certain point of view on - different problems and I try to express my opinion through my collections," Gaultier said to the *Washington Post*. His inspiration comes from a particular vision of an African immigrant in cities such as Paris or New York; this regal woman kept many of the vibrant colors and fabrics of her homeland but also adopted many of the styles of her new country. As a result his collection celebrated the African diaspora in a sensitive and intelligent way, something that had rarely been accomplished in the past.

That same year, designer John Galliano created a collection for Dior that had been inspired by the style of dress of the Masai. Indeed, 1997 was a year in which a host of designers looked to Africa for new ways of combining colors and patterns. But more than simply appropriating the traditional dress of those in Africa, the fashion industry seemed to finally take a sincere interest in getting things right. The clothes that came out of this new black chic were far more sophisticated and more subtly ethnic than such attempts at black style had been in the past.

The impact of Asia also was significant, and designers were inspired by such disparate influences as the growing strength of the Asian market, the Westerners' search for more exotic inspiration, and the popularity of Arthur S. Golden's book *Memoirs of a Geisha* (1997). (Even Madonna adopted a geisha style for several television appearances and magazine photo spreads.) The Asian-American designer Tam captured the limelight with her "Buddha" collection and with other collections inspired by trips to Bhutan, a tiny country near Nepal.

The finale to the industry's ethnic panoply has been Bohemian Chic, a hodge-podge of cultural references brought together in a sort of gilded, hippie style. Design houses Fendi and Marni have been the leaders of this style. At Fendi the company's famous baguette shoulder bags have been studded with mirrors and stones to create a mosaic pattern reminiscent of Islamic mosques. Marni has offered skirts and jackets with embroidery inspired by Native Americans. And American designers such as John Bartlett (b. 1964), Michael Kors (b. 1959) and Marc Jacobs have recreated traditional serapes and ponchos in luxurious cashmere or high-tech coated nylon.

The result of designers' cultural meandering is that the notion of global fashion has been vividly realized in collections that merge ethnic sensibilities with a broadly accessible commercial style.

Robin Givhan

01

02
03

"AS INTERPRETED BY FASHION, THE ETHNIC LOOK REPRESENTS ENTERTAINMENT,
NOT AN ATTITUDE TO LIFE AND CERTAINLY NOT THE *ZEITGEIST*." (GERDA BUXBAUM, 1999)

04
05

LIVING ON THE EDGE IN XXL

HIP-HOP

Hip-Hop fashion belongs to the tradition of street style. It represents fashion for urban spaces, for big cities and is an expression of the socially marginalized. The principle of "living on the edge," of a life poised between danger and pleasure, is visualized in a clothing style. The origin of this style lies in functional clothing born out of financial hardship: extra large sizes are chosen so that younger children can grow into them while workwear is chosen because it is robust and durable. Clothing that previously conveyed social stigma—oversized garments and workwear—has now been adapted and reinterpreted as positive stylistic features. The look of Hip-Hop, however, has not remained a fashion for the inner-city streets. It has been absorbed and copied by suburban youth and by international couturiers.

Oversized clothing is a characteristic feature of the Hip-Hop style. The garments enlarge the entire body silhouette and make it into a threatening gesture. The thick, bulky material, in the form of multiple-woven cotton fabrics or down jackets in big sizes, is intended to bulk up the material volume and serves as a warning to possible opponents. The symbol "XXL" not only indicates size but also suggests danger. This look also includes baggy pants worn so low that the crotch hangs down as far as the knees (in order to show off brand-name boxer shorts). This type of clothing does not have smooth surfaces; the removal of straight-stitch seams produces artificial bulges and folds which are further exaggerated by phenomena such as the pushed-up pant leg.

Hip-Hop openly makes references to, appropriates, and adopts elite symbols of haute couture as well as emblems of popular culture (television shows, famous sportsmen, video games). The style favors simple, graphically concise logos (the Mercedes star, Gucci or Chanel logos). These symbols of affluence and power are exaggerated by enlargement, which was also the case with "Zoot" suits in the 1940s. The excessive emphasis on consumer products in Hip-Hop alludes to social differences and hierarchies in the cultural terrain.

Street space is marked by graffiti as a sign of "ownership" and by actual physical presence—in other words, gangs that take over the area. This image is emphasized by voluminous Hip-Hop clothing, which, because of its bright colors, makes the wearer stand out from his surroundings and signifies that he or she "belongs."

Birgit Richard

01

02

03

04

05

06

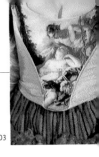

03

"FASHION DOES NOT REFLECT A NOSTALGIA FOR THE PAST BUT AN ETERNAL PRESENT THAT LIES BEYOND THE PAST." (BARBARA VINKEN, 1993)

01

Time travel—probably the most current theme in fashion—lists and combines various elements from the past. The "unknown" comes through as an accumulation of vaguely familiar pieces and details from bygone eras. The popularity of Neo-Classicism and the Directoire period, with its myth of Purism, were followed by the use of symbols of heraldry, medieval, chain-link, shirt constructions, ruche collars, lace insets, pageboy suits, Romeo panels, and jerkins for women. Futurism is just as popular with designers and is expressed by attempts to overcome traditional norms, above all in the selection of materials.

Historicism—a style characterized by the use of traditional forms and elements—is one that can be used as an effective method for overcoming transience through revival. Romanticism, whose origins are in knightly poetry, recurs as a sign of crisis in society. The yearning for tradition, for better times, is always revived when tomorrow seems to hold little promise. There are two possible responses: an introspective search or a retreat back into the past. Wartime crinolines, *robes de style* during World War I, and evening gowns made of crushed tulle, as well as poke-bonnets and white lace blouses during the Nazi era, were expressions of a yearning for revival, to extinguish transience.

In 1990 Karl Lagerfeld devoted his entire collection to the eighteenth-century Louis Quinze period. A series of grand evening gowns in manteau style by Gianni Versace in 1990/91—usually worn with thigh-high boots—made reference to the same historical period. Christian Lacroix chose to design a bustier dress with a lace-trimmed petticoat and a jacket with netted lace—in the style of the sixteenth century—and drew inspiration from the subtle palette in the paintings of Jan Vermeer (1632–75).

In 1992, Krizia used props from the Habsburg era to create an alpine, folkloric look: dirndl skirts, Tyrolean hats, and Loden jackets with braid overwork and trimming personified the look of the popular Empress Elisabeth "Sisi" of Austria (1837–98). By using these sentimental, historical figures, fashion infused the previously disdained folkloric style with a new romanticism.

The stiff, Elizabethan, lace collar was Anna Molinari's theme in 1993, and in the same year Chloé presented crocheted, wide, swinging coats and embroidered tulle tunics. Dolce & Gabbana reinterpreted the muslin dress and boa (a long, fluffy scarf made of feathers). In 1994 Hervé Léger revisited the *Directoire* and Neo-Classic eras. While in the same year, Gianfranco Ferré went a step further by transferring the Empire cut into leather. In 1995 Retro merged with the "Glam" look, as it is now called, creating references to the pomp and glory of the bygone days of Imperialism.

Gerda Buxbaum

02

RETRO-MODERNISM

04
05

01

"MY ROLE IS THAT OF A SEDUCER." (JOHN GALLIANO, 1998)

JOHN GALLIANO

The historicism and romanticism of John Galliano's designs are rivaled only by the spectacular and theatrical nature of his fashion shows. One of the great image-makers of the twentieth century, he is largely responsible for the media feeding frenzy which has typified the coverage of collections in the 1990s. Compared to France, the infrastructure of the British fashion industry is less developed, so a spectacular show may be a designer's only passport to media coverage. Yet, in recent years, the more conservative French couture houses have hired three British designers to help revive their flagging fortunes: Galliano at Givenchy and later at Dior; Alexander McQueen at Givenchy; and Stella McCartney at Chloé.

Galliano produces twelve collections a year for his own label and for Dior, where, as chief designer, he designs both the haute couture and ready-to-wear. Each collection has a narrative theme or structure based on a fictional character. The shows are designed to include the audience in the fantasy scenario as the models move through a series of elaborately staged tableaux dressed like film sets. The models wear only one outfit (very different from the quick changes of the conventional fashion show) and are encouraged to act their character's part. Galliano creates composite figures, from doomed beauties to *grandes horizontales,* based on cinema, art, and a range of historical characters. Stylistically promiscuous, his designs bring together Colonial and Belle Époque references and impressionistically fuse cultures and peoples. His exotic style is antithetical to the casual, minimalist and Deconstructionist looks which have typified most 1990s design.

Everywhere the leitmotifs of fantasy and excess are maintained. The set designer makes a snowy rooftop for *la vie bohème,* a stable for an American show, a circus ring, or a café concert. A suburban sports stadium became an enchanted forest filled with forty-foot-high spruce trees, and at the Gare d'Austerlitz a steam train delivered models to a platform that had been transformed into a Moroccan souk where the seated spectators were served fresh mint tea. Galliano's obsession with detail even extends to the invitations—a red ballet slipper, a rusty key, a charm bracelet inside a Russian doll, or a mischievous (St. Trinian's style) school report.

Behind these theatrical tactics lie Galliano's formidable tailoring skills. His greatest influence on recent fashion has been his revival of the bias cut, originating from his admiration of Madeleine Vionnet's designs. Although his aesthetic is luxurious and Parisian, his pursuit of transformation harks back to the elaborate staging of the London club scene of the 1980s, when Galliano was a student at St. Martin's College of Art. In the late 1990s, he still talks of the attitude and energy of London and imports House, Techno, and Jungle music into the sober couture house, mixing funk with finesse and street irreverence with seduction.   *Caroline Evans*

JOHN GALLIANO

1960	Born on November 28 in Gibraltar
1984	Graduates with honors from St. Martin's College of Art and Design, London; final-year collection "Les Incroyables," inspired by the French Revolution, causes a sensation
1985	Introduces women's collection, "The Ludic Game," during British Fashion Week
1986	Spring/Summer collection "Fallen Angels"; Autumn/Winter collection "Forgotten Innocents"
1987	Receives British Designer of the Year Award (also in 1994, 1995, and 1997 jointly with Alexander McQueen)
1988	Spring/Summer collection "A Streetcar Named Desire," inspired by Blanche Dubois
1987–89	Ready-to-wear collection for Balenciaga
1990	Ready-to-wear in Paris at the invitation of the Chambre Syndicale de la Couture Parisienne
1992	"Napoleon and Josephine" collection
1994	Spring/Summer collection "Princess Lucretia," inspired by the 1930s: crinolines, obliquely cut evening gowns, pajama suits
1995	Spring/Summer collection "Misia Diva": modern glamor
1996	Spring/Summer collection "La Papillon et la Fleur"; first haute couture and prêt-à-porter collection for Givenchy
FROM 1997	Chief designer at Dior for haute couture and prêt-à-porter; first collection is a mixture of Belle Époque, Massai princess, bird-of-paradise dresses
1998	Spring/Summer collection for Dior, inspired by decadent Berlin nightlife of the 1920s; CFDA International Award
1999	Autumn/Winter collection for Dior, inspired by Africa and the Maori

02
03

01 John Galliano, "Olivia the Filibuster" collection, Spring/Summer 1993 ••• 02 John Galliano, final year show at St. Martin's College, London, 1984 ••• 03 John Galliano for Dior Haute Couture, grand evening dress, Autumn/Winter 1997/98 ••• 04 John Galliano for Dior, advertising campaign, Autumn/Winter 1997/98

04

HIGH-TECH CHIC

03
04

"SOME DAY WE WILL BLOW CLOTHES THE WAY WE BLOW GLASS. IT'S RIDICULOUS THAT FABRIC SHOULD BE CUT UP TO MAKE A FLAT THING TO GO ROUND A ROUND PERSON."
(MARY QUANT, 1967)

Advances in fabric technology increasingly drive the look of clothes. Designers take their cues from new-fangled fabrics that reflect light, that stretch, that have been adorned with sequins (not by hand, but by computer), and that have threads of metal or plastic woven into their surfaces. Fabric shows such as the acclaimed Premiere Vision in Paris are ground zero for the next big trends in fashion.

Designers have long been enamored of the possibilities that technology affords them. Nicole Miller used Scotchguard—the same material used to create reflective stripes on road crews' uniforms—to make her dresses glow in the dark. The designer Miuccia Prada embroidered shirts made of latex and used mirrors, in lieu of sequins and rhinestones, to adorn her dresses. Donna Karan used non-rip paper—best known in the form of Federal Express envelopes—to create cocktail dresses. Yet this experimentation with high-tech fabrics is often little more than a gimmick. After all, who really needs a $1,000 dress that glows in the dark?

As designers became more comfortable with technology, using it as another tool rather than as an enticing toy, they began to use it in ways that both benefited and enticed consumers. Fabric innovations offered greater practicality to fashion with the introduction of washable silks and dry-cleanable mink. Also, protective resins such as Teflon rendered fabrics stain resistant. Yeohlee Teng and David Chu of Nautica applied Teflon coatings to their pristine white cotton garments, making them more resilient to the assaults of urban living. The combination of Spandex with fabrics such as cotton and wool introduced unprecedented levels of comfort to tailored jackets and slim pants in both the men's and the women's markets, while in the sportswear industry new fabrics such as Nike's Dri-Fit could keep athletes warm in the winter and cool in the summer.

Textile technology has even been applied to fur. Designer Karl Lagerfeld, working for the House of Fendi, shaved mink and sable so close to the skin that it could be manipulated like any other fabric, thus expanding the looks that could be achieved with fur. Cynthia Steffe brought glitz and glamour to her clothes—without all of the expensive and time-consuming hand beading—by using computer-generated sequins. The Italian design house Marni, a proponent of the new Hippie Chic look, created felt garments, thus combining a genre of haute bohemia with a made-at-home quality.

The importance of this new textile market has also increased the tendency for fashion to look the same. Designers shopped at the same fabric markets, became entranced with the same innovations, and often were driven to create the same silhouettes. However, this fury for techno-textiles signals the fall of certain limitations, enabling designers to realize their wildest fantasies.   *Robin Givhan*

05

"THE FUTURE OF FASHION? IT HAS NONE. THE TREND IS NO FASHION. WE ARE GETTING NAKEDER AND NAKEDER." (THIERRY MUGLER)

NEW MILLENNIUM

02

John Galliano claims that "The only way to get forward in fashion is to return to construction," while Karl Lagerfeld has expressed the opinion that the only thing that can be new about fashion is the material. The twentieth-century French philosopher Jean Baudrillard (b. 1929) takes the view that the body no longer exists and has said, "in this new erotic world every illusionistic element is missing.... The body is present, even over-exposed, but only as part of the technical equipment."

We are plunging into a new millennium. How will we dress for it? Designers of all nationalities are inventing clothes and props for an imaginary future in which men and women primarily wear whatever marvels the chemical industry produces. What is not a fiction is that the suitcases of our increasingly nomadic society are getting smaller. Since irons are becoming superfluous, most of the space is taken up by cosmetics and fragrances—now that body maintenance is the focus of attention. In fact, many traditional fashion categories have become meaningless, and "seasonless dressing" has become the motto; casual clothes adorned with sequins or evening wear made from paper or nylon have become status quo. For example, Donna Karan often refers to "liquid tailoring" and places sensuous comfort at the top of her list of requirements.

Has fashion overlooked anything in this last decade? We are already familiar with cross-dressing, sadomasochistic and "hooker" fashions, bodices worn over suits, exterior construction seams, "Barbie-doll" dresses, Minimalism, Purism, New Naturalism (one that even Oscar Wilde would have thought irritating), Romanticism, High-Tech, "Collage" dresses of cotton, lace, plastic, paper, and tulle, and the Glam look that harks back to the splendor and magnificence of past centuries through ruched collars, lace inserts, pageboy suits, Romeo caps, and *justeaucorps*.

However, in the immediate future, will our clothing be enriched with digital functions? Will deficiencies in human nature be eradicated, urged on by a sophisticated techno-fashion culture? What would be needed to establish this on the mass market is true "softwear," fashionable computer clothing—wearable computing—which could be thrown into the washing machine. As Jakob Steurer has noted: "We run around like packhorses saddled with information devices of all kinds. However, I believe we should feel better in the saddle—and not under it."

Whether this clothing—and we will probably need to find a new term for it—is transparent, shiny, slit high, executed in gaudy colors, made from leather and covered with metal studs, or retro in style will no longer be of concern. Perhaps all that we will need are sophisticated pieces of Lycra that conform to our bodies as though they were undressed.

Gerda Buxbaum

01

APPENDIX

DESIGNER BIOGRAPHIES

AZZEDINE ALAÏA

1940	Born in Tunisia, circa 1940
	In Tunis, apprentices as tailor and studies sculpture at the École des Beaux Arts
1957	Moves to Paris
1957–70	Works as assistant to various designers, including Guy Laroche and Thierry Mugler
1970	Opens a studio in Paris, primarily for show business clients
1980	Receives international attention with a studded, oversized, patent leather coat
1982	Conquers the U.S. market after a fashion show at the department store Bergdorf-Goodman, New York
1985	Designs a pink corsage-Latex dress for Grace Jones's attendance at the Oscar Awards, earning him the title "King of Stretch"
1986	Collection with skintight dresses out of patent leather, latex, and Lycra, with wide buckles, openwork, and inserts with tattoo designs
1992	Collaborates with photographer Jean-Paul Goude by creating custom designs for his photographs
1996	Designs costumes for Massai warriors for a fashion spread in the French magazine *Elle*

GIORGIO ARMANI

1934	Born on July 11 in Piacenza, Italy
1960	Works as a menswear buyer and window designer for the Milan department store La Rinascente
1964–70	Works as assistant to Nino Cerutti
1970–75	Works as a freelance designer for various fashion houses
1975	Founds Giorgio Armani S.p.A., together with Sergio Galeotti
1975–81	Introduces the lines Giorgio Armani Le Collezioni, Mani Uomo and Donna, Armani Junior, Armani Underwear, Armani Swimwear, Emporio Armani, and Armani Jeans
1982	Becomes first fashion designer, after Christian Dior, to appear on the cover of the *Times*
1987–97	Introduces lines for eyeglasses, hosiery, skiwear, golf accessories, and watches
1991	Receives honorary doctorate from the Royal College of Art
PERFUMES	Armani (1982), Armani Men's Cologne (1984), Gió (1992), Aqua di Gió (1995), Emporio Armani (1998)

CHRISTOBAL BALENCIAGA see p. 66

PIERRE BALMAIN

1914	Born on May 18 in Saint-Jean-de-Maurienne, France
	Studies architecture at the École des Beaux Arts, Paris
1934–39	Works as assistant to Edward Molyneux
1939–45	Together with Christian Dior, responsible for the collection of the House Lucien Lelong
1945	Opens a house of couture in Paris
1947	Opens his first boutique for accessories, Le Kiosque des Fantasies as well as his first boutique in New York
1953	Expands into the United States where he shows his collections for the first time under the name Jolie Madame
1977	Sells his business for financial reasons but remains responsible for the design
1982	Dies on June 29; his former assistant Erik Mortensen assumes artistic direction
FROM 1992	Oscar de la Renta responsible for all collections of the House of Balmain
PERFUMES	Elysées (1946), Vent Vert (1947), Jolie Madame (1949), Miss Balmain (1960), Ivoire (1979), Ebène (1983)

GEOFFREY BEENE see p. 111

BENETTON see p. 114

BIBA

1936	Born Barbara Hulanicki on December 8 in Warsaw, Poland
1948	Moves to London
1953–54	Studies at the Brighton College of Art
1955	Wins the *Evening Standard* design competition for the design of a bathing costume
1960	Founds a small mail-order fashion company named Biba's Postal Boutique, after her sister
1964	Opens a small boutique in a side street off King's Road, London
1968	Launches a mail-order catalogue and opens a larger store in the Kensington High Street that becomes a cult store in the late 1960s and early 1970s; in particular, has great success with dresses flattering the figure known as the "Slinky" look
1972	Purchases the department store Derry & Toms opposite the Biba boutique and develops it into the Art Deco retreat Big Biba
1975	Closes the department store and emigrates to Brazil
1975–80	Works as a freelance designer for the Fiorucci and Cacharel labels, among others
FROM 1980	Moves to Florida and works as an interior designer

MANOLO BLAHNIK

1943	Born in Santa Cruz, Canary Islands, Spain
	Studies languages and fine arts in Geneva, Switzerland
1968	Moves to Paris, where he works as a set designer
1970	Visits New York and shows his theater designs to Diana Vreeland, who applauds his shoe designs
1971	Starts working as a shoe designer in London
1972	Designs shoes for Ossie Clark and the fashion chain, Midas
1973–99	Opens flagship store under his own name in London's Chelsea district and boutiques in the United States and Asia
1987	Receives his first award by the CFDA
1999	Becomes first shoe designer to receive the Houston Museum of Fine Art's Silver Slipper Award

PIERRE CARDIN

1922	Born on July 1 in Venice, Italy
1939	Apprentices as a tailor in Vichy
1945–50	Works as assistant to Madame Paquin, Elsa Schiaparelli, and Christian Dior
1947	Designs costumes for Jean Cocteau's film *Beauty and the Beast*
1950	Opens a small studio in Paris where he designs primarily costumes for theater productions
1953	First haute couture collection for women
1954	Opens his first boutique in Paris; designs his "Robes Belles"
1958	Unisex collection
1965	Designs a women's ready-to-wear line for French department store Printemps
1966	Futuristic "Space" collection inspired by Yuri Gagarin's flight in space
1967	Sleeveless vests with asymmetrical zippers and low-riding metal belts
1968	Skirts with squares that stick out; shift dresses with superimposed geometric shapes and stark black-and-white graphic style
1969	Uses vinyl, plastic, and silver-dyed leather
1977	Opens Evolution gallery in Paris which carries exclusive furniture and accessories
1979	Becomes first Western couturier to expand into China
1988	Creates new body shapes with wire-reinforced seams and tutu skirts shaped like discs
1991	*Pierre Cardin: Past-Present-Future*, retrospective, Victoria and Albert Museum, London

PERFUMES Singulier (1955), Pierre Cardin pour Monsieur, Cardin de Pierre Cardin, Bleu Marine (1965), Men's Cologne (1972), Cardin (1976), Choc de Cardin (1981), Paradoxe de Cardin (1984), Maxim's de Paris (1985), Bleu Marine de Cardin (1986)

HUSSEIN CHALAYAN

1970	Born in Nicosia, Cyprus
1982	Moves to England
1989–93	Studies fashion design at Central St. Martin's College of Art and Design, London; sells his final-year collection to Brown's, London's leading fashion house
1994	Introduces ready-to-wear line Hussein Chalayan; first collection features dresses printed with poetic texts and an avant-garde runway presentation

GABRIELLE "COCO" CHANEL see p. 27

ANDRÉ COURRÈGES

1923	Born on March 9 in Pau, France Technician and civil engineer (bridge construction); studies fashion design
1950–61	Assistant to Cristobal Balenciaga
1960	Opens his "White" salon in Paris
1965	"Space" collection; the "Moon Maiden" look
1967	Introduces three lines: Prototype (made-to-measure), Couture Future (expensive luxury prêt-à-porter), and Hyperbole (inexpensive prêt-à-porter)
1969	Knitted catsuits
1972	Outfits the French team at the Summer Olympic Games in Munich; changes style to be more feminine, with gathers and use of pastel colors
1973	Presents first menswear collection
1985	Business goes to the Japanese group Itokin
FROM 1994	Jean-Charles de Castelbajac designs collections for Courrèges

PERFUMES Empreinte, Eau de Courrèges (1971), Courrèges pour Hommes (1977)

ANN DEMEULEMEESTER

1959	Born on December 29 in Courtai/ Kortrijk, Belgium
FROM 1973	Studies fashion design in Antwerp; works for a Belgian ready-to-wear company
1981	Receives diploma from the Académie des Beaux Arts, Antwerp; participates in "Groupe des Six," a joint fashion show in London
1985	Founds own production company together with husband Patrick Robyn
1987	Presents first collection in London
1990	Introduces own footwear collection
FROM 1992	Presents collection in Paris at Ecole des Beaux-Arts
1993	Oversized, white tops; long, black robes
1994	"Grunge" look; "Layered" look
1996	Presents first menswear collection
1996–97	"Transparent" look

CHRISTIAN DIOR see p. 63

DOLCE & GABBANA

1958	Domenico Dolce born on August 13 in Palermo, Italy

Apprentices as a tailor and joins his father's business

1962	Stefano Gabbana born on November 14 in Milan, Italy Studies graphic arts and works as graphic artist
1982	They begin their career together by opening their own studio
1986	Present first own collection and "Real Woman" fashion show
1987–95	Open a new showroom in Milan followed by two more there and one in New York
1989	Introduce first swimwear and lingerie collection, the latter as an essential part of their women's outerwear
1990	Present first menswear collection
1990–94	Additionally work as fashion consultants for collections by Complice
1993	Design a collection for Madonna, whom both admire greatly
1994	Open flagship store in Milan; introduce D&G, a successful, secondary line for young people; add jeans, accessories, and eyeglasses to their expanding product range
1996	Develop legendary "Animal Prints" collection

PERFUMES Dolce & Gabbana Parfum (1992), Dolce & Gabbana pour Homme (1996), By Dolce & Gabbana (1997), D&G Feminine and D&G Masculine (1999)

ERTÉ see p. 30

ESCADA

1933	Founder Margaretha Ley born on February 13 in Själevad, Sweden Apprentices as a tailor at the Stockholm fashion house Leja; later works as a model, including for the sophisticated Viennese tailor Fred Adlmüller and Jacques Fath in Paris
1937	Founder Wolfgang Ley born on October 11 in Cologne, Germany
1974	Found company in Munich
1976	Introduce Escada label, named after a race horse
1980	Launch Laurèl label
1982	Expand into the American market
1992	Margaretha Ley dies on June 4; Michael Stolzenburg succeeds her as head designer
1993–97	American designer Todd Oldham is consultant to Escada as "creative partner"
1994	Stolzenburg dies; Scotsman Brian Rennie becomes new head designer; Escada Sport label is launched
1998	Introduction of new Escada line The Todd Oldham for Apriori Collection

PERFUMES Escada by Margaretha Ley (1990), Escada pour Homme (1993)

JACQUES FATH

1912	Born on September 12 in Vincennes, France
1937	Opens a small fashion boutique in Paris, and rapidly acquired a reputation as one of the leaders in French fashion
1947	Launches famed "pencil" skirt
1948	Conquers the American market through cooperation with ready-made designer Joseph Halpert; opens a store for reasonably priced clothing and accessories in Paris
1954	Dies at the height of his career on November 13
1957	The fashion house closes; perfume company is retained
1991	The Banque Saga Group purchases the name "Jacques Fath, Maison de Couture"
1992	House reopens under artistic direction of Dutch designer Tom van Lingen
1997	New York-based Russian designer Elena Nazaroff assumes artistic direction

PERFUMES Iris Gris (1946), Canasta (1950), Fath de Fath (1953), Green Water (1967), Ellipse (1971), Expression (1977)

FENDI

1925	The parents of the five Fendi sisters Paola (b. 1931), Anna (b. 1931), Franca (b. 1935), Carla (b. 1937), and Alda (b. 1940) found a workshop for leather goods and furs in Rome
1945–55	The five sisters successively enter the family business
1955	Present first fashion show with furs, leathers, and accessories
1965	The sisters engage the young Karl Lagerfeld as head designer of fur coats and jackets, making Fendi the international leader in haute fourrure (fur fashions)
1969	Produce first series of limited issue, ready-to-wear furs
1977	Present first women's wear collection
1983	Found the secondary Fendissime line, focusing on youth-oriented, affordable furs
1984	Expand product range with jeans, scarves, sunglasses, and ties
1989	Open first flagship store in New York
1990	Introduce menswear and swimwear

PERFUMES Fendi (1986), Fendi uomo (1989), Asja (1993)

SALVATORE FERRAGAMO see p. 46

GIANFRANCO FERRÉ

1944	Born on August 15 in Legnano, Italy
1969	Completes doctorate of architecture but immediately begins to design jewelry and accessories
1969–77	Works as a consultant to Italian textile and clothing companies
1978	Begins a freelance career as a fashion designer with the thrilling "Alta-Moda-Pronta" collection, produced jointly with the textile producer Franco Mattioli
1982	Introduces less expensive Oaks by Ferré women's wear line and first menswear collection
1989–97	Works as artistic director for the House of Dior

MARIANO FORTUNY

1871	Born Mariano Fortuny y Madrazo in Granada, Spain. Trains as painter and stage designer
1901	Opens a technical studio in Paris; invents indirect lighting
1907	Devotes himself to dyeing and pleating silks in his Venetian palazzo; creates his first Delphos robes
1919	Founds a textile plant in Venice; produces unique "Delphos" robes
1920	Opens boutiques in Paris and New York; shows overgarments in the form of Coptic tunics; designs velvets with oriental and Renaissance motifs
1920–42	Participates in all art biennials
1949	Dies on May 2 in Venice; has appointed princess Gozzi as heiress who continues the business and has fabrics manufactured after Fortuny's designs

JOHN GALLIANO see p. 168

JEAN-PAUL GAULTIER see p. 138

RUDI GERNREICH

1922	Born on August 8 in Vienna, Austria
1938	Immigrates to the United States with his mother
1938–42	Studies at Los Angeles City College and Los Angeles Art Center School

1949–60	Designs demonstration models for various textile companies in New York
1960	Founds his own company in Los Angeles for fashion, furniture, and household articles; presents a complete look that integrates clothing, hairstyle, and make-up
1964	Attracts much attention with his "Monokini," a bathing suit without a top
1965	Collaborates with hair designer Vidal Sassoon; makes dramatic impact on lingerie industry with the "no-bra bra," made of see-through, thermoplastically preformed material
1966	Attracts attention again by covering the body of his muse Peggy Moffitt with black vinyl triangles
1970	Propagates a unisex look which rejects any type of body hair; collection with wild mix of different patterns and styles, stripes, checks, polka dots, and clashing colors
1985	Dies on April 20 in Los Angeles

ROMEO GIGLI

1949	Born on December 12 in Faenza, Italy. Studies architecture; apprentices as a tailor in New York
1977	Works as a freelance designer for various fashion companies
1981	Founds his own company in Milan with the support of Carla Sozzani, editor in chief of Italian *Vogue*
1984	Shows first collection under his own name
1985	Introduces secondary line, G by Gigli
FROM 1985	Designs collections for Callaghan line of the Italian company Zamasport
1986	Has international breakthrough with Spring/Summer collection inspired by the early Italian Renaissance; Autumn/Winter collection inspired by the Byzantine Empire and Empress Theodora; Gigli's voluminous silhouettes become trademark "Cocooning" style of fashion
1989	Presents his collection for the first time at the ready-to-wear shows in Paris

PERFUMES Romeo Gigli (1991), Romeo Gigli per Uomo (1992)

HUBERT DE GIVENCHY

1927	Born on February 21 in Beauvais, France. Studies at the École des Beaux Arts, Paris
1945–52	Works as assistant to Jacques Fath, Robert Piquet, and Lucien Lelong; designs boutique fashions for Elsa Schiaparelli
1951	Opens own house of couture in Paris; designs the famous "Bettina" blouse, named after model Bettina Graziani

1953 First encounter with Cristobal Balenciaga, with whom he develops a close friendship and collaboration

FROM 1954 Works as personal stylist to actress Audrey Hepburn; designs costumes, including for the movies *Funny Face* and *Breakfast at Tiffany's*

1968–75 Introduces ready-to-wear collection "Givenchy Nouvelle Boutique" and a Givenchy menswear line

1988 Company purchased by LVMH group

1991 *40 Ans de Création* retrospective, Musée de la Mode et du Costume, Paris

1996 British designer John Galliano is appointed artistic director

FROM 1997 Within one year, artistic directorship is transferred to Alexander McQueen

MADAME GRÈS

1903 Born Germaine Krebs in Paris, France Studies sculpture; apprentices at the Paris fashion house Premet

1931 Opens salon Alix in Paris

1934–41 Designs costumes for Hollywood

1939 Gives up salon and works as a freelance designer for various fashion companies

1942 Opens another salon in Paris under the name Grès; designs collections in the French national colors, blue-white-red, whereupon the Nazis immediately close her salon

1945 Reopens salon; develops her trademark style inspired by ancient Greece: white garments with asymmetrical lines, extravagantly gathered and draped

1965 Presents her designs for the first time at a fashion show in New York

1980 Launches first ready-to-wear line; stays true to her style

1993 Dies in Paris; company is bought by a Japanese group

1994 Major Madame Grès retrospective, Metropolitan Museum of Art, New York

PERFUMES Cabochard (1959), Grès pour Homme (1965), Qui pour quoi (1976), Grès Monsieur (1980)

RENÉ GRUAU see p. 70

GUCCI

1904 Master saddler Guccio Gucci (1881–1953) founds a workshop in Florence, Italy to produce leather goods; initially the company specializes in leather goods, particularly bags and baggage

1960 Launches the famous Gucci loafer, a comfortable, moccasin-style shoe

1961–77 Gradually expands product range to include silk scarves, ties, watches, and perfumes

1978 Presents first ready-to-wear collection for women

1989 Sells family business to the Arab finance company Investcorps, because of financial difficulties

1994 American Tom Ford (b. 1962 in Texas, see photo) becomes head designer and, in the following years, turns Gucci into the hottest insider fashion-tip; Mario Gucci, the grandson of the company's founder and current head of Gucci, is shot

1995–97 Great success with collections in so-called Mod style; "Hipsters" pants in shiny velvet become legendary

PERFUME Envy (1997)

KATHERINE HAMNETT

1947 Born in Graves End, Kent, Great Britain

1955–59 Studies at St. Martin's College of Art & Design, London

1969 Founds fashion label Tuttabankem and works as a freelance designer

1979 Founds company and label Katherine Hamnett

1983 Attracts attention with her "Message" T-shirts with political statements

1984 Wears a T-shirt bearing the slogan "58% Don't Want Pershing" to a reception hosted by Prime Minister Margaret Thatcher

1985 Becomes first designer to launch ripped, pre-worn jeans

1986 Opens first boutique in London

1989 Shows collection in Paris for the first time

1990–99 Introduces a menswear line and the lines Katherine Hamnett Classics, Hamnett Active, and Denim

HERMÈS

1837 Master saddler Thierry Hermès founds company in Paris; initially store sells bridles, gauntlets, boots, and gloves; later, expands to include suitcases, bags, and briefcases; becomes famous in aristocratic circles throughout the world

1930 Creation of prototype for the "Kelly" bag cult handbag

1937 Expansion of product range with famous Carré Hermès, hand-printed silk scarves

1988–97 Former journalist and fashion editor Claude Brouet assumes responsibility for the women's ready-to-wear line; makes Hermès a cult label in this area

1990 Introduces new handbag design, "Dumbo"

1998 Belgian Martin Margiela is appointed ready-to-wear designer

PERFUMES Calèche (1961), Equipage (1970)

CHARLES JAMES see p. 51

DONNA KARAN see p. 135

REI KAWAKUBO see p. 127

KENZO TAKADA see p. 112

LAINEY KEOGH

1957 Born on September 20 in Ireland Studies textile design and textile technology

1989 Receives the Prix de Coeur from Christian Lacroix for her work with Irish linens

1989–92 Studies fine arts and commerce

1995 Costume design for the film *Two Nudes Bathing*, for which she receives the Cable Ace Award

1997 Presents her work at the Fashion Week, London

1998 Designs and produces the fabrics for the Christian Dior Autumn/Winter haute couture collection

1999 Presents first own collection "Wildlife, Sex and Survival" at the Natural History Museum for the Fashion Week, London

CALVIN KLEIN

1942 Born on November 19 in New York, United States

1960–62 Studies at the Fashion Institute of Technology, New York

1968 Founds Calvin Klein Ltd. in New York, together with Barry Schwartz

1970 "Pea Coat," a double-breasted short coat with wide lapels becomes a sales hit

1980 Receives attention for his advertising with Brooke Shields in Calvin Klein jeans

1982 Breakthrough with Calvin Klein underwear; provocative advertising campaign with Marky Mark

1992–93 Designs Spring/Summer collection in the "Layering" look

1995 *Obsession—The Lives and Times of Calvin Klein* by Steven Gaines and Sharon Churcher is published in New York

1995–96 Pioneers the "Transparent" look in his Autumn/Winter collection

PERFUMES Obsession (1985), Eternity (1989),
Escape (1991), cK one (1994), cK be
(1997), Contradiction (1998)

KRIZIA

1933 Founder Mariuccia
Mandelli born in
Bergamo, Italy

1954 Begins to design
youth fashions in col-
laboration with her
friend Flora Dolci

1963 Attracts attention with an ensemble of
shorts and tops that expose the midriff

1964 Presents a noted collection in the "Op
Art" look at the shows in Florence

1967–69 Introduces the Kriziamaglia and
Kriziababy lines

1970 Makes "Hot" pants fashionable; introduces fabric prints in animal and plant
motifs that become her trademark

1983 Presents her famous "Chrysler Building" overalls in silver plissé fabric;
launches the Krizia Uomo line

1989–92 Introduces the lines K of Krizia, KM by
Krizia (for men), and MM by Krizia

PERFUMES K de Krizia, Krizia Uomo, Teatro alla
Scala

CHRISTIAN LACROIX

1951 Born on May 16 in
Arles, France

1973–76 Studies art history at
Montpellier Univer-
sity and museum
studies at the Sor-
bonne

1976–78 Sells fashion drawings to various fashion houses

1978 Joins the Hermès design team

1979–81 Works as assistant to Guy Paulin in the
House of Chloé

1981–87 Responsible for haute couture at the
House of Patou

1987 Opens a couture salon in the prestigious Rue du Faubourg St. Honoré,
Paris with the assistance of the luxury
group LVMH; attracts much attention
with first fashion show with bright colors, unconventional pattern mixes, and
baroque forms

1988 Presents first ready-to-wear collection

1989–94 Introduces an accessories line, the less
expensive Bazaar line, and a jeans line

PERFUME C'est la vie! (1990)

KARL LAGERFELD see p. 128

HELMUT LANG see p. 157

JEANNE LANVIN

1867 Born on January 1
in Paris, France

1880 Begins apprentice-
ship as a milliner

1889 Opens a millinery
shop in Paris; designs
dresses for children
and young girls on the side

1909 Opens a boutique in the Rue du
Faubourg St. Honoré where she sells
haute couture for women

1918 Launches the robe de style, based on
eighteenth-century designs

1919–26 Expands her collections with sporty
women's wear, a menswear collection,
and children's wear

1939 Presents her couture collection in New
York

1946 Dies in Paris; her daughter takes over
the business

1950–96 Over the years a number of designers
are commissioned, including Giorgio
Armani and Claude Montana

FROM 1998 Designer Cristina Ortiz is responsible
for artistic direction

PERFUMES My Sin (1925), Arpège (1927), Scandal
(1931), Monsieur Lanvin (1933),
Crescendo (1965), Chiaro (1969), Via
Lanvin (1971), Lanvin Homme (1977),
Claire de Jour (1983)

RALPH LAUREN

1939 Born Ralph Lipschitz
on October 12 in New
York, United States

1967 Founds Polo label
with tie collections

1968 Introduces Polo by
Ralph Lauren line of
high-quality menswear

1971 Introduces Polo pony logo at the same
time as first women's wear line

1972 Introduces Polo Ralph Lauren footwear

1974 Introduces sportswear line CHAPS by
Ralph Lauren and Ralph Lauren Eye-
wear for men and women

1980 Introduces Ralph Lauren underwear
and leather goods

1981 Becomes first American designer to
open a flagship store in Europe on New
Bond Street, London

1986 Receives the CFDA Designer of the Year
Award (also in 1995, 1996)

1992 Receives the Lifetime Achievement
Award by the Council of Fashion

1994 Introduces the Polo Sports line

1996 Introduces Polo Jeans, Lauren by Ralph
Lauren (women's sportswear), and
Ralph Lauren Home Collection

1998 Introduces Ralph Lauren Swimwear,
Ralph Lauren Infants and Toddlers,
Ralph Lauren Girls, and Ralph Lauren
Boys

1999 Introduces the Polo RLX running shoe;
launches Ralph Line, a less expensive
department store collection for young
women

PERFUMES Polo (1989), Safari (1991), Safari for
Men (1995), Polo Sport (1996), Ralph
Lauren Polo Sport Woman (1997),
Extreme Polo Sport (1998)

HERVÉ LÉGER

1957 Born on May 30 in
Bapaume, France

1975 Studies sculpture
but abandons studies
after a brief period;
thereafter, works first
as a hairdresser, then as an accessories
designer for Swarovski, the Austrian
manufacturer of fine glassware, among
others

1980–82 Works as assistant to Karl Lagerfeld at
Fendi

1982–83 Designs for several couturiers including
Chanel, Lanvin, and Chloé

1985 Founds own company but continues to
work as a freelance designer

1992 Has sensational success with the
presentation of "robes à bandés," his
"Bandage" dresses made out of
stretch-bands

1993 Presents first ready-to-wear collection

1994–95 Famous collection of cocktail dresses
made out of rainbow-colored stretch-
bands, publicized in all major fashion
magazines

1996 Adds transparent stretch-lace to range
of materials

MARTIN MARGIELA

1957 Born on April 9 in Genk, Belgium

1979 Receives diploma from the Académie
des Beaux Arts, Antwerp

1984–87 Works as design assistant to Jean-Paul
Gaultier

1988 Founds the company Sarl Neuf, together with Jenny Meirens; presents first
women's ready-to-wear collection in
Paris

1989 Presents collection with models walking
across white material in socks saturated
with red paint

1990 Presents first garments made from lin-
ing material with seams on the outside

1991 1950s ball gowns overdyed in gray, worn
with old jeans

1992 Aprons and tops made from old head-
scarves; pleated polyester T-shirts with
Prince of Wales check

1993 Spring/Summer collection: reconstruct-
ed stage costumes; Autumn/Winter
collection: used, cut-up costumes from
the 1940s assembled in new ways

1996 "Photoprint" collection; participates in
the Florence Art & Fashion Biennale

1997 Has first solo exhibition in Rotterdam; presents collection jointly with Comme des Garçons in Paris

1998 Designs Hermès' women's ready-to-wear range; introduces first menswear collection

CLAIRE McCARDELL see p. 59

ALEXANDER McQUEEN

1969 Born on March 17 in London, Great Britain

Apprentices as a tailor and studies at Central St. Martin's College of Art & Design, London

1992–94 Works as assistant to Romeo Gigli in Milan

1994 Founds his own label

1995 Establishes his reputation as creative bad boy by presenting first wild collections, including Spring/Summer collection "Highland Rape" (not commercially viable even in designer's own view); invents rave pants known as Hipsters

1996 Receives much attention in the fashion media for his Autumn/Winter "Gothic" collection

1997 Succeeds John Galliano as head designer for French haute couture house Givenchy; first collection in Greek style, featuring a headdress of golden ram horns

MISSONI

1921 Ottavio Missoni born on February 11 in Dubrovnik, Croatia

1931 Rosita Jelmini, later Missoni, born on November 20 in Golasecca, Italy

1948 Rosita and Ottavio meet at the Olympic Games in London; he is a Games participant in the hurdles race, she a language student

1953 Shortly after marrying, the Missonis open a small, knitting workshop in Milan, Italy

1955 Sell first collection of vertically striped sweaters to the department store chain La Rinascente

1961 Develop new knitting patterns; create the typical "Missoni" pattern mosaics, mixtures of straight, zigzag, and wavy stripes

1964 Designer Emmanuelle Khan joins as artistic consultant

1967 Missoni fashion show in Florence causes a scandal when the models wear see-through blouses without bras

1978 *25 Years Missoni*, retrospective, Metropolitan Museum of Art, New York

1979 Present first menswear collection at the shows in Florence

FROM 1980 Introduce several lines for home textiles, wall hangings, decoration, and upholstering fabric

PERFUMES Missoni (1980), Aria (1984), Molto Missoni (1990), Noi (1996)

ISSEY MIYAKE see p. 144

CLAUDE MONTANA

1949 Born on June 29 in Paris, France

1971 Begins to design fashion in London and produces fashion jewelry

1973 Designs for the French leather firm MacDouglas

1976 Makes leather fashionable for women with his collections of waist-pleated, nappa leather pants combined with high-heels; the "Oversize" look featuring voluminous jackets with generously padded shoulders

1976–79 Designs "Claude Montana pour Ferrer Y Sentis" collection for the Spanish firm Ferrer y Sentis

1978 Designs a collection for Ferrer y Sentis consisting of black leather and metal chains; it outrages the press and is claimed to be reminiscent of the Nazi era

1980 Founds Claude Montana S.A.

1990–93 Also responsible for the haute couture collection of the House of Lanvin

1992 Introduces secondary line, State of Claude Montana

1997 Partially closes the House of Montana because of financial difficulties

PERFUMES Montana (1987), Just Me (1996)

FRANCO MOSCHINO see p. 136

THIERRY MUGLER

1948 Born in Strasbourg, France

1962–64 Trains as a dancer and studies at the École des Arts Décoratifs, Strasbourg

1968 Moves to Paris; works as a freelance designer for various fashion companies

1973 Presents his first collection under the brand name Café de Paris

1974 Founds the ready-to-wear company Thierry Mugler

1977 Presents his first collection "Spectacle"

1984 Has legendary show at the Zenith palace in Paris with falling snow and roses and madonnas, dominatrices, and angels that float down onto the runway

1986 "Gouvernante" two-piece suits with jagged seams become Mugler's trademark; broad-shouldered, narrowly belted, leather jackets worn with leggings and high-heeled boots; paste embroidery in star and comet shapes

1987 Menswear collection in the "Macho" look: skin-tight, leather outfits and muscle T-shirts

1988 Publishes *Thierry Mugler Photograph*

1994 20th anniversary fashion show, "Extraterrestrial Porn Opera," with Milky Way runway, galactic princesses in chromium-plated corsets, and see-through full-length vinyl suits

1997 Presents first haute couture collection, an homage to woman as exotic bird of paradise, with extravagant corsets inspired by insect carapaces

PERFUMES Angel (1993), A-Men (1997)

JEANNE PAQUIN

1869 Born Jeanne Becker in Paris, France

Trains as a dressmaker at the Paris fashion salon Drecoll

1891 Founds her own salon in the Rue de la Paix, Paris

1900 Chairs fashion show organization at the Paris World Exposition; temporary President of the Chambre Syndicale de la Couture Parisienne

1912 Opens salons in London, Madrid, and Buenos Aires as well as a fur boutique in New York; receives international attention for her fur-trimmed suits and coats

1913 Presents a collection with tango dresses which receives much attention

1920 Withdraws from the business; her main house in the Rue du Faubourg St. Honoré continues on until 1954

1936 Dies in Paris

JEAN PATOU

1880 Born in Normandy, France

Trains as a tailor

1908 Works as a freelance tailor in Paris

1912 Opens the women's and fur fashion store Parry in Paris; his entire first collection is purchased by a New York department store

1919 Opens an haute couture salon in the Rue St. Florentin, Paris

1921 Causes a stir with his design for a Wimbledon tennis dress for tennis player Suzanne Lenglen

1924 Becomes first European designer to present his collection on models from the United States; collections with athletic daywear

1925 Shifts the dress waist back to its natural place

1929 Has his most successful year with calf-length day dresses and ankle-length evening robes

1936 Dies in Paris; business continues under changing artistic leadership (including Marc Bohan, Karl Lagerfeld, and Christian Lacroix)

PERFUMES Sublime (1922), Amour-Amour (1924), Joy (1926), Moment Suprême (1933), Monsieur Net (1955), Câline (1964), Eau de Sport (1969), Mille (1972), Eau de Patou (1976), Patou pour Homme (1980), Ma Liberté (1987)

PAUL POIRET see p. 21

MIUCCIA PRADA see p. 161

EMILIO PUCCI

1914 Born Marchese Emilio Pucci di Barsento on November 20 in Naples, Italy

Studies political science; serves as pilot in Word War II, afterwards flies passenger aircraft

1947 A fashion photographer for *Harper's Bazaar* discovers Pucci skiing in a self-made ski suit; the ski suit with new tapered pants is produced in the United States

1949 Presents women's wear summer collection on Capri and opens a studio in Florence

1950 Presents a collection with ski, tennis, and golf wear

1954 "Capri" pants become an international success; also designs matching loose shirt-blouses and silk scarves in bright colors and new patterns, which quickly become known as "Pucci Patterns"

1958 Works on improving stretch-weaves for sporty pants; discovers elastic Shantung silk for tight pants and bodysuits

1985 Experiences a major comeback through a renewed interest in his style, colors and patterns, leggings and bodysuits

1992 Dies on November 30 in Florence; daughter Laudomia carries on the company

PERFUMES Vivara (1965), Signor Vivara (1970), Miss Zadig, Monsieur Zadig (1971), Pucci (1980)

MARY QUANT

1934 Born on February 11 in Blackheath, Great Britain

1952–55 Studies at the Goldsmith's College of Art, London

1955 Together with her husband, opens a small boutique, Bazaar, on King's Road, London

1959 Opens a second Bazaar boutique in Knightsbridge; designs very short dresses, as if in a children's style

1963 Breaks through with the invention of the miniskirt; "Lolita" and "Schoolgirl" looks; "Wet" collection with raincoats and low-heeled PVC boots; introduces shoulder bags with long straps as an alternative to handbags

1965 Begins designing nylon stockings

1966 Introduces a cosmetics series for teenagers; awarded the Order of the British Empire

1976 Retires from running her own company and continues to work as a freelance designer for various companies

PERFUME Havoc (1974)

PACO RABANNE

1934 Born Francisco Rabaneda-Cuervo on February 18 in San Sebastián, Spain

Studies architecture in Paris

1963 Attracts attention with his sculptures; designs accessories for Dior, Balenciaga, and Givenchy

1966 Presents twelve experimental dresses made of plastic, metal, and paper

1967 Founds his own house of couture in Paris; presents "Molded" dresses—one of a kind dresses molded to the body and made out of metal parts

1968 Designs costumes for the movie *Barbarella* with Jane Fonda; collection with dresses made out of aluminum-knitted threads and imitation fur coats

1988 Revival of experimental "Rabanne" look; dresses in materials such as Plexiglas and holographic fabrics

1989 Introduces ready-to-wear line for women; carries futuristic style over into wearable clothing in metallic materials and colors

1990 Introduces ready-to-wear line for men

1991 Publishes *Trajectory*, followed by *The End of Times* (1992) and *Le Temps Présent* (1994)

PERFUMES Calandre (1969), Paco Rabanne pour Homme (1973), Métal (1979), Soin pour Homme (1984), La Nuit (1985), Sport (1986), Ténéré (1988)

ZANDRA RHODES

1940 Born on September 11 in Chatham, Great Britain

1959–63 Studies textile design, textile printing, and lithography at the Medway College of Art, Kent and at the Royal College of Art, London

1964 Establishes herself as a freelancer by designing wallpaper and fabrics for upholstery and clothing

1967 Begins to design dresses; unusual forms with curved or zigzag seams, sewn-on bits, and appliqué work

1970 Designs costumes for the musical *Georgy Girl*; makes multi-colored hair and "Rag" dresses with decorative holes fashionable

1972 Has spectacular fashion show models at the Roundhouse Theatre, London

1974 Founds Zandra Rhodes Ltd.; distributes underwear, eye glasses, furs, shoes, and a sari collection

1978 Introduces the "Rag" look: rags of material are held together with safety pins and perforated stones

1979 Launches collection Zandra Rhodes II line, first in Australia and later in England

1980 Poses for a poster collection

1982 Introduces Zandra Rhodes sportswear collection

MARCEL ROCHAS

1902 Born on February 24 in Paris, France

1925 Opens an haute couture salon in the Rue du Faubourg St.-Honoré, Paris

1931 Presents collection with broad-shouldered women's suits, influenced by the garments worn by Balinese dancers

1935 Shortens hemline from previously fashionable calf-length

1943 Designs costumes for Cocteau's film *L'Éternel Retour*

1945 Presents collection with three-quarter-length coats and redingotes (riding coats); introduces a decorative white dove as his trademark

1955 Dies on March 14 in Paris; his wife Hélène continues the company's perfume and cosmetics lines

1980 Introduction of an accessory line

1989 Introduction of a ready-to-wear line for women and men designed by Peter O'Brien

PERFUMES Madame Rochas (1966), Monsieur Rochas (1969), Eau de Roche (1970), Audace (1971), Mystère, Mister de Rochas (1978), Macassar (1980), Byzance (1987), Globe (1991), Eau de Rochas (1993), Tocade (1994)

YVES SAINT LAURENT

see p. 104

JIL SANDER

1943 Born on November 27 in Wesselburen, Germany

Trains in textiles in Germany and the United States

Works as editorial assistant at the magazines *McCall's* in New York and *Brigitte* in Hamburg

1968	Opens first shop Hamburg-Pöseldorf, including own designs
1969	Founds marketing company Jil Sander Moden in Hamburg
1973	Presents first collection under own name
1976	Creates a sensation with multi-layered "Onion" look
1979	Jil Sander Cosmetics
1983–85	Professor at the Hochschule für angewandte Kunst, Vienna
1984	Jil Sander Leder (leather goods)
1985	Becomes first German designer to present her collections in Milan rather than in Germany
1993	Opens flagship store in Paris
1994	Jil Sander Spa. Italia, Milan, and Jil Sander America Inc., New York
1995	Jil Sander Eyewear; awarded Order of the Federal Republic of Germany
1996	Receives Fashion Group Award, New York
1997	Presents Jil Sander Men's Collection
1998	Opens flagship store in Milan
PERFUMES	Jil Sander Woman Pure (1978), Jil Sander Women, Jil Sander Men (1979), Jil Sander Men II (1981), Jil Sander Women II (1983), Jil Sander Women III (1986), Jil Sander Sun (1989), Jil Sander No. 4 (1994), JIL (1998)

ELSA SCHIAPARELLI see p. 42

LEVI STRAUSS

1829	Born on February 26 in Buttenheim, Germany
1847	Emigrates to the United States
1850	Works in a textile shop in New York
1853	Moves to San Francisco; joins brother-in-law David Stern to expand the family's textile business and supplies gold prospectors with underwear, shirts, tents, and blankets
1855	Sews and designs the first pants made out of brown canvas and sells them to prospectors
1857	Replaces the canvas with a durable cotton called serge from Nîmes, France, and dyes pants made from this fabric with indigo
1860	Adds copper rivets to pants to make them more durable
1872	Takes out a patent on his indigo-dyed serge pants
1873	Jacob Davis, a tailor from Carson City, Nevada, joins Strauss' enterprise; together they add a patent for the copper rivets
1890	Founds Levi Strauss & Company in San Francisco
1902	Dies; his nephews take over the business

ANNA SUI

1955	Born on August 4 in Dearborn Heights, Michigan, United States
	Studies at Parson's School of Design, New York
1973–90	Works as a freelance fashion designer and stylist for fashion photographer Steven Meisel, among others
1983	Founds own fashion company in New York
1991	Has first runway show in New York; pioneers retrospective 1960s "Hippie chic"
1992	Opens first, large, in-store boutique at Macy's, New York; introduces menswear line
1995	Breaks through in Europe by launching a secondary line, Sui by Anna Sui, in cooperation with the Italian Gilma group
1996	Turns away from the stylistic elements of the 1960s for the first time with a 1920s-style collection
PERFUME	Anna Sui (1998)

PHILIP TREACY

1966	Born in Ireland
	Studies fashion design at the Royal College of Art, London
1987	While at college, works on hat projects for the London department store Harrods
1990	Founds a company as hat designer; makes hats for designers including Galliano and Karl Lagerfeld; clientele includes celebrities and supermodels

EMANUEL UNGARO

1933	Born on February 13 in Aix-en-Provence, France
1951–54	Apprentices as a tailor in his father's shop
1955–61	Moves to Paris and is assistant to Cristobal Balenciaga
1961–62	Works as assistant to André Courrèges
1965	Opens a small studio and a large haute couture salon in Paris
1968	Begins to design fabric patterns, typically with exaggerated flowers and polka dots; invents the "pattern mix" from a variety of designs and colors
1969	Introduces ready-to-wear line under the name Ungaro Parallèle
1970–80	Intoduces several new lines: Solo Donna, Ungaro Ter, Emanuel (United States only), and Ungaro Uomo

1996	Sells business to Ferragamo S.p.A. but remains artistic director
1997	Robert Forrest joins as head designer
PERFUMES	U de Emanuel Ungaro (1977), Diva (1983), Senso (1987)

VALENTINO

1932	Born Valentino Clemente Ludovico Garavani on May 11 in Voghera, Italy
	Studies fine arts in Milan
1950	Studies at the École de la Chambre Syndicale de la Couture Parisienne; wins competition organized by the International Wool Secretariat
1951–56	Works as assistant to Jean Dessès and Guy Laroche
1959	Returns to Italy; opens an haute couture salon in Rome
1962	First fashion show at the Palazzo Pitti, Florence
1967	Has great success with an all-in-white collection; one season later presents dresses in "Valentino" red, a custom Valentino color
1968	Designs Jackie Kennedy's dress for her wedding to ship-owner Aristoteles Onassis
1970	Introduces a ready-to-wear line
1972	Introduces menswear line and Valentino Più line for decorative materials
1985–88	Founds secondary labels Miss V, Oliver Homme, and Oliver Femme
1990	Opens the Accademia Valentino, an art exhibition center in Rome
1992	Retrospective, Metropolitan Museum of Art, New York
1998	Sells his business
PERFUMES	Valentino (1978), Valentino de Valentino (1985), Vendetta (1993), Very Valentino (1997)

GIANNI VERSACE see p. 143

MADELEINE VIONNET see p. 38

LOUIS VUITTON

1821	Born in the Jura mountains, France
1835	Goes to Paris where he works as a packer at the court of Napoleon III
1854	Opens a shop with leather products, especially luggage, in the Rue Neuve des Capucines, Paris; quickly becomes a high society favorite
1890	Invents a theft-proof lock which makes it possible to lock an entire series of luggage with just one key
1892	Dies in Paris

1896 The heirs to the House of Vuitton invent the "monogram canvas" with the LV symbol

1959 A new production method makes it possible to expand the luggage range

1960–96 Product range is increased with every imaginable article from saddles and umbrellas to soccer balls

1996 Introduction of a ready-to-wear line designed by Marc Jacobs

VIVIENNE WESTWOOD

see p. 119

YOHJI YAMAMOTO

1943 Born in Tokyo, Japan
Studies law

1964–69 Studies fashion design at the Bunka Gakuin Academy, Tokyo

1972 Founds own fashion business

1977 Presents his ready-to-wear collection in Tokyo for the first time

1981 Presents his collection in Paris featuring purist, formless garments in bleak colors; it is described as a "nuclear bomb explosion" and the "end of fashion" by the European press

1984 Introduces menswear line whose unusual, soft appearance and collarless jackets are very well received

1989 Is the focus of the movie-documentary *Aufzeichnungen zu Kleidern und Städten* (Notes on Clothes and Cities) by film-maker Wim Wenders

1991 Introduces an underwear line

1993 Designs costumes for the Bayreuth Opera Festival production of Wagner's *Tristan and Isolde*

PERFUME Yohji Yamamoto (1996)

SELECT BIBLIOGRAPHY

I. General Reference Works

Arnold, Janet. *Patterns of Fashion vol. 3: Englishwomen's Dresses and Their Construction, c. 1860–1940*, London 1977.

Boucher, Francois. *20,000 Years of Fashion: The History of Costume and Personal Adornment*, expanded edition, New York 1987.

Dictionnaire de la Mode au XXe siècle, Paris 1996.

Ewing, Elizabeth. *History of Twentieth-Century Fashion*, New York 1992.

The Fashion Book, London 1998

Hayward Gallery. *Addressing the Century: 100 Years of Art and Fashion* (exhib. cat.), London 1998.

Laver, James. *Costume and Fashion, A Concise History*, London 1985.

Loschek, Ingrid. *Accessoires: Symbolik und Geschichte*, Munich 1993.

———. *Die Modedesigner. Ein Lexikon von Armani bis Yamamoto*, Munich 1998.

———. *Mode im 20. Jahrhundert*, Munich 1995.

Martin, Richard (ed.). *Contemporary Fashion*, Detroit 1995.

———. *The St. James Fashion Encyclopedia. A Survey of Style from 1945 to the Present*, Detroit 1997.

Mulvey, Kate and Melissa Richards. *Decades of Beauty: The Changing Image of Women 1890s–1990s*, New York 1998.

O'Hara, Georgina. *The Thames and Hudson Dictionary of Fashion and Fashion Designers*, London 1986.

———. *The Encyclopedia of Fashion*, London 1986.

Rennolds Milbank, Caroline. *Couture: The Great Designers*, New York 1985.

———. *New York Fashion: The Evolution of American Style*, New York 1989.

Schmid, Beate Dorothea and Ingrid Loschek (ed.). *Klassiker der Mode: Die Erfolgsgeschichte legendärer Kleidungsstücke und Accessoires*, Augsburg 1999.

Steele, Valerie. *Women of Fashion: Twentieth-Century Designers*, New York 1991.

Tucker, Andrew. *The London Fashion Book*, New York 1998.

Waugh, Norah. *The Cut of Women's Clothes 1600–1930*, London 1968.

Wilson, Elizabeth and Lou Taylor. *Through the Looking Glass: A History of Dress from 1860 to the Present Day*, London 1989.

II. Fashion Theory

Barthes, Roland. *Die Sprache der Mode*, Frankfurt am Main 1985.

Benstock, Shari and Suzanne Ferriss. *On Fashion*, New Jersey 1994.

Breward, Christopher. *The Culture of Fashion. A New History of Fashionable Dress*, Manchester/New York 1994.

Davis, Fred. *Fashion, Culture, and Identity*, Chicago 1992.

Hollander, Ann. *Sex and Suits*, London 1995.

Lipowetsky, Gilles. *The Empire of Fashion. Dressing Modern Democracy*, Princeton 1994.

McDowell, Colin. *Dressed to Kill: Sex Power & Clothes*, London 1992.

———. *The Designer Scam*, London 1994.

Poschardt, Ulf. *Anpassen*, Hamburg 1998.

Richard, Birgit. *Todesbilder: Kunst, Subkultur, Medien*, Munich 1995.

Steele, Valerie. *Fetisch: Mode, Sex und Macht*, Berlin 1996.

1900–1914 Between Dream and Reality

Buxbaum, Gerda. *Mode aus Wien 1815 bis 1932*, Salzburg/Vienna 1986.

Crowninshield, Frank. "An Elegance of Another Era," in: *Rita de Acosta Lydig*, New York 1940.

Deslandres, Yvonne. *Paul Poiret 1879–1944*, Paris 1986.

Fukai, Akiko. *Japonism in Fashion*, Kyoto 1994.

Iribe, Paul. *Les Robes de Paul Poiret raconté par Paul Iribe*, Paris 1908.

Kirke, Betty. *Madeleine Vionnet*, San Francisco 1998.

Lepape, Georges. *Les choses de Paul Poiret vues par George Lapape*, Paris 1911.

Martin, Richard and Harold Koda. *Orientalism: Visions of the East in Western Dress*, New York 1994.

Museen der Stadt Wien. *Traum und Wirklichkeit Wien, 1870–1930* (exhib. cat.), Vienna 1986

Newton, Mary Stella. *Health, Art and Reason: Dress Reformers of the 19th Century*, London 1974.

Pozharskaia, M.N. *The Art of the Ballets Russes: The Russian Seasons in Paris, 1908–1928*, New York 1991.

Reeder, Jan Glier. "Historical and Cultural References in Clothes from the House of Paquin," in: *Textile and Text* 3:4 (1991).

———. "The House of Paquin," in: *Textile and Text* 12:14 (1990).

———. *The Touch of Paquin: 1891–1920*, Master's Thesis, Graduate Program in Museum Studies, Fashion Institute of Technology, New York 1990.

Said, Edward W. *Orientalism*, New York 1979.

Schouvaloff, Alexander. *Léon Bakst: The Theater Art*, London 1991.

Sirop, Dominique. *Paquin*, Paris 1989.

Steele, Valerie. *Paris Fashions: A Cultural History*, London 1989.

Vinken, Barbara. *Mode nach der Mode: Geist und Kleid am Ende des 20. Jahrhunderts*, Frankfurt am Main 1993.

Völker, Angela. *Textiles of the Wiener Werkstätte, 1910–1932*, New York 1994.

Voss, Ursula. *Szenische Collagen: Theaterexperimente der europäischen Avantgarde zwischen 1913 und 1936*, Bielefeld 1998.

White, Palmer. *Poiret*, London 1973.

Wichmann, Siegfried. *Japonisme: The Japanese Influence on Western Art Since 1858*, London 1981.

1915–1921 Crinolines and Masculine Clothing

Barthes, Roland. "Erte or A la lettre," in: *The Obvious and the Obtuse*, New York 1985.

Blum, Stella. *Designs by Erté: Fashion Drawings and Illustrations from Harper's Bazaar*, New York 1976.

Bowman, Sara and Michel Molinare. *A Fashion for Extravagance*, New York 1985.

Charles-Roux, Edmonde. *Chanel and Her World*, London 1982.

Da la Haye, Amy. *Chanel: The Couturière at Work*, London 1994.

Damase, Jacques. *Sonja Delaunay: Mode und Design*, Zurich 1991.

Erté. *Erté Fashions*, New York 1972.

———. *Things I Remember*, New York 1975.

Framke, Gisela (ed.). *Künstler ziehen an – Avantgardemode in Europa 1910–1939*, Heidelberg 1998.

Leymarie, Jean. *Chanel*, New York 1987.

Spencer, Charles. *Erté*, New York 1970.

Stern, Radu. *Gegen den Strich: Kleider von Künstlern 1900–1940*, Bern 1992.

1922–1929 A Stylized Masquerade

Chapsal, Madeleine. *La Chair et la Robe*, Paris 1989.

Demornex, Jaqueline. *Madeleine Vionnet*, Paris 1990.

Fabo, Sabine. *Kunstforum* 9 (1998).

Hall, Carolyn. *The Twenties in Vogue*, New York 1983.

Holman Edelmann, Amy. *The Little Black Dress*, London 9.

Kamitis, Lydia. *Vionnet: Memoire de la Mode*, Paris 1996.

Kirke, Betty. *Madeleine Vionnet*, Tokyo 1991.

Lee-Potter, Charlie. *Sportswear in Vogue since 1910*, London 1984.

Robinson, Julian. *The Golden Age of Style: Art Deco Fashion Illustrations*, London 1976.

Tinel, Brigitte. *Sportswear. Zur Geschichte und

Entwicklung der Sportkleidung, Kiefeld 1992.
Vionnet, Madeleine. *Les Années d'innovation, 1919–1939* (exhib. cat.), Lyon 1995.

1930–1938 New Illusions

Coleman, Elizabeth A. *The Genius of Charles James*, New York 1982.
Etherington-Smith, Meredith. *Patou*, New York 1983.
Ferragamo, Salvatore. *Il clazolaio dei sogni*, Sansoni 1971.
———. *Shoemaker of Dreams*, London 1957.
Homage à Elsa Schiaparelli (exhib. cat.), Paris 1984.
Mariano Fortuny 1871–1949. Der Magier des textilen Designs (exhib. cat.), Vienna 1985.
Martin, Richard. *Fashion and Surrealism*, New York 1987.
Schiaparelli, Elsa. *Shocking Life*, London 1954.
White, Palmer. *Elsa Schiaparelli: Empress of Paris Fashion*, London 1986.

1939–1946 Between Uniformity and Glamour

Engelmeier, Regine and Peter W. (eds.). *Fashion in Film*, Munich/New York 1990.
Farneti Cera, Deanna (ed.). *Glanzstücke. Modeschmuck vom Jugendstil bis zur Gegenwart*, Munich 1991.
Fox, Patty. *Star Style: Hollywood Legends as Fashion Icons*, Santa Monica 1995.
Kohle, Yohannan and Nancy Nolf. *Claire McCardell: Redefining Modernism*, New York 1998.
Lee, Sarah Tomerlin. *American Fashion*, New York 1975.
Tapert, Annette. *The Power of Glamour*, New York 1998.

1947–1949 The "New Look"

Chariau, Joëlle (ed.). *René Gruau*, Munich 1984.
De Marly, Diana. *Christian Dior*, London 1990.
———. *The History of Haute Couture 1850–1959*, London 1980.
Dior by Dior, Harmondsworth 1958.
Garnier, Guillaume (ed.). *Pierre Balmain, 40 années de création* (exhib. cat.), Paris 1986.
Giroud, François and Sascha van Dorssen. *Dior*, Munich 1987.
Guillaume, Valérie. *Jacques Fath*, Paris 1993.
Healy, Robyn. *Balenciaga: Masterpieces of Fashion Design*, Melbourne 1992.
Jouve, Marie-Andrée. *Cristobal le Magnifique*, Paris 1989.
Keenan, Brigid. *Dior in Vogue*, London 1981.
Pochna, Marie-France. *Dior*, Munich 1997.
———. *Christian Dior*, Paris 1994.

1950–1960 New Departures and Rediscoveries

Bottero, Amelio. *Il potere e la Moda*, Amelio Bottero, Il Pungolo 1990.
Casadio, Mariucca. *Emilio Pucci*, New York 1998.
Cinquant'anni di moda (exhib. cat.), Rome 1985.
L'Elegance des Années 50, photographié par Henry Clarke, Paris 1986.

Italian Fashion. Vol. 1: The Origins of High Fashion and Knitwear, Vol. 2: From Anti-Fashion to Stylism, Milan 1987.
Kennedy, Shirley. *Pucci. A Renaissance in Fashion*, New York 1991.
Lépicard, José Marie and Susan Train. *Givenchy: 40 Years of Creation*, Paris 1991.
O'Keeffe. *Schuhe. Eine Hommage an Sandalen, Slipper, Stöckelschuhe*, Cologne 1997.
Vergani, Guido. *Maria Pezzi: Una vita dentro la moda*, Milan 1998.
———. *The Sala Bianca: The Birth of Italian Fashion*, Milan 1992.
Wilcox, Claire. *A Century of Rags: Icons of Style in the 20th Century*, London 1997.

1961–1967 Pop Music, Space Race, Bodysuits, and Secondhand

Andy Warhol Museum. *The Warhol Look: Glamour Style Fashion*, Boston 1997.
Booker, Christopher. *The Neophiliacs: The Revolution in English Life in the Fifties and Sixties*, London 1969.
Pierre Cardin: Past-Present-Future, London/Berlin 1990.
Hulanicki, Barbara. *From A to Biba*, London 1983.
Kenzo, Tokyo 1985.
Lobenthal, Joel. *Radical Rags: Fashion of the Sixties*, New York 1990.
Melly, George. *Revolt into Style: The Pop Arts in Britain*, London 1970.
Moffitt, Peggy and William Claxton. *The Rudi Gernreich Book*, New York 1999.
Palmer, Alexandra. "Paper Dresses: The Ultimate Ready-To-Wear," in: *Per una Storia della Moda Pronta*, Milan 1990.
Polhemus, Ted. *Pop Styles*, London 1984.
———. *Street Style*, London 1994 (published as an addition to the exhibition at the Victoria and Albert Museum, November 1994–February 1995).
Quant, Mary. *Quant by Quant*, London 1966.
Rabanne, Paco. *Trajectoire*, Paris 1991.
Rhodes, Zandra and Dune Knight. *The Art of Zandra Rhodes*, London 1984.
Wilson, Elizabeth. *Adorned in Dreams: Fashion and Modernity*, Berkeley 1985.

1968–1979 The Looks

Benetton, Luciano and A. Lee. *Io e i miei fratelli*, Milan 1990.
Krell, Gene and Maud Molyneux. *Vivienne Westwood*, New York 1997.
Mantle, Jonathan. *Benetton: The Family, The Business, The Brand*, London 1999.
Metropolitan Museum of Art. *Yves Saint Laurent* (exhib. cat.), New York 1983.
McRobbie, Angela (ed.). *Zoot Suits and Second-Hand Dresses*, Basingstoke 1989.
Mezger, W. *Discokultur: Die jugendliche Superszene*, Heidelberg 1980.
Perry, Charles. *The Haight-Ashbury: A History*, New York 1984.
Poschardt, Ulf. *DJ Culture*, London 1998.
Rudotsky, Bernard. *The Unfashionable Human Body*, New York 1971.

Vermorel, Fred. *Vivienne Westwood: Fashion, Perversity and the Sixties Laid Bare*, New York 1996.
Wolfe, Tom. *Radical Chic and the Man Maning the Flak Catchers*, New York 1974.
Yves Saint Laurent: Images of Design 1958–1988, New York 1988.
Yves Saint Laurent und die Modephotographie, Munich 1992.

1980–1990 Dress for Success / No Future

Benaïm, Laurence. *Issey Miyake*, New York 1997.
Casadio, Mariucca. *Moschino*, London 1997.
Chenoune, Farid. *Jean-Paul Gaultier*, Paris 1996.
Delbourg-Delphis, Marylene. *La Mode pour la vie*, Paris 1983.
Fondacion Cartier pour l'art contemporain, Paris. *Issey Miyake: Making Things* (exhib. cat.), Paris 1998.
Grand, France. *Comme des Garçons*, New York 1998
La Mode pour la vie, Paris 1983.
La Mode selon les créateurs (exhib. cat.), Paris 1991.
Martin, Richard and Grace Mirabella. *Versace*, New York 1997.
Miyake, Issey. *Issey Miyake/Mark Holborn*, Cologne 1995.
Miyake, Issey. *Issey Miyake by Irving Penn*, Tokyo 1995.
Molloy, John. *Dress for Success*, New York 1975.
———. *The Woman's Dress for Success Book*, New York 1977.
Sischy, Ingrid. *Donna Karan*, London 1998.
Soli, Pia and Sergio Salaroli. *Moda: L'immagine coordinata*, Zanichelli 1990.
Versace, Gianni. *Bare Witness*, New York 1996.

1991–2000 Global Village at the End of the Millennium

Braddock, Sarah E. and Marie O'Mahony. *Techno Textiles: Revolutionary Fabrics for Fashion and Design*, London 1998.
De la Haye, Amy and Cathie Dingwall. *Surfers, Soulies, Skinheads & Skaters: Subcultural Style from the Forties to the Nineties*, Stuttgart 1996.
Gan, Stephen and Alix Browne (ed.). *Visionaire's Fashion 2000: Designers at the Turn of the Millennium*, New York 1997
Givhan, Robin. "Black Chic: After a Fashion, Haute Couture is Finally Catching up with Far-Flung Influences of the African Diaspora," in: *The Washington Post*, 1 December 1997.
Herman, Valli. "The Next Generation: Culture Comes Naturally to a New Crew of Designers on the Rise" (Series: "Faces of Change"), in: *The Dallas Morning News*, 17 August 1994.
McDowell, Colin. *Galliano*, London 1997.
Menkes, Suzy. "The Comeback of Glamour: New Materials for the New Woman," in: *The International Herald Tribune*, 12 April 1994.
O'Brien, Joanne. "Born November 1992, Died June 1993. No Flowers; Grunge," in: *The Times of London*, 6 June 1993.
Quintanilla, Michael. "Premiere Vision," in: *The Los Angeles Times*, 26 March 1999.
Tucker, Andrew. *Dries van Noten. Shape, Privat and Fabric*, London 1999.

THE AUTHORS

Andrea Affaticati works as a freelance journalist specializing in culture and society. She writes primarily for *Vogue Italia, Uomo Vogue, Carnet,* and *Secolo XIX.*

Rebecca Arnold lectures on fashion history and cultural theory at Central St. Martin's College of Art and Design, London. Her book on late twentieth-century fashion entitled *Fashion, Desire & Anxiety* will be published in spring 2000.

Christopher Breward is Reader in Historical and Cultural Studies at London College of Fashion, The London Institute. He is the author of *The Culture of Fashion* (1995) and *The Hidden Consumer* (1999).

Gerda Buxbaum holds a doctorate in fashion history and is the director of the Modeschule der Stadt Wien (Fashion Institute of the City of Vienna). She has written numerous books on the history of fashion and was the editor of the Prestel publications *Glanzstücke. Modeschmuck vom Jugendstil bis zur Gegenwart* (1991) and *Die Hüte der Adele List* (1995).

Joëlle Chariau is joint proprietor of the Munich art gallery Bartsch & Chariau, which specializes in fashion illustrations.

Farid Chenoune teaches French Literature and has published several books including *A History of Men's Fashion* (1993), *Jean-Paul Gaultier* (1996), and *Hidden Femininity: Twentieth-Century Lingerie* (1999). He is the author of numerous articles on cultural and social history and is currently working on a study of the nightlife in Paris between 1919 and 1939.

Elizabeth Ann Coleman is presently the department head and the David and Roberta Logie Curator of Textiles and Costumes at the Museum of Fine Arts, Boston. She is an internationally recognized scholar in several fields; in fashion, her work has included exhibitions and publications on Charles James and the Houses of Worth, Doucet, and Pingat.

Carlo Ducci worked as an attorney before taking up journalism in 1984, when he became the London-based correspondent for Italian magazines, newspapers, and television stations. He returned to Italy in 1987 and has been working since then as a features editor for *Vogue Italia.* He is currently a senior writer for Condé Nast.

Caroline Evans is Senior Lecturer in Cultural Studies at Central St. Martin's College of Art and Design, London. She specilizes in fashion and fine art and has published widely in these fields.

Deanna Farneti Cera is an international expert on imitation jewelry, costume jewelry, and Bijoux de couture. She is the author of numerous books including *Joys of Hollywood* (1987), *Glanzstücke: Modeschmuck vom Jugendstil bis zur Gegenwart* (1991), and *Dictionnaire International du Bijou* (1998). She lives and works in Milan.

Anna Gloria Forti has worked in the fashion sector ever since she completed her doctorate in literary studies. In 1981 she joined *Vogue Italia* as fashion editor and has been head of the *L'Uomo Vogue* editorial office since 1999.

Gisela Framke is an historian who has been Deputy Director of the Museum für Kunst und Kulturgeschichte, Dortmund, since 1988 and curator of urban history and textiles. She has researched and organized exhibitions on the history of women and the phenomenon of lace in the nineteenth and twentieth centuries.

Robin Givhan is the fashion writer for the *Washington Post.* She has also written for the *International Herald Tribune* and *Runway Madness,* a collection of fashion photography by Lucian Perkins.

Ingrid Loschek teaches history and theory of fashion at the Hochschule für Gestaltung, Technik und Wirtschaft in Pforzheim. From 1994–95 she was also guest lecturer at Harvard University. Her extensive academic work and role as an exhibition consultant have earned her respect as a fashion and costume historian. Her numerous publications on the subject of fashion and cultural history are considered seminal works.

Margit J. Mayer has been writing about fashion for Condé Nast magazines (German and French *Vogue* and *Gentlemen's Quarterly*) since 1986—including three years as a New York correspondent—and has been the fashion editor of *Stern* magazine since April 1999.

Patricia Mears is the curator of the costume and textile collection at the Brooklyn Museum of Art. She has organized and written the accompanying publications for the exhibitions *Fancy Feet* (1993), *A Slice of Schiaparelli* (1995), and *Japonism in Fashion* (1998). She is also an adjunct professor at the Fashion Institute of Technology, where she lectures on the history of twentieth-century fashion.

Jane C. Milosch is an independent curator and art journalist. She has worked as a curator for the Detroit Institute of Arts and the Davenport Museum of Art and is a regular contributor to *ARTnews.*

Jane Mulvagh joined British *Vogue* in 1981 as a fashion historian and worked there for eight years. She is the author of several books including *The Vogue History of Twentieth-Century Fashion* and *Newport Houses.* She writes regularly for the *Financial Times* and *The Art Newspaper* and is tutor for Masters of Art in Fashion Journalism at Central St. Martin's College of Art, London.

Alexandra Palmer is the Nora E. Vaughan Fashion Costume Curator at the Royal Ontario Museum, Toronto, Canada, and adjunct faculty member in the Graduate Program in Art History, York University.

Jan Glier Reeder holds a master's degree in Museum Studies in Costume and Textiles from the Fashion Institute of Technology, where she conducted her research on the work of Madame Paquin. She taught courses on the history of couture and textiles and is currently staff specialist in the Couture Department at William Doyle Galleries, New York City.

Caroline Rennolds Milbank is a fashion historian and the author of *Couture: The Great Designers* (1985) and *New York Fashion: The Evolution of American Style* (1989). She is currently working as a curatorial consultant.

Birgit Richard teaches new media in theory and practice in the Department of Classical Philology and Aesthetics (Institut für Kunstpädagogik) at the Johann Wolfgang Goethe University, Frankfurt am Main.

Beate Dorothea Schmid holds a degree in fashion design from the Fachhochschule Pforzheim. She works as a freelance fashion journalist for the *Frankfurter Allgemeine Zeitung* and the Agentur Select in Koblenz, among others, and is a freelance editor and book author. Her first book, written jointly with Ingrid Loschek, was published in September 1999.

Valerie Steele holds a doctorate from Yale University and is the Chief Curator of the museum at the Fashion Institute of Technology in New York. She is the author of numerous books including *Women of Fashion: Twentieth Century Designers* (1991) and *Fetish: Fashion, Sex and Power* (1995). She is also the founding editor of *Fashion Theory: The Journal of Dress, Body & Culture.*

Julia Szabo is a freelance journalist who has written about culture and style for a variety of publications including *Elle Decor, I.D., The New York Times, The New York Daily News, Harper's Bazaar,* and *Travel and Leisure.* She lives in New York City.

Elizabeth Wilson is a professor of cultural studies at the University of North London and the author of a number of books including *Adorned in Dreams: Fashion and Modernity, The Sphinx in the City: The City, Urban Disorder and Women,* and *The Lost Time Café.* She is currently writing a book about bohemians and artists.

Gundula Wolter holds a doctorate in art history and the history of costume. Her publications on the history of European clothing and fashion include *Die Verpackung des männlichen Geschlechts* and *Hosen, weiblich. Kulturgeschichte der Frauenhose.* Since 1998 she has been a visiting professor at the Institut für experimentelles Textil- und Bekleidungsdesign at the Hochschule der Künste in Berlin.

ACKNOWLEDGMENTS

First and foremost, I would like to thank the twenty-six authors for their contributions to the content and success of this book. Their expertise and insightful observations reveal concurrent methodologies in writing about fashion, and their stimulating texts entice the reader to learn more about the history of twentieth-century fashion.

The importance of obtaining the best photographic materials and reproduction rights for this book proved to be a greater challenge than initially anticipated. We relied heavily on the cooperation of fashion houses, designers, private and museum collections, picture archives, photographers, artists, and magazines to provide us with high-quality photographic materials that best represent the work of twentieth-century designers and photographers. It was not always possible to obtain *the* iconic image or perfect shot. When these were unavailable in some cases it led to the discovery of an excellent alternative, the uncovering of a lesser-known, yet outstanding example. What was disappointing, however, was that quite a few major fashion and media companies, such as *Vogue* France and *Vogue* Germany, were unable to provide us with a single image. In the future we hope to win their cooperation.

My particular thanks go to Sabine Thiel-Siling and Jane Milosch at Prestel for their enthusiasm and commitment, friendly help, and cooperation in the planning and production of this book. I am especially grateful to Nino Pavlek, chief picture researcher, who worked relentlessly to obtain photographic materials and secure reproduction rights. I am also indebted to Amélie Haas, Agnes Schorer, and Christof Cremer in Vienna for their invaluable assistance with picture research and many administrative details.

I would like to thank the following individuals and organizations for their interest and professional cooperation in this project: Action Press, Hamburg: Ute Joos; A.D.A.G.P., Paris: Janet Kabidayan; AFDPP, Paris: Anna C. Biedermann; Azzedine Alaïa, Paris: Ms. Farida; Amster Rothstein & Ebenstein, NYC: Karen Ash; Giorgio Armani, Milan: Deirdre McCready and Isabel Kaus at Schoeller & von Rehlingen Public Relations, Munich, Hamburg; Art Department, NYC: David Maloney; Art Partner, New York: Candice Marks; Richard Avedon Studio, NYC: Sharyl DeAlva; Balenciaga, Paris: Didier Hesse and Hanne Andrée Jouvre; Benetton S.p.A.: Richard Gerbert at Paola Gräfin Balbo; Bartsch & Chariau collection, Munich: Andreas Bartsch; François Berthoud; Laura Biagiotti-Cigna, Rome;

Dirk Bikkembergs, Paris: Beatrice Novy; Manolo Blahnik: Duagnan Michael; The Brooklyn Museum of Art: Ruth Jansen; Burberry Limited, London: Alannah Weston; Camera Press, London: Elizabeth Kerr; Patricia Canino, Paris; Pierre Cardin, Paris: Marion Brenot; Center for Creative Photography, Arizona, USA: Dianne Nilsen; Hussein Chalayan, London: Annika McVeigh; Chambre Syndicale du Prêt-à-Porter des Couturiers et des Créateurs de Mode, Paris: Denise Dubois; Chanel: Katja Wilde, Marika Genty and Odile Premel; Comme des Garçons, Paris: Jelka Music; Condé Nast Publications/ Permissions, NYC: Michael Stier; Jean-Charles de Castelbajac, Paris: Pascal Collet; Esther de Jong, Paris; Ann Demeulemeester, Paris: Michèle Montag; Demont Photo Management, Los Angeles: Thierry Demont; Christian Dior, Paris: Soizic Pfaff; Fashion Center/Business Improvement District, NYC: Andrea De Vaynes; Fashion Institute of Technology, NYC: Irving Solero; Ferragamo, Florence: Raffaella Spadoni and Alexandra Degel at Schoeller & von Rehlingen Public Relations, Munich, Hamburg; Fabrizio Ferri; Hans Feurer, Paris; Michele Filomeno, Paris: Hélène Rossignol; Dr. Hans Frensch, Frankfurt; John Galliano, Paris: Mesh Chhiber; Jean-Paul Gaultier, Paris: Lionel Vermeil and Nathalie Limonta; Marilyn Gaultier Agency, Paris: Robert and Jean-Marc; Gmurzynska gallery, Cologne: Ms. Kotrouzinis; Grès, Paris: Madame Casiez; Gucci: Christine Sticken at Network Public Relations GmbH, Shirin von Wulffen, Hamburg and Aurora Fiorentini/ Gucci Archives, Florence; Guerlain, Paris: Elisabeth Sirot; Prof. F. C. Gundlach, Hamburg; Mats Gustafson, New York; Frank Habicht; Hamiltons Photographers Agency, London: Leigh Yule and Fiona; Hermès, Paris: Marie-Claude Poirier; Reiner Hosch, Vienna; Hiro, NYC: Shelley M. Dowell; Margaret Howie, South Africa; Hulton Getty Picture Collection, London: Charles Merullo; IMG, NYC: Laura McKenna and Ivan; Donna Karan, Milan: Federica Sheean; Kenzo S.A., Paris: Ruth Obadia; Lainey Keogh, Dublin; Betty Kirke, New York; Calvin Klein, Inc., NYC: Eric Delph; CK Cosmetics Co., NYC: Melissa Falk; KL Gallery, Paris: Caroline Lebar; Nick Knight, Surrey, England: Emma Wheeler; The Kobal Collection, London: Sheryl Thomas; Christian Lacroix, Paris: Elizabeth Bonnel; Helmut Lang, New York: Hannah Lawrence; La Chemise Lacoste, Paris: Agnès Colonna D'Istria; Lanvin, Paris: Hania Destelle

and Odile Fraigneau; Ralph Lauren, Paris: Alekha; Lesage, Paris: Nathalie Vibert; Lighthouse Artists Management, Paris: Patrick Deedes Vincke; Peter Lindbergh; Lord & Taylor, NYC: Sunny Lebowitc; *L'Officiel*, Paris: Marie-José Susskind; Christin Losta, Munich; Marek & Associates, NYC: Michael Costa and Amen; Niall McInerney, London; Martin Margiela, Paris: Patrick Scallon; Guy Marineau; Willy Maywald Association, Paris: Jutta Niemann; The Metropolitan Museum of Art/The Costume Institute: Stephan Houy-Towner; Sandro Michahelles; Issey Miyake, Paris: Valérie Lebérichel and Yann; Sarah Moon, Paris: Renate Gallois-Montbrün; Moschino, Milan: Stefania Vismara; Andreas Münchbach; Musée de la Mode et du Textile, Paris: Marie-Hélène Poix; Musée Galliera, Musée de la Mode de la Ville de Paris: Sylvie Lécaillier; Museum at the Fashion Institute of Technology, NYC: Irving Solero; Museum für Kunsthandwerk, Frankfurt am Main: Dr. Sabine Runde; Nike, Oregon, USA: Andrea Corso; Stefano Pandini; Jean Patou, Paris: Valérie Dufournier and Platon; Prada, Milan: Verde Visconti; Mary Quant Ltd., London: Camilla Twigg; Paco Rabanne, Paris: Alexandre Boulais; Eugène Rubin and Mme Alla Ter-Abramoff; Yves Saint Laurent: Eleonore de Musset (YSL Couture), Maryvonne Numata (YSL Rive Gauche), Catherine Chevalier (YSL Parfums); Jil Sander, Hamburg: Doris B. Franze; Sorelle Fontana, Rome: Maria-Elenne Parissi; Staatliche Museen zu Berlin/ Preussischer Kulturbesitz, art library: Dr. Adelheid Rasche and Ms. Schwichtenberg (picture archives); Ray Stevenson; Levi Strauss & Co. Archives, USA: Lynn Downey; Vivienne Tam, NYC: Lisa Mercer; Mario Testino; Philip Treacy, London: Jessica; Union Centrale des Arts Décoratifs, Paris: Sonia Edard and Mme Perez; Versace, Milan: Daniel Marks and Loew, Munich; VG Bild-Kunst, Bonn: Uta Raschke and Eva Neuroth; Roger Viollet, Paris: Michèle Lajournade; *Vogue* Germany: Susanne Niessen; Veroushka von Lehndorff, New York; Warnaco, Inc., NYC: Stanley Silverstein; Vivienne Westwood, London: Barbara Galliano, Andrea Cameroni, and Alexander Krenn; Staley Wise, NYC: Matthew Marden; Wolford AG, Bregenz: Alina Zimmerhaeckel; *Women's Wear*, Berlin, Melissa Drier; Zahm collection, Berg/Mörlbach: Volker Zahm and Veronica Peter; Rascoff Zysblatt Organization, NYC: Tom Cyrana.   *Gerda Buxbaum*

PHOTO CREDITS

Every effort has been made by the Publisher to acknowledge all sources and copyright holders. In the event of any copyright holder being inadvertently omitted, please contact the Publisher directly. The numbers listed below refer to pages where illustrations are located.

t. = top; c. = center; b. = bottom; l. = left; r. = right

INDEX

PUBLICATION DATA

Front cover: Jil Sander, advertising campaign (Photo: Nick Knight)
Frontispiece: Jeanne Lanvin Haute Couture (Photo: Christin Losta
and © Christin Losta and Frankfurter Allgemeine Zeitung Magazin)
Photo p. 174: Hommage à Dior (Photo: Sarah Moon)

Prestel Verlag
Königinstrasse 9, 80539 Munich
Tel. +49 (89) 38 17 09-0; Fax +49 (89) 38 17 09-35
www.prestel.de

Prestel Publishing Ltd.
4, Bloomsbury Place, London WC1A 2QA
Tel. +44 (20) 7323-5004; Fax +44 (20) 7636-8004

Prestel Publishing
900 Broadway, Suite 603, New York, NY 10003
Tel. +1 (212) 995-2720; Fax +1 (212) 995-2733

www.prestel.com

Library of Congress Control Number is available

The Deutsche Bibliothek holds a record of this publication in the
Deutsche Nationalbibliografie; detailed bibliographical data can
be found under: http://dnb.ddb.de

Prestel books are available worldwide. Please contact your nearest
bookseller or one of the above addresses for information concerning
your local distributor.

PROJECT DIRECTORS: Sabine Thiel-Siling and Jane C. Milosch
MANAGING EDITOR: Jane C. Milosch
PRODUCTION EDITING: Claudia Hellmann, Courtenay Smith, and Danko Szabó

DESIGNER BIOGRAPHIES by Beate Dorothea Schmid, Munich
CONTRIBUTIONS TRANSLATED FROM THE GERMAN by Jenny Marsh except
for the following pages by Elizabeth Schwaiger (pp. 14, 32, 36, 44, 52, 112,
154, 16, pp. 176–83)
CONTRIBUTIONS TRANSLATED FROM THE FRENCH by David Radzinowicz
(pp. 39, 63, 65, 70)
CONTRIBUTIONS TRANSLATED FROM THE ITALIAN by Marguerite Shore
(pp. 42, 56, 73, 114, 136, 143, 161)
PHOTO RESEARCH: Nino B. Pavlek, Agnes Schorer, Amélie Haas, and Christof Cremer

DESIGN FOR LAYOUT: Hans Schmid/Beisenherz, Munich
COVER DESIGN: LIQUID | www.liquid.ag
LAYOUT AND TYPESETTING: Matthias Liesendahl, Munich
PRINTING AND BINDING: MKT Print d.d., Ljubljana, Slovenia

Printed in Slovenia on acid-free paper.

ISBN 3-7913-3312-7